THOMAS WYLTON

ON THE INTELLECTUAL SOUL

AUCTORES BRITANNICI MEDII AEVI · XIX

THOMAS WYLTON

ON THE INTELLECTUAL SOUL

Edited by
LAUGE O. NIELSEN
AND
CECILIA TRIFOGLI

English translation by
GAIL TRIMBLE

Published for THE BRITISH ACADEMY
by OXFORD UNIVERSITY PRESS

Oxford University Press, Great Clarendon Street, Oxford OX2 6DP
Oxford New York
Auckland Cape Town Dar es Salaam Hong Kong Karachi
Kuala Lumpur Madrid Melbourne Mexico City Nairobi
New Delhi Shanghai Taipei Toronto

With offices in
Argentina Austria Brazil Chile Czech Republic France Greece
Guatemala Hungary Italy Japan Poland Portugal Singapore
South Korea Switzerland Thailand Turkey Ukraine Vietnam

Published in the United States
by Oxford University Press Inc., New York

© The British Academy 2010

Database right The British Academy (maker)

All rights reserved. No part of this publication may be reproduced,
stored in a retrieval system, or transmitted, in any form or by any means,
without the prior permission in writing of the British Academy,
or as expressly permitted by law, or under terms agreed with the appropriate
reprographics rights organization. Enquiries concerning reproduction
outside the scope of the above should be sent to the Publications Department,
The British Academy, 10 Carlton House Terrace, London SW1Y 5AH

You must not circulate this book in any other binding or cover
and you must impose the same condition on any acquirer

British Library Cataloguing in Publication Data
Data available

Printed in Great Britain
on acid-free paper by
CPI Antony Rowe,
Chippenham, Wiltshire

ISBN 978–0–19–726461–4

CONTENTS

Acknowledgements	vi
Introduction	
1. Life and writings of Thomas Wylton	vii
2. Manuscript tradition and editorial principles	xii
2.1. Manuscripts	xii
2.2. Quality of the manuscripts and their relationships	xv
2.3. Criteria of the edition	xxxi
3. Senko's edition	xxxi
4. Presentation of the text	xxxvii
5. The main doctrinal points of Thomas Wylton's *Quaestio de anima intellectiva*	xxxix
5.1. The structure of Wylton's question	xl
5.2. The nature of the material intellect and the role of the agent intellect	xliv
5.3. The material intellect as the form of the human body	xlviii
5.4. The realist assumption in Wylton's interpretation	li
5.5. Averroes' view and the Catholic view	lv
5.6. Cognition of universals and cognition of singulars	lix
QUAESTIO DE ANIMA INTELLECTIVA	1
Index Auctorum	124
Index Nominum	126
Index Verborum Potiorum	127

ACKNOWLEDGEMENTS

We sincerely thank:

Professor Jenny Ashworth for her judicious and useful suggestions on the work;

Professor David d'Avray, London, for reading the first draft of our edition and his suggestions for the presentation of the apparatus;

the librarians of Balliol College, Oxford, for their unfailing support and facilitation of our work with the manuscripts in their care;

Professor Christopher Schabel, Nicosia, for letting us use his microfilm of the Pelplin manuscript;

Professor Jean-Baptiste Brenet, Paris, for giving us access to his then forthcoming article on John Jandun's use of Wylton's question (since published in *Freiburger Zeitschrift für Philosophie und Theologie*, 56.2 (2009), 309–40);

Professor William J. Courtenay, Madison, for giving us access to his then forthcoming article on MS Balliol 63 (since published in *Vivarium*, 47 (2009), 375–406);

the universities of Oxford and Copenhagen for providing stimulating and congenial working conditions.

Lauge O. Nielsen thanks the Danish Research Council for the Humanities for financial support in the initial stages of the work.

Lauge O. Nielsen, *University of Copenhagen*
Cecilia Trifogli, *University of Oxford*
Gail Trimble, *University of Oxford*

INTRODUCTION

1. Life and writings of Thomas Wylton

Thomas Wylton, an early fourteenth-century philosopher and theologian, was fellow of Merton College from about 1288 to 1301, and he taught as Master of Arts at Oxford until 1304. At this point he moved to Paris in order to study theology, and he incepted as Master of Theology in 1312. During the following ten years Wylton appears to have been teaching theology at Paris University. He was appointed chancellor of St Paul's Cathedral in London in 1320, although it is likely that he took up this position only in 1322. The position of chancellor was vacant in 1327, so Wylton must have died by that date.[1]

Our knowledge of Wylton's activity as Master of Arts in Oxford is strictly limited. There is little doubt, however, that he was in Oxford when he composed his two extant Aristotelian works: a question-style commentary on the *De anima* and a question-style commentary on the *Physics*.

The *De anima* commentary is transmitted in a single manuscript preserved in the library of Balliol College, Oxford.[2] This copy is very corrupt and incomplete. It stops abruptly in the course of question 42 of book 2, which discusses whether there are only five senses.[3] There are no explicit indications that this commentary also originally included questions on book 3. A first reading of the commentary suggests the influence of Thomas Aquinas on Wylton's interpretation of Aristotle's doctrine of the intellect.[4] Wylton's discussion of the relationship between the soul and its powers, however, shows realist assumptions which are typical of Wylton.[5] This commentary has not yet been studied in any detail.[6]

The *Physics* commentary contains a complete set of questions on the eight

---

[1] On Wylton's biography see especially A. B. Emden, *A Biographical Register of the University of Oxford to A.D. 1500*, 3 vols. (Oxford, 1957–9), iii. 2054–5. For a list of Wylton's works see R. Sharpe, *A Handlist of the Latin Writers of Great Britain and Ireland before 1540* (Turnhout, 1997), 691–3.

[2] Oxford, Balliol College, MS 91, fols. 247ra–277vb.

[3] The title of the question is 'Utrum sit ponere in animali alium sensum praeter quinque'. It stops at line 11 of fol. 277vb and the rest of the column is left blank.

[4] See especially bk. 1, q. 8, 'An intellectivae coniunctae corpori sit intelligere propria operatio vel sit totius coniuncti primo' (fol. 251rb, lin. 14 ab imo–^{va}, lin. 1 ab imo).

[5] See bk. 2, q. 8, 'Utrum potentia animae sit de essentia animae' (fols. 260rb, lin. 1–261vb, lin. 4 ab imo).

[6] A very short presentation of Wylton's view on the intellect and on intellectual knowledge in this commentary is given by Z. Kuksewicz, *De Siger de Brabant à Jacques de Plaisance: la théorie de*

books of Aristotle's *Physics*. It is preserved in four manuscripts.[7] Some questions from this commentary about motion, time, place, and the *incipit–desinit* problem have been edited over the last twenty years by C. Trifogli, who has also published studies of Wylton's physical theories. These have revealed both some fundamental aspects of Wylton's thought and his influence on some of his contemporaries. For example, they show Wylton's ontological realism. In his discussion of the ontological status of motion and time Wylton rejects Averroes' reductive view and supports a realist view according to which motion and time are two distinct successive things, not reducible to permanent things. In particular, he argues that it is necessary to posit motion as a successive thing inhering in the mobile substance during its change and distinct from the mobile substance itself and the formal determinations acquired and lost by it during a change.[8] Similarly, he thinks of time as a successive quantity inhering in motion and really distinct from motion, in no way dependent on the human soul.[9] Wylton's realist assumptions about motion and time are remarkably similar to those of Walter Burley, and it is very likely that Wylton was an actual source for Burley's views.[10] There is no doubt that Wylton's question on the *incipit–desinit* problem had a strong influence on Burley, for in the latter's famous treatise *De primo et ultimo instanti* there are several passages which can be found almost verbatim in the corresponding question in Wylton's *Physics* commentary.[11] We know that there was an institutional connection between Wylton and Burley, since Burley refers to Wylton as to his teacher.[12] With regard to the nature of place and the question of its

---

l'intellect chez les Averroïstes latins des XIIIe et XIVe siècles (Wrocław, Warsaw, and Cracow, 1968), 177–81.

[7] Cesena, Biblioteca Malatestiana, MS Plut. VIII sin. 2, fols. 4[r]–141[v]; Madrid, Biblioteca Nacional, MS 2015, fols. 1[r]–217[v]; Vatican City, Vatican Library, MS Vat. Lat. 4709, fols. 1[r]–143[r]; Erfurt, Stadtbibliothek, MS Ampl. Fol. 178, fols. 57[r]–73[v] (only bks. 7 and 8). C. Trifogli is preparing a critical edition of this work.

[8] The edition of Wylton's questions on the ontological status of motion is in C. Trifogli, 'Due questioni sul movimento nel commento alla *Fisica* di Thomas Wylton', *Medioevo*, 21 (1995), 31–73. For a study of Wylton's position see C. Trifogli, 'Thomas Wylton on Motion', *Archiv für Geschichte der Philosophie*, 77 (1995), 135–54.

[9] The edition of the relevant question on time is in C. Trifogli, 'Il problema dello statuto ontologico del tempo nelle *Quaestiones super Physicam* di Thomas Wylton e di Giovanni di Jandun', *Documenti e studi sulla tradizione filosofica medievale*, 1 (1990), 491–548.

[10] On Burley's views on motion and time see C. Trifogli, 'Burley on Motion and Time', forthcoming in the *Brill Companion to Walter Burley*.

[11] For the edition of Wylton's question and the textual parallelisms with Burley's *De primo et ultimo instanti* see C. Trifogli, 'Thomas Wylton's Question "An contingit dare ultimum rei permanentis in esse"', *Medieval Philosophy and Theology*, 4 (1994), 91–141.

[12] This reference to Wylton occurs in Burley's so-called *Tractatus primus*; see J. A. Weisheipl, 'Ockham and Some Mertonians', *Medieval Studies*, 31 (1969), 163–213 at 184–6. An edition of Burley's *Tractatus primus* is being prepared by E. D. Sylla.

immobility, Wylton adopts some of the salient points of Duns Scotus' understanding.[13]

We know more about Wylton's activity as Master of Theology at Paris. His major extant work from this period is a *Quodlibet*, discussed at Paris very probably during Advent 1315 (although Lent 1316 remains a possibility).[14] The majority of the questions in Wylton's *Quodlibet* are preserved in the form of a *reportatio* in a single manuscript, Vatican City, Vatican Library, MS Borgh. Lat. 36 (eighteen questions).[15] With a few exceptions, all these questions have been published but the editions are scattered among various publications.[16] The topics of these questions are very heterogeneous. Questions dealing with theological issues are predominant, but there are also questions in natural philosophy, metaphysics, and theory of knowledge. The theological problems addressed are the infinite power of God, the nature of the beatific vision, the distinction between the divine attributes, eternity of the world, and divine relations. The questions in natural philosophy discuss final causality, the instant of time, and the problem of indefinite dimensions. The metaphysical questions deal with the problem of the simultaneous existence of accidents of the same species in the same subject, and with the ontological status of number. The epistemological questions are about the knowledge of singulars and the common sensible. Five questions on the intension and remission of forms, which most probably belonged to the *Quodlibet* but are missing from the Vatican manuscript, have been discovered by S. D. Dumont in two other manuscripts.[17] Dumont is preparing an edition of these questions.

Studies devoted to Wylton's quodlibetal questions indicate that Wylton enjoyed a prominent career as a Master of Theology at Paris, engaging in disputes with the most important of his contemporaries over a number of controversial issues. For example, he debated with Peter Auriol on the nature of relations,[18] on the problem of the infinite power of God,[19] and on the nature of theology and

---

[13] For an edition of Wylton's question on the immobility of place and a study of its contents and of its relation to Scotus see C. Trifogli, 'Thomas Wylton on the Immobility of Place', *Recherches de théologie et philosophie médiévales*, 65 (1998), 1–39.

[14] On the evidence for dating Wylton's *Quodlibet* see the survey paper by C. Trifogli, 'The *Quodlibet* of Thomas Wylton', in C. Schabel (ed.), *Theological Quodlibeta in the Middle Ages: The Fourteenth Century* (Leiden and Boston, 2007), 231–66 at 234–5.

[15] On fols. 47ra–96va.

[16] For precise references see Trifogli, 'The *Quodlibet*', 237–66.

[17] See S. D. Dumont, 'New Questions by Thomas Wylton', *Documenti e studi sulla tradizione filosofica medievale*, 9 (1998), 341–81 at 346–7. The two manuscripts are Tortosa, Archivo Capitular de Tortosa, MS 88, and New Haven, Yale University Library, Beinecke General, MS 470. The Tortosa manuscript also contains Wylton's *Quaestio de anima intellectiva* and a number of other theological questions by Wylton. See below, pp. xiv–xv.

[18] See M. G. Henninger, 'Thomas Wylton's Theory of Relations', *Documenti e studi sulla tradizione filosofica medievale*, 1 (1990), 457–90.

[19] A. Maier, 'Das Lehrstück von den *vires infatigabiles* in der scholastischen Naturphilosophie',

virtue;[20] with William of Alnwick on the issue of the eternity of the world;[21] with Henry of Harclay on the infinite;[22] with the Carmelite Sibert of Beek on the nature of the beatific vision;[23] with Guy Terreni on the problem of final causality;[24] with Durand of St-Pourçain on the nature of intellection.[25]

Salient aspects of Wylton's thought also appear in his quodlibetal discussions. One of them is his strong realism in the understanding of relations. Wylton holds not only that a relation is a real thing distinct from the *relata*, but also that the extra-mental existence and the distinction of the *relata* are not necessary conditions for the extra-mental reality of a relation.[26] Another characteristic of Wylton's thought is that, following Scotus, Wylton supports the formal distinction and claims that this type of distinction holds between divine attributes.[27]

Wylton first became known to historians of medieval philosophy for being a prominent exponent of Parisian Averroism. In the *Quaestio de anima intellectiva* he defends Averroes' view on the unity of the intellect, and it is in this work that Wylton's Averroism is most apparent. Anneliese Maier was the first to call the attention of scholars to Wylton's *Quaestio*, in her paper 'Wilhelm von Alnwicks Bologneser Quaestionen gegen den Averroismus (1323)', first published in 1949.[28] On the basis of a marginal annotation, Maier was able to identify the Averroistic opinion on the intellect rejected by Alnwick in his questions disputed in Bologna in 1323 with that of Thomas Wylton in his *Quaestio de anima intellectiva*. The only witness of Wylton's *Quaestio* known to Maier was the fragmentary copy in Oxford, Balliol College, MS 63.[29] A complete copy was later discovered by

---

Archives internationales d'histoire des sciences, 5 (1952), 6–44 at 25–8; and ead., *Metaphysische Hintergründe der spätscholastischen Naturphilosophie* (Rome, 1955), 247–50.

[20] See L. O. Nielsen, 'The Debate between Peter Auriol and Thomas Wylton on Theology and Virtue', *Vivarium*, 38 (2000), 35–98.

[21] See A. Maier, 'Wilhelm von Alnwicks Bologneser Quaestionen gegen den Averroismus (1323)', in A. Maier, *Ausgehendes Mittelalter: Gesammelte Aufsätze zur Geistesgeschichte des 14. Jahrhunderts* 2 vols. (Rome, 1964–7), i. 1–40 at 23–6.

[22] A. Maier, 'Diskussionen über das aktuelle Unendliche in der ersten Hälfte des 14. Jahrhunderts', in Maier, *Ausgehendes Mittelalter*, i. 41–85 at 55–7.

[23] See L. O. Nielsen and C. Trifogli, 'Questions on the Beatific Vision by Thomas Wylton and Sibert de Beka', *Documenti e studi sulla tradizione filosofica medievale*, 17 (2006), 511–84.

[24] See C. Trifogli, 'Thomas Wylton on Final Causality', in A. Fidora and M. Lutz-Bachmann (eds.), *Erfahrung und Beweis: Die Wissenschaften von der Natur im 13. und 14. Jahrhundert* (Berlin, 2007), 249–64.

[25] See Dumont, 'New Questions', 367–73.

[26] See Henninger, 'Thomas Wylton's Theory', 468–90.

[27] See L. O. Nielsen, T. B. Noone, and C. Trifogli, 'Thomas Wylton's Question on the Formal Distinction as Applied to the Divine', *Documenti e studi sulla tradizione filosofica medievale*, 14 (2003), 327–88.

[28] In *Gregorianum*, 30 (1949), 265–308. All subsequent references to this paper are to the reprint in *Ausgehendes Mittelalter* (n. 21 above).

[29] Maier, 'Wilhelm von Alnwicks Bologneser Quaestionen', 15–19.

Władysław Senko in Pelplin, Seminarium Duchowne, MS 53/102. In 1964 Senko edited Wylton's *Quaestio* on the basis of the Oxford and Pelplin manuscripts.[30] More recently another complete copy was discovered by Girard J. Etzkorn and Robert Andrews in Tortosa, Cathedral Library, MS 88.[31] Wylton's authorship of the *Quaestio* is attested in the Oxford manuscript.[32] This manuscript contains only about a third of the text, but given the highly unitary character of the *Quaestio*, the evidence provided by it can be regarded as conclusive.

With regard to the dating of the question, a *terminus post quem* is established by Wylton's *Quodlibet*, which appears to have been completed around Advent 1315. In his question on the intellectual soul Wylton explicitly refers to an earlier question of his, entitled 'An possibile sit formare verbum de singulari materiali'. This question was included in Wylton's *Quodlibet* according to the table of contents as reconstructed by A. Maier.[33] A *terminus ante quem* is provided by John of Jandun's questions on the *De anima*, since in this work Jandun relies on and uses Wylton's *Quaestio* extensively.[34] Jandun's questions have been placed in the years between 1315 and 1318,[35] but recent research suggests that the work was completed a little later, in the period 1317–19.[36]

In the case of someone such as Guy Terreni it is clear that his question on the intellectual soul as the form of man was prompted by university debates on epistemology—debates in which Wylton and Auriol appear to have taken part.[37]

---

[30] W. Senko, 'Tomasza Wiltona "Quaestio disputata de anima intellectiva"', *Studia mediewistyczne*, 5 (1964), 3–190 at 75–116. See also id., 'Jean de Jandun et Thomas Wilton: contribution à l'établissement des sources des "Quaestiones super I–III De anima" de Jean de Jandun', *Bulletin de philosophie médiévale*, 5 (1963), 139–43; id., 'La quaestio disputata de anima intellectiva de Thomas Wilton dans le ms 53/102 de la bibliothèque du Grand Séminaire de Pelplin', *Miscellanea mediaevalia*, 2 (1963), 464–71; id., 'Les opinions de Thomas Wilton sur la nature de l'âme humaine face à la conception de l'âme d'Averroès', *Rivista di filosofia neoscolastica*, 56 (1964), 581–604.

[31] G. J. Etzkorn and R. Andrews, 'Tortosa Cathedral 88: A "Thomas Wylton" Manuscript and the Question on the Compatibility of Multiple Accidents in the Same Subject', *Mediaevalia philosophica Polonorum*, 32 (1994), 57–99 at 57–64.

[32] See below, p. xiii.

[33] See below, pp. 116–18, para. 197. This quodlibetal question is edited in Senko, 'Tomasza Wiltona Quaestio', 117–21. Cf. Trifogli, 'The *Quodlibet*', 256–7.

[34] See especially the excellent study by J.-B. Brenet, 'Jean de Jandun et la *Quaestio de anima intellectiva* de Thomas Wilton', *Freiburger Zeitschrift für Philosophie und Theologie*, 56.2 (2009), 309–40. Brenet has carefully collected all the passages in Jandun's questions where he uses, in most cases almost verbatim, Wylton's *Quaestio*. For some examples of this use, see also below, pp. xxii, xxvii, xxix–xxx.

[35] See L. Schmugge, *Johannes von Jandun (1285/89–1328): Untersuchungen zur Biographie und Sozialtheorie eines lateinischen Averroisten* (Stuttgart, 1966), 123–5.

[36] See J.-B. Brenet, *Transferts du sujet: la noétique d'Averroès selon Jean de Jandun* (Paris, 2003), 13, who in note 3 refers to the forthcoming edition of Kuksewicz, *De Siger de Brabant à Jacques de Plaisance*.

[37] See L. O. Nielsen and C. Trifogli, 'Guido Terreni and his Debate with Thomas Wylton', *Documenti e studi sulla tradizione filosofica medievale*, 20 (2009), 573–663.

Wylton's reference to his question on the intellectual cognition of singulars may be taken to imply that his question had its roots in similar circumstances.[38] At any rate, it must be admitted that we do not find any explicit references to the immediate occasion for Wylton's authoring of the question on the intellectual soul. It is probably warranted to link Wylton's strong defence of the rationality of Averroes' stance and his emphasis on the fact that the Catholic perception is simply a matter of faith with the passing of the constitution *Fidei catholicae* at the Council of Vienne in 1312.[39] At the Council it was established as a point of Christian doctrine that the intellectual soul as a substance is truly the form of the human body. Seen against this background, Wylton's question comes across as a highly sophisticated and multifaceted exposition of what is implied by this doctrinal decision. In this sense, Wylton's defence of Averroes and his exploration of the reasonableness of Church doctrine take on the guise of an exercise in theology, which is not surprising in view of Wylton's position in the university at the time.

2. Manuscript tradition and editorial principles

2.1. *Manuscripts*

Wylton's *Quaestio de anima intellectiva* is preserved in three manuscripts, two of which (P, T) give a complete copy of the text and one (O) only a fragment amounting to about the first third of the text (paras. 1–74):

O = Oxford, Balliol College, MS 63[40]
Parchment, fourteenth century (not long after 1330). 13¼ × 9¼ in. i + 171 fols., medieval foliation which uses 91 twice. Two columns (except fols. 67–85), with

---

[38] This does raise the question of why the question on the intellectual soul was not included in Wylton's *Quodlibet*. Perhaps the 'expanded' question list in BAV, MS Borgh. lat. 36 (fol. 46^{va-b}), was partly intended as an answer to this.

[39] See Henricus Denzinger (ed.), *Enchiridion symbolorum, definitionum et declarationum de rebus fidei et morum*, rev. A. Schönmetzer, 34th edn. (Rome, 1967), § 902, p. 284.

[40] Described by R. A. B. Mynors, *Catalogue of the Manuscripts of Balliol College Oxford* (Oxford, 1963), 43–9. Recent articles on this highly interesting manuscript and its contents are L. O. Nielsen, 'The Intelligibility of Faith and the Nature of Theology: Peter Auriol's Theological Programme', *Studia theologica*, 53 (1999), 26–39; id., 'Peter Auriol and Thomas Wylton on Theology and Virtue'; id., 'Peter Auriol's Way with Words: The Genesis of Peter Auriol's Commentaries on Peter Lombard's First and Fourth Books of the *Sentences*', in G. R. Evans (ed.), *Medieval Commentaries on Peter Lombard's* Sentences (Leiden, 2002), 149–219; and id., 'The *Quodlibet* of Peter Auriol', in Schabel (ed.), *Theological Quodlibeta in the Middle Ages*, 267–331. In an article entitled 'Balliol 63 and Parisian Theology around 1320' (*Vivarium*, 47 (2009), 375–406) William J. Courtenay succeeds in identifying several of the authors whose works are contained in this manuscript, and he concludes that the first half of the manuscript reflects discussions in the Parisian faculty of theology in the years 1318–22, which agrees well with the dating implied by Jandun's use of Wylton's text. In his article Courtenay also provides an exhaustive and analytic table of contents for the first half of the manuscript.

varying number of lines. No signatures, and very few catchwords. Many hands, all English, some very small and crabbed; space sometimes left for capitals, which have nowhere been filled in.

Contents: Peter Auriol, questions on *Sentences* 2 (fols. 1^r–17^v); five questions by Peter Auriol and one by Thomas Wylton (*Utrum habitus theologicus sit practicus vel speculativus*) (fols. 19^r–21^v); anonymous question on *Sentences* 1 (fol. 22^{r-v}); anonymous question (unfinished) (fol. 23^r); anonymous commentary on *Ecclesiastes* (fol. 23^{r-v}); Denis de Burgo, *Utrum finis per se sacrae scripturae in via sit amare deum* (fols. 24^r–26^r); Peter Auriol's conclusions regarding time (fol. 27^v); John of Bologna (de Lana), questions on the soul (fols. 28^r–51^v); anonymous short introduction to *Sentences* 1–2 (fol. 51^v); Thomas Wylton, *Quaestio de anima intellectiva* (fols. 52^r–53^r); Peter Auriol, excerpt from his commentary on *Sentences* 1 (fols. 54^v–56^v); Giles of Rome and others, *Recollectiones* on *Sentences* 2 (fols. 57^r–59^r); anonymous introduction to *Sentences* (fol. 59^{r-v}); anonymous questions (around 20) (fols. 60^r–66^r); anonymous questions on *Sentences* 1, dist. 1–3 (fols. 67^r–85^v); questions by Peter Auriol (fols. 86^r–87^v); Gerald, questions on the beginning of *Sentences* 3 (fols. 87^v–88^r); anonymous introduction to *Sentences* (fol. 88^v); two questions by Robert Beverley (fols. 89^r–99^v); anonymous quodlibetal questions (fols. 100^r–111^v); Robert Winchelse, disputed questions (fols. 112^r–131^v); Robert Winchelse, quodlibetal questions (fols. 132^r–143^v, 150^r–154^v); anonymous quodlibetal questions (fols. 144^r–149^v); Robert Winchelse, quodlibetal questions (fols. 155^r–161^v); Giles of Rome, *Quaestiones de cognitione angelorum* (fols. 162^r–169^v).

The fragment of Wylton's *Quaestio de anima intellectiva*. *Incipit*: 'An intellectivam esse formam corporis humani possit ratione necessaria probari et convinci evidenter' (fol. 52ra). *Explicit*: 'et hoc solo quando est denudatus ab omni potentia. Similiter 5' (fol. 53rb). The final part of fol. 53rb is left blank as well as fols. 53^v and 54^r. In the bottom margin of fol. 52^r the same hand as that of the main text writes: 'An intellectivam esse formam corporis possit ratione necessaria et evidenti convinci. Wyltona'. Marginal annotations and corrections by various hands.

P=Pelplin, Seminarium Duchowne, MS 53 (102)[41]
Parchment, first half of the fourteenth century. 320×230 mm. ii+230 fols. Two columns. Many hands. Written in a *littera textualis cursiva* of the fourteenth century.

Contents: Magisterial Act of the Paris Faculty of Theology (fols. 2^v–13^v); anonymous commentary on *Sentences* 1 (fols. 14^r–130^v); Francis Mayron, commentary on *Sentences* 1 (fols. 131^r–196^v); anonymous questions (fols. 197^r–200^v);

---

[41] Described by Senko, 'Tomasza Wiltona Quaestio', 68–71; id., 'La Quaestio disputata', 464–5.

anonymous fragment of *De vita Christiana* (fol. 201ʳ); John Baconthorp, questions from *Quodlibet* 3 (fols. 201ʳ–207ʳ); anonymous question *Utrum Deus sit virtutis infinitae in vigore* (fols. 209ʳ–213ʳ);[42] anonymous question *Utrum sint septem liberales artes* (fols. 213ᵛ–214ʳ); Giles of Rome, *De erroribus philosophorum* (fragment) (fols. 214ʳ–216ʳ); list of errors condemned by Robert Kilwardby (fol. 216ʳ); list of errors condemned by Étienne Tempier (fol. 216ʳ⁻ᵛ); Thomas Wylton, *Quaestio disputata de anima intellectiva* (fols. 217ᵛ–223ʳ); Durand of St-Pourçain, *Quodlibet* 3, quaestio 1 (fols. 225ʳ–230ᵛ).

Wylton's *Quaestio de anima intellectiva. Incipit*: 'An intellectivam esse formam humani corporis possit ratione necessaria et evidenti convinci' (fol. 217ᵛ). *Explicit*: 'nihil est aeternum ex parte post quin sit aeternum ex parte ante et econverso' (fol. 223ʳ). Marginal corrections by various hands.

T = Tortosa, Cathedral Library, MS 88[43]
Parchment, mid fourteenth century. 180 × 255 mm. 156 fols. Two columns. Probably a French hand. The codex is made up of two manuscripts and so now has two parts: (i) fols. 1ʳ–120ᵛ and (ii) fols. 121ʳ–156ᵛ.

Contents: The first part contains twenty-eight theological questions, which are all anonymous. Two of these are known to be by Henry of Harclay (fols. 74ᵛᵃ–94ᵛᵃ).[44] Many others have been proved to be by Thomas Wylton. These are the following (according to the numbering in Etzkorn and Andrews's description of T):[45]

1. *Utrum cum unitate specifica speciei athomae alicuius qualitatis stet distinctio graduum infra illam naturam sic specifice unam* (fol. 1ʳᵃ⁻ᵛᵃ)
2. *Utrum eadem qualitas numero suscipiat magis et minus vel quilibet gradus novus constituat unum individuum* (fol. 1ᵛᵃ–3ᵛᵃ)
3. *Utrum minus calidum opponatur magis calido* (fols. 3ᵛᵃ–4ʳᵇ)
4. *Utrum intensio fiat in huiusmodi formis per additionem* (fol. 4ʳᵇ⁻ᵛᵇ)
5. *Utrum gradus isti sint simpliciter indivisibiles* (fols. 4ᵛᵇ–5ʳᵇ)
6. *Utrum essentia divina sit perfectio infinita intensive* (fols. 5ʳᵇ–15ᵛᵃ)
7. *Utrum ista stent simul quod aliquid sit obiectum per se et primum et adaequatum alicuius potentiae et cum hoc stet quod aliquid cognoscatur ab illa potentia quod non continetur per se sub illo* (fols. 15ᵛᵃ–16ʳᵇ)

[42] This question has been ascribed to John of Jandun and edited by Z. Kuksewicz in Z. Kuksewicz, 'Johannis de Janduno *De infinitate vigoris Dei*: édition critique', *Studia mediewistyczne*, 24 (1985), 77–152.
[43] Described by Etzkorn and Andrews, 'Tortosa Cathedral 88', 58–62.
[44] These are questions 22 and 23 in Etzkorn and Andrews's list. They are now edited (with an English translation) in Henry of Harclay, *Ordinary Questions*, ed. by Mark G. Henninger, English translation by Raymond Edwards and Mark G. Henninger, 2 vols. (Oxford, 2008): q. xiii (i. 514–93); q. xxix (ii. 1008–97).
[45] On Wylton's authorship see Etzkorn and Andrews, 'Tortosa Cathedral 88', 58–61, and Dumont, 'New Questions', 357–81.

8. *Utrum ubicumque excessus unius arguit excessum alterius in duplo et sic ulterius secundum proportionem ex excessu unius in infinitum sequatur alterius in infinitum* (fols. 16rb–17rb)
12. *Utrum intellectus possit formare aliud verbum de singulari a verbo sui universalis vel utrum intellectus noster possit de duobus singularibus formare duo verba* (fols. 23ra–24rb)
13. *Utrum possit convinci evidenti ratione animam intellectivam esse formam corporis* (fols. 24va–36rb)
14. *Utrum in una proprietate relativa constitutiva divinae personae sint aliquae realitates quae non omnibus modis sint eaedem ex natura rei* (fols. 36rb–39va)
15. *Utrum propter cognitionem creaturarum Dei perfectam et distinctam productionem earum necesse sit ponere in Deo rationes distinctas ideales correspondentes creaturis cognitis* (fols. 39va–46ra)[46]
17. *Utrum possint simul esse plures intellectiones in intellectu* (fols. 48rb–52rb)
18. *Utrum plura accidentia eiusdem speciei possint simul esse in eodem subiecto* (fols. 52rb–59ra)
21. *Utrum in lumine naturali ex rebus sensibilibus possimus scientifice aliqua investigare de Deo* (fols. 62vb–74va)
24. *Utrum ista stent simul quod mundus sit aeternaliter a Deo productus* (fols. 94va–111va)
26. *Utrum praedestinatus possit damnari* (fols. 113ra–117ra)

The second part of the manuscript contains an incomplete *tabula Scoti* (it ends in the middle of the letter 'S'), i.e. an index by James of Ascoli of Scotus' *Ordinatio*, *Quodlibet*, *Collationes*, and *Questions* on the *Metaphysics* (fols. 121^r–156^v). In addition to the *tabula Scoti*, James includes at least five references to his own *Quaestiones*.

Wylton's *Quaestio de anima intellectiva* is at fols. 24^v–36^r. *Incipit*: 'Utrum possit convinci evidenti ratione animam intellectivam esse formam corporis' (fol. 24^v). *Explicit*: 'nihil est aeternum ex parte post quin sit ex parte ante et econverso etc.' Marginal annotations and corrections by various hands.

2.2. *Quality of the manuscripts and their relationships*

Although each of the three manuscripts has a good number of errors, it has always been possible to correct the errors of a manuscript either with the reading of another manuscript or (less frequently) by minor and straightforward emendations, and to give an intelligible text throughout.

We classify the types of variant which emerge in the collation into four general categories: omissions, additions, substitutions, and inversions. Inversions, understood broadly as variants involving word order, are frequent in our textual

---

[46] Dumont has pointed out that this question extends only to fol. 43vb and that it is followed by an incomplete discussion by Wylton on relations (*Replicationes quaedam quod non quaelibet relatio in actu requirat terminum in actu*) at fols. 43vb–46ra. See Dumout, 'New Questions', 362–4.

tradition—there are around 200 cases. They all, however, seem to us acceptable readings rather than errors, and so they are of no help in establishing the relative quality of the three manuscripts and their relationships. Accordingly, in the following discussion we leave inversions aside and concentrate on the other three types of variant. For each of these we shall distinguish variants from errors, where variants are understood as variations from our edition of the text rather than from a provisional text, and so already reflect our editorial choices.

Omissions

Following a common practice, we divide omissions into long omissions (omissions of three or more words) and simple omissions (omissions of one or two words) and further classify long omissions into pure (i.e. unconditioned) omissions and homoeoteleuta. From the qualitative point of view, we classify an omission as an error if it results in a corruption of the sense of the passage or at least makes the passage read much less smoothly or makes it somewhat incomplete.

We first consider omissions which are errors. Of the two complete copies of the text, T is considerably more faulty than P. T has 14 errors of long omission, of which 7 are homoeoteleuta (paras. 23, 70, 78, 107, 125, 168, 208) and 7 pure (paras. 8, 69, 78, 120, 137, 145, 161) against the 7 of P, of which 4 are homoeoteleuta (paras. 23, 124, 145, 183) and 3 pure (paras. 42, 113, 125). The erroneous long omissions of T are mainly concentrated in the second part of the text (paras. 75–208), whereas in the first part (paras. 1–74) the three manuscripts have essentially the same value: O has 3 errors of long omission, which are all homoeoteleuta (paras. 60, 70), P has 2 (1 homoeoteleuton and 1 pure), and T has 4 (2 homoeoteleuta and 2 pure). As to simple omissions, there is no significant quantitative (or qualitative) difference between the manuscripts: P and T have both around 60 errors of simple omission and O around 20 (in a third of the total text).

As to the relationship between the three manuscripts, the test of common errors of (long) omission is not of great help in our case. The only long omission common to two manuscripts is a homoeoteleuton of P and T (para. 23), and so it could well have occurred independently. Some slight evidence of a closer connection between O and P is offered by the study of simple omissions. Overall there are 9 simple omissions common to OP, 6 to OT, and 2 to PT. While the 6 simple omissions common to OT are all variants, 3 of the 9 common to OP are significant errors in our judgement: the omission of *visus* in para. 27, that of *caelo* in para. 49, and that of *generabilis nec* in para. 57.

We now consider pure long omissions that are acceptable readings, i.e. variants rather than errors. What is striking here is the comparatively high number of omissions of this kind in T: in the first part of the text T has 11 (paras. 10, 20, 23, 27, 40, 45, 48, 64, 67, 70), O has 3 (paras. 12, 21, 64), and P has 1 (para. 6);

in the second part T has 11 (paras. 80, 88, 91, 92, 95, 105, 149, 177, 179, 197, 207) and P has none. So, comparing the two complete copies, T has a total of 22 variants of pure long omission and P only 1. This high number of cases shows that T has a tendency to shorten the text. The alternative explanation of these cases as expansions in the other witnesses (OP in the first part of the text and P in the second part) is not plausible, as the examples below will show. As to the typology of the abbreviations of T, we can distinguish three main types:

(1) Some of them occur in quotations from or references to passages from Aristotle and Averroes. Here are two examples (the omissions of T are in italics):

Para. 40: Sed in primo instanti productionis hominis intellectus materialis nobis coniungitur ut forma et perfectio nostra in actu, ut patet per Commentatorem, 1 commento 3 De anima, *qui dicit nos per illum intellectum ab aliis speciebus distingui.*

Here T gives the reference to a passage in Averroes' commentary but omits the report of the relevant claim of Averroes in that passage. Note that this claim of Averroes' had already been presented earlier in the text (para. 14), and at that point T did not shorten the text.

Para. 88: Primum etiam patet ex illo capitulo 3 De anima 'Quoniam aliud est magnitudo *et magnitudinis esse*'

Here T gives a shorter quotation of the initial passage of the chapter of the *De anima*. The same shorter quotation is found in para. 95. A similar case of shorter quotation is in para. 177.

(2) Other abbreviations occur in (2.1) the references to topics under discussion; (2.2) comments on the value or nature of an argument; (2.3) mention of an opinion.

Example of 2.1:

Para. 48: Et ideo non sequitur quod intellectus agens sit perfectio informans intellectum materialem. Quo modo autem sit forma et perfectio *intellectus materialis et non solum agens respectu eius, et etiam forma informans eum* dicetur inferius in articulo de intellectu adepto.

A similar abbreviation is found in para. 64.

Example of 2.2:

Para. 23: Ad tertiam auctoritatem, *quae plus inter alias ponderatur*, cum dicit . . .

Similar abbreviations occur in paras. 149, 179, 197.

Example of 2.3:

Para. 67: Est etiam intelligendum quod non est sua intentio quod intellectus noster materialis coniunctus ... intelligat substantias separatas solum ut relucent in phantasmatibus et in intellectis speculativis, *ut quidam dicunt*, sed ...

(3) Other abbreviations occur inside an argument as omission of some explanatory part of it. Here are the most extensive abbreviations of this type:

Para. 10: Hanc autem passionem intellectus vocat Commentator, 2 De anima, commento 57, 'evasionem', et hoc sive procedat intellectus ab ignorantia in scientiam, sive ab habitu in actum secundum. *Utroque modo patitur intellectus, pro quanto recipit passive suam perfectionem*, sed neutro modo patitur passione qua aliqua eius perfectio ab ipso abiciatur.

Para. 27: Et esset valde simile, si diaphanum esset potentia cognoscitiva colorum, et cum hoc intellectus agens esset forma informans intellectum materialem sicut lumen informat diaphanum, et simul cum his colores non haberent actum in se per quem immutant visum, *sicut nec phantasmata per quem immutant intellectum*.

Para. 45: ... ita nec intellectus materialis intelligit res materiales nisi praesente lumine intellectus agentis, *quod lumen est ipse intellectus agens*.

Para. 91: Ergo species quam recipit erit singularis et in essendo et in repraesentando *ex eadem causa qua in sensu*.

Para. 92: Igitur per eandem rationem ab illis duabus speciebus abstractis contingit abstrahere aliam speciem, *quae per eandem rationem esset alia et alia, abstracta per intellectum tuum et meum*.

Para. 207: Exemplum: ad hoc quod ignis sit calefaciens aquam in actu, multa praesupponuntur, ... quorum nullum est de intellectu essentiali ignis calefacientis in quantum huiusmodi, nec aquae in quantum est sub calefieri, *necessario tamen requiruntur non tamquam consequentia actionem istam, sed aliquo ordine praecedentia*.

Similar but less extensive abbreviations occur in paras. 20, 70, 80.

Another omission of T, which is formally a homoeoteleuton, may also be regarded as an abbreviation of the third type distinguished above. It occurs in the reply to an objection to the claim that the agent and the corresponding patient are in the same genus. The objection is based on the counter-example of the first mover, God, and the first mobile. They belong neither to the same physical genus nor to the same logical genus (para. 52). The reply is the following:

Para. 53: Dicendum quod non oportet agens secundum suam substantiam esse in eodem genere cum patiente nec physico nec logico, ut probat ista ratio, sed sufficit quod sit in eodem genere analogo. *Unde licet Deus et homo non sint in aliquo uno genere, nec logico nec physico, sunt tamen in uno genere analogo*, puta entis.

Here T cuts the sentence that explains how the reply applies to the counter-example.

Abbreviations of the third type are found almost exclusively in T. The only real exception is the pure omission in P of the explanatory remark *licet aliter et aliter* in para. 6.

We shall see later that some of the substitutions of T are also abbreviations.

We consider it rather unlikely that Wylton is the author of these abbreviations and have adopted the fuller version of the text.[47]

In conclusion, the study of omissions reveals that (1) P is more correct than T; (2) there is some slight evidence of a couple OP; (3) T has the tendency to shorten the text, especially in the first part, and so is less reliable.

Additions

As in the case of omissions, we divide additions into long (three or more words) and short (one or two words), and further distinguish long additions as pure or conditioned, i.e. dittographies.

In our tradition we have only one dittography, in O, of three words (para. 23). A case of quasi-dittography in O will be discussed in the section on substitutions. Pure long additions are relatively more frequent: P has 2, of which 1 is isolated (para. 111) and 1 is replicated in O (para. 19); T has 8, which are all isolated (paras. 15, 20, 22, 31, 70, 108, 111, 125); and O has 1, which is shared with P. So there are in total 10 pure long additions in our tradition and we have classified 6 of them as errors and 4 as variants. In what follows we first discuss the 6 cases that we regard as errors and then the 4 that we regard as variants.

The isolated pure addition of P is in fact an addition supplied in the margin by the scribe of P. The relevant passage is the following:

> Para. 111: Nec aliqua alia substantia aeterna est causa huiusmodi copulationis, quoniam haec copulatio est nova, et ab aeterno et **immutabilis** *a tali autem substantia immutabili* non procedit actus novus secundum eum.

We have printed in italics the marginal addition of P and in bold the erroneous reading *immutabilis* of P, from which the marginal addition seems to originate. The original text of P does not make grammatical sense and the scribe realized this. In fact, the marginal addition restores grammar. The further problem is that the scribe did not realize that neither the original text nor the text with the addition makes conceptual sense since in both versions the incompatible properties of being *nova*, on the one hand, and *ab aeterno* and *immutabilis*, on the other, are ascribed to the *copulatio*. The scribe missed the simple point that the original text of P needs only a very minor emendation of *immutabilis* to *immutabili*, and he wrongly surmised that something had been omitted. This case reveals the poor understanding

---

[47] One might consider the possibility that T is a very defective copy of the text in a later revision and that this revision was to all appearances slight as compared with OP.

of the scribe of P, which is also confirmed by a study of the erroneous substitutions in P, as we shall see below.

Two of the pure additions of T seem to be straightforward cases of an erroneous reading in a model of T transmitted in addition to the correct reading in T. These are:

> Para. 15: intentiones *accidentales sive intentiones* intelligibiles
>
> Para. 70: Sciendum quod *modus ultimus et* intentio ultima Commentatoris

In the first case the erroneous reading is *intentiones accidentales* and in the second it is *modus ultimus*. Both erroneous readings are conditioned by the context in which they occur.

The other two pure additions of T are quite straightforward cases of quasi-repetition:

> Para. 31: quod in intellectu agente hoc est proprium, ut *in intellectu agente quod* scientia in actu sit eadem cum scito
>
> Para. 111: Substantiae autem aeternae sunt immutabiles *et aeternae immutabiles* et per se et per accidens

One major addition of T, however, is much more relevant. It occurs in the section of Wylton's question devoted to the arguments against Averroes' claim of the unity of the material intellect in all men (paras. 96–111). Wylton first presents the arguments that Averroes himself raised against his own position (paras. 96–103), then the arguments of Albert the Great (paras. 104–7), and finally the arguments of some philosophers quoted anonymously (paras. 108–11). For the sake of brevity they will be called 'anonymous arguments'. While the text of P contains four anonymous arguments, the text of T contains five: the additional argument of T appears between the first and second arguments in the text of P and is here printed in italics:

> Paras. 108–9: Iterum arguunt alii dicentes hoc esse ficticium quod aliquid per se subsistens et separatum sit forma et perfectio alicuius quod est per se unum, quia per se unum fit ex duobus quia hoc actu, hoc potentia, ex 7 et 8 *Metaphysicae*.
>
> *Praeterea, unumquodque movens determinat sibi certam proportionem mobilis. Unde si essent plures stellae, non moverent nisi cum fatigatione. Intellectus vero determinat sibi certum numerum corporum.*
>
> Praeterea, ficticium videtur esse quod aliquid unum per se subsistens copuletur tot corporibus loco et tempore distantibus et distinctis.

The additional argument of T, unlike the other anonymous arguments, is not very clear. We have not identified the adversaries of Averroes who advanced these arguments and so we cannot check the exact nature of the additional argument of T. It seems, however, that the argument as reported in T is incomplete. In our interpretation, the original argument actually contained two arguments. The first argument applies to the intelligences as movers and to the stars as moved. The conclusion of this argument is not spelt out but only implied in T—that is, there cannot be more stars than there actually are. The second argument is the parallel argument as applied to the lowest intelligence as the mover of the human bodies. Only the first premiss of this argument is stated in T (*intellectus vero determinat sibi certum numerum corporum*), and the parallel conditional and the conclusion are left out—i.e. therefore, if there were more humans, then the intelligence would be worn out by all these humans. Consequently, there cannot be more human bodies than what is determined by the lowest intelligence, which is absurd. The obscurity of this argument is a slight indication that it is spurious. But there are two more compelling reasons for rejecting this argument, one internal and the other external.

The internal reason is that the section of the text which is devoted to replying to the arguments against Averroes' position (paras. 112–34), and which follows immediately after the presentation of the arguments, provides replies to each of the arguments in the preceding section with the sole exception of the additional argument found in T. So the additional argument of T is the only argument of the series left without a reply. Although it is not at all unusual in medieval questions for some arguments to be left unanswered, so that the lack of a reply to an argument is in general not a sufficient reason for rejecting an argument as spurious, in this case there is additional evidence for disregarding this particular argument. Later in the question Wylton returns to the opinion which the anonymous arguments against Averroes belong to, and in referring to the article of the unity of the intellect he remarks:

> Para. 144: Contra istum articulum etiam adducunt multas rationes, quarum efficaciores sunt superius positae et solutae.

Here Wylton explicitly states that he has answered all the arguments of this opinion which he presented earlier. So if the additional argument of T had been included among those presented by Wylton, it should have received a reply, which is not the case. On the other hand, Wylton's remark does not exclude the possibility that the additional argument of T could in fact have been an argument presented by this group of Averroes' opponents, although clearly not one of the more effective. Accordingly, one can speculate that T or most probably its model had access to the arguments of the opinion but not precise indications about which of these arguments should be included. Furthermore, in support of the reliability of the criterion of the 'missing reply' one must notice that in Wylton's question all arguments (not only those of the series to which the additional argument of T belongs) which need a reply are in fact answered. Accordingly, Wylton's question is complete in its argument–reply pairings and the additional argument of T is the only exception. The alternative explanation, that the other manuscript P is responsible for the omission of both the argument and its reply, is highly implausible, and, as we shall see, it is not supported by external evidence.

The external evidence comes from the question about the unity of the intellect in John of Jandun's *Questions* on Aristotle's *De anima*, book 3 (q. 7: *Utrum intellectus sit unus numero in omnibus hominibus*).[48] In q. 7 Jandun copies, in many cases almost verbatim, long passages of Wylton's question.[49] In particular, Jandun devotes a section of his question to the arguments against the position of Averroes. This section is essentially a copy of the corresponding section in Wylton, containing the arguments against Averroes by Averroes himself, those of Albert, and the anonymous arguments. But the additional anonymous argument of T is not present in Jandun, where the passage that is parallel to Wylton's text quoted above, and which contains the first two anonymous arguments, is as follows:

> Item, aliqui obloquuntur contra Commentatorem dicentes hoc esse ficticium quod aliquid per se subsistens et separatum sit forma et perfectio alicuius quod est unum per se. Nam ex aliquibus duobus fit unum per se eo quod unum illorum est actus et reliquum potentia, ut patet in 2 huius et 8 *Metaphysicae*; quare etc.
>
> Praeterea, videtur esse ficticium quod aliquid per se subsistens copuletur tot corporibus loco et tempore distantibus et distinctis. (ed. cit., col. 261)

This is a very faithful copy of the passage in Wylton—it could in fact be used as another witness of Wylton's text—and this does not support including the additional argument of T.

Moreover, some of the short additions of T which we have regarded as erroneous reveal the weakness of this witness. The isolated additions of *duae* after *substantiae* in para. 49 and of *intellectus* after *quando* in para. 73 are perfectly in order from the grammatical and conceptual points of view, and as a matter of fact they clarify the passages in which they occur. The problem, however, is that these passages are quotations from Averroes and the additions of T are not found in the text of Averroes himself. So in these two cases T is less reliable than OP in the quotations from a historical source.

A similar and more deceptive case of addition is in the reference to Aristotle's *Physics* at the end of the following passage:

> Para. 151: materia hominis et intellectiva, quae fuit eius forma, manent homine corrupto. Illa unio . . . non manet. Ergo haec unio est res alia a principiis hominis. Sic arguit Philosophus, 1 *Physicorum*, ad probandum quod privatio sit aliud a materia *et forma*.

---

[48] All references to Jandun's *Questions* on *De anima* are to the 1587 Venice edition (repr. Frankfurt a.M., 1966).

[49] On the extent of the influence of Wylton's question on Jandun's *Questions* on *De anima* see Brenet, 'Jean de Jandun'.

The addition of *et forma* looks very plausible because it makes the argument of Aristotle in *Physics* 1 about the principles of change (matter, form, and privation) a complete parallel to the argument about the principles of man (matter of man, intellectual soul, i.e. the form of man, and union between the two), but it is in fact a mistake. The problem is that while it is true that Aristotle applies the argument from 'separation in being' (*x* persists and *y* does not; therefore *x* is not the same thing as *y*) to the case of matter and privation (matter, e.g. man, persists in a change, and privation, e.g. non-musical, does not), he does not and cannot apply the argument to the case of privation and form because the form in Aristotle's sense in *Physics* 1, unlike the intellectual soul of the Christian tradition, does not persist in a change involving that form.

Another deceptive addition of T is that of *non* in para. 18 ('album *non* est nigrum'), which completely spoils the sense of the argument.[50]

In conclusion, the study of additions confirms that T is less reliable than the other two witnesses.

Let us now turn to the four cases of pure additions that we have relegated to the critical apparatus, although we do not think that they originate from marginal glosses or that they are obviously mistaken. One is the addition in OP of *ex parte intelligentis* in para. 19. This addition seems to us conceptually redundant. Another is the addition in T of *nisi quo primo* in para. 125, which does not seem to fit in the context of the discussion. Finally, there are two much more relevant additions in T. They both occur in the same context, namely Wylton's defence of the claim that the material intellect is not a pure potency but is a kind of act, although it is initially without any concept and in potency to all of them. In the passage with the first addition Wylton illustrates the compatibility of the properties of being an act and in potency with example(s):

> Para. 20: ... quod intellectus materialis in se sit actus, licet sit in potentia ad intentiones intelligibiles, sicut superficies in se est actus, licet sit in potentia ad colores, *et sicut potentia visiva in se est quidam actus, licet sit in potentia ad actum visionis*.

In the passage with the second addition Wylton remarks that Averroes' definition of the material intellect as in potency to the *intentiones* of all material things is a natural definition rather than a definition in an absolute sense, and illustrates this point with example(s) of natural definition:

> Para. 22: Iuxta quod intelligendum quod haec definitio intellectus materialis est definitio naturalis quae datur per notiora nobis, non simpliciter, cuiusmodi definitio est haec 'natura est principium motus' etc. *et illa 'anima est actus corporis organici'* etc.

Both passages occur in the first part of the text where there are three witnesses,

---
[50] For an explanation of the argument see below, p. xlv.

and the two major additions of T in italics are absent from the other two manuscripts OP. The two cases are exactly parallel. In both instances OP give only one example to illustrate the relevant claim: that of the surface in the first case and the definition of nature in the second. In both cases T adds another: the example of the visual power in the first case and that of the definition of the soul in the second. Furthermore, the two additional examples are also very similar from the conceptual point of view. While the examples common to all three manuscripts are taken from doctrinal contexts radically distinct from that of the claim they are supposed to illustrate, the two additional examples are taken from the same doctrinal context and are as a result more relevant to the discussion: in the first case, while the intellect and a surface have little in common, the intellect and the visual power are both cognitive powers; similarly, in the second case, motion, the thing defined in the definition of the first example, has nothing in common with the intellect, whereas the thing defined in the second example, viz. the soul, contains the intellect as one of its powers. So both additional examples of T seem to serve the purpose of giving more conceptual unity to the discussion and making it more accessible. They are obvious improvements on the text and could be the work of Wylton himself or his secretary. Since they are only in T, however, we have chosen to put them in the apparatus.

Substitutions

We divide variants consisting of substitutions into conditioned and pure substitutions.[51] A conditioned substitution is replacement of some word with a word different from it but palaeographically similar—that is, a substitution that can be explained on palaeographical grounds as the result of a copyist's misreading of his model or by a slip of his pen (examples: natura/materia, intellectiva/intelligentia, ergo/igitur, ista/illa, alia/aliqua, huiusmodi/huius, dicitur/dicatur/dicetur/dicuntur). A pure substitution in its simplest form is replacement of some word with a different word that is not palaeographically similar (corpus/materia, opinio/fides, substantia/intelligentia). We have also classified as pure substitutions all the cases of complex substitutions involving more than one word and typically an entire phrase or clause in a sentence.

As is usual in textual traditions of our kind, conditioned substitutions are very numerous and more frequent than pure substitutions: in this text there are around 700 conditioned and 300 pure substitutions.

Looking at the substitutions that are errors and focusing on the first part of the text (where all three manuscripts are available), the fragmentary copy O turns out to be the most correct of the three witnesses. O has a total of around 45 errors

---

[51] Following A. G. Judy in his edition of Robert Kilwardby's *De ortu scientiarum* (Oxford, 1976), p. xxxiii.

by substitution, T around 70, and P around 85. There is, however, one major (conditioned) error of substitution in O, which has no analogue in the other two witnesses. This occurs in the following difficult passage:

> Para. 54: (1) Unde ad eundem pertinet determinare *de corpore mobili in quantum mobile et de primo movente, qui Deus est. Et eodem modo ad eundem pertinet determinare de intellectu possibili in quantum receptivus est huiusmodi actus naturalis qui est intelligere, et de intellectu agente in quantum est agens et movens talem potentiam ad actum*, (2) ita quod sicut in corporalibus ad eundem pertinet determinare *de motu* et etiam de Deo in quantum primum movens*, ita ad eundem pertinet determinare de intellectu materiali, qui est quoddam mobile intellectualiter, et de intellectu agente, non quidem secundum suam quidditatem, sed secundum quod est quoddam principium reductivum talis potentiae ad actum.
>
> * *motu*] fortasse *mobili* scribendum

This is the version of the passage transmitted with some variants (negligible for our discussion) by P and T and which we have accepted. We think, however, that this passage is the most unsatisfactory of the whole question because part (2), although different in its linguistic formulation from part (1), is from the conceptual point of view largely a repetition of part (1). The only relevant conceptual difference between the two parts is in the description of the material/possible intellect: as receptive of the act of understanding in part (1) and as some kind of mobile in part (2). The most plausible way to make sense of the passage is to connect the two descriptions: being receptive of the act of understanding is what makes the possible intellect a kind of mobile and therefore makes the relation between the possible intellect and the agent intellect a case of the relation between a mover and the thing moved by it, analogous to the relation between the first mover, i.e. God, and the bodies moved by it. This connection, however, is not made clear in the actual version of the passage.

In O the portion of part (2) starting with *de motu* until the end of part (2) is replaced with the portion of part (1) starting with *de corpore mobili* until the end of part (1) (the two portions involved are in italics above). That is, approximately, the resulting passage in O is a dittography of part (1) without part (2). Both the dittography of the portion of part (1) and the omission of the portion of part (2) are by homoeoteleuton. Adding to these two cases 3 omissions by homoeoteleuton, it turns out that O has a total of 5 homoeoteleuta, whereas (in the initial part of the question where there are three witnesses) P has only 1 homoeoteleuton and T has 2. Accordingly, of the three witnesses O is the most correct in respect of errors of substitution but the most erroneous in respect of homoeoteleuta.

As to the two complete copies P and T, from the quantitative point of view P has the highest number of errors by substitution: P around 270 as against around 200 in T. The great majority of the erroneous substitutions of P, however, are conditioned (around 240 out of 270). Furthermore, P has the smallest number of pure errors of substitution: around 30 against around 40 in T. Accordingly, with its high number of conditioned errors and small number of pure errors P can be regarded as a bad representative of a very correct tradition and better than that to which T belongs. From the practical point of view, it would be easier to reconstruct a correct text having P rather than T as the unique witness. A characteristic conditioned error of P is the misreading of *sicut*: there are 28 cases in which instead of the correct reading P has the erroneous, palaeographically conditioned readings *sed* (24 cases), *sic* (3 cases), and *aliud* (1 case). This confirms the carelessness of the scribe of P, which we pointed out in the discussion of additions. In the case of the characteristic error with *sicut*, it must certainly have been the case that the model of P wrote the word in an unintelligible way, but it is indicative of the scribe's lack of understanding that he fails to guess the correct reading in such a high number of occurrences. We may also add that in a couple of cases the scribe of P deliberately replaces the correct reading with a wrong one (the 'correction' of *mixtum* to *immixtum* in para. 11 and that of *sicut* to *sed* in para. 60).

The test of common errors of substitution yields some slight evidence of a closer relationship between O and P than between any other pair of witnesses, adding to the evidence provided by the errors of omission. There are 6 errors of substitution common to OP (paras. 3, 16, 43, 49, 56, 58) against the 3 common to PT (paras. 57, 62, 73) and 1 common to OT (para. 11). While all the errors of PT and OT are very trivial conditioned errors and so of no weight in establishing relationships, two of the OP errors are pure and so have some weight. The first of these two occurs in the following passage:

> Para. 49: . . . intelligentia movens est anima et forma caeli, cum tamen illa intelligentia solum uniatur *caelo* ut movens *caelum* appropriatum.

OP have *saltem* instead of *caelum*. This substitution, which does not seem immediately explicable on palaeographical grounds, gives a worse sense to the passage. OP also omit *caelo* earlier in the passage, and we considered this as a relevant common error of omission.

The second error occurs in the quotation of a proposition from Averroes' commentary on *De anima* 3, t. c. 4.[52] The proposition is stated twice in t. c. 4 in slightly different formulations:

> (1) Omne recipiens aliquid necesse est ut *sit denudatum* a natura recepti (385. 67–8)
>
> (2) Recipiens debet *esse denudatum* a natura recepti (386. 93)

---

[52] All references to Averroes' Long Commentary on *De anima* are to the edition of F. Stuart Crawford in the Corpus Commentariorum Averrois in Aristotelem, 6/1 (Cambridge, Mass., 1953).

The relevant phrase here is the construction with the past participle *denudatum*, which is preserved in T but changed to the present infinitive *denudari* in OP:

Para. 58: omne recipiens oportet *esse denudatum/denudari* a natura recepti

The reading *denudari* deviates from the two formulations in Averroes, makes worse sense, and is not straightforwardly conditioned.

We now turn to some relevant cases of pure (isolated) variants of T. In the study of the omissions we pointed out that most of the long omissions of T are abbreviations rather than errors. Furthermore, a significant number of the major substitutions of T are also abbreviations. We list these cases here and then add some comments:

(1) Para. 23: Dicit igitur contra opinionem Empedoclis *quod intellectus 'non est aliquod entium', scilicet aliorum a se, 'antequam intelligat', id est antequam receperit intentionem obiecti, per quam assimilatur obiecto. Tunc enim fit omnia entia, puta intentionaliter*. Unde Philosophus dicit in 3 *De anima* quod anima est quodam modo omnia, quod intelligendum est intentionaliter, non realiter, ut posuit Empedocles. *Hanc puto esse intentionem Commentatoris* de intellectu materiali.

T: Dicit igitur contra opinionem Empedoclis *illa verba*. Unde in 3 *De anima* dicit Philosophus quod anima est quodam modo omnia, quod intelligendum est intentionaliter, non realiter, ut posuit Empedocles. *Hic** de intellectu materiali.

   * *Hic*] fortasse *Haec* legendum

(2) Para. 27: *Cuius contrarium dicit Commentator, 2 De anima, commento 67, ubi dicit cum Philosopho* quod color est per se visibilis . . .

T: *Licet contrarium communiter teneant, scilicet* quod color est per se visibilis . . .

(3) Para. 106: Tertia ratio sua est ultima *ratio supra posita quam allegat Commentator contra se, et ideo transeo.*

T: Tertia ratio est ultima *Commentatoris supra posita.*

Jandun (q. 7, col. 260): Tertia ratio est ultima ratio quam tangit Commentator contra se.

(4) Para 111: Igitur ista copulatio *non est nisi ficticium, quia dictum sine omni ratione.*

T: Igitur ista copulatio *impossibilis.*

Jandun (q. 7, col. 261): Igitur huius⟨modi⟩ copulatio non est nisi ficticium quia dictum sine omni ratione.

(5) Para. 184: Aliter potest dici, *cum dicitur, si extrema sint idem, quod medium est idem cum extremis, verum* est de medio copulante extrema ad invicem in esse naturae, non intentionaliter solum. Sed intellectio *non copulat intelligibile cum intellectu nisi* intentionaliter.

T: Aliter potest dici *quod propositio vera* est de medio copulante extrema in esse naturae, non intentionaliter solum. Intellectio autem *solum* intentionaliter.

(6) Para. 197: Quomodo autem intellectus possibilis primo recipit speciem singularis . . .

dixi *in quadam quaestione quam determinavi de verbo singulari, qua quaerebatur 'An possibile sit formare verbum de singulari materiali'.*

T: Quomodo autem intellectus possibilis primo recipit speciem singularis ... dixi *alias.*

(7) Para. 198: Et ideo inter intellectum et speciem singularis materialis est proportio secundum opinionem fidei, sed non secundum opinionem *Commentatoris, quam puto esse opinionem Philosophi.*

T: Et ideo inter intellectum et speciem singularis materialis est proportio secundum opinionem fidei, licet non secundum opinionem *Philosophi et Commentatoris.*

We have printed the relevant parts in italics. The first two cases occur in the initial section of the text where all three witnesses are available, and the expanded version that we have accepted is present with minor variants in both O and P; in the remaining cases the expanded version is that of P. In all these cases, except perhaps (3) and (5), the abbreviations of T are not simply more concise linguistic formulations of the same sentence, leaving its content unchanged, but affect the meaning.

From the conceptual point of view, case (1) is the most significant. The passage in (1) is the final part of Wylton's reply to an objection against his view that the possible intellect is an actual being even before it understands anything—that is, also at the stage at which it is a blank slate. The objection appeals to the claim of Aristotle and Averroes that the possible intellect is not a being before it understands. Wylton rightly considers this claim as the major textual evidence against his view. In the initial part of his reply to this objection he clarifies the context of Aristotle's claim but does not explicitly show how the claim can be reconciled with his own view. This is done only in the literal explanation in the final part of his reply, the part omitted by T. In particular, the crucial point in Wylton's literal explanation is to take the beings Aristotle refers to in his claim as not including all beings but only those different from the intellect (*aliorum a se*), so that, in Wylton's interpretation, Aristotle is saying that the intellect is not one of the beings different from the intellect itself.

The abbreviation in case (4) likewise weakens the passage from the conceptual point of view. It occurs at the end of one of the four 'anonymous' arguments (see above, p. xx) against Averroes' view of the unity of the intellect. The argument starts from the premiss that in Averroes' view one cannot find a cause of the copulation between the possible intellect and an individual man, and so it seems that the conclusion to be drawn from this premiss is that the copulation is left without an explanation and is therefore fictitious, as in the expanded version of P, rather than that the copulation is actually impossible, as in the abbreviation of T. Furthermore, in support of the reading of P we have the external evidence of Jandun.

Case (6) contains an explicit self-reference by Wylton, the only one in the whole question. T has only the indeterminate reference *alias*, whereas P provides the full title of the question. Now one may think that the original text by Wylton had only *alias* and that at some point in the transmission of the text a marginal annotation supplying the reference was added and later incorporated into the main text. On this hypothesis, the text of P would be secondary and the result of a later expansion. We are, however, reluctant to accept this hypothesis. The text of P does not only include the title of the question, which would be consistent with its having originally been nothing more than a marginal gloss, but is also couched in the first person (*quam determinavi* . . .), and there is no reason to consider this inauthentic. Similarly, in cases (1) *ad fin.*, (3), and (7) we are reluctant to accept the abbreviations of T because they imply the omission of first-person sentences. As for case (3) in particular, the external evidence for the omission of *et ideo transeo* given by Jandun is much weakened by the fact that this is a first-person sentence.

As for case (2), the abbreviation of T eliminates the precise reference to a passage in Averroes' commentary on the *De anima*, which runs counter to the accuracy of reference to the two main historical sources, Aristotle and Averroes, that is a general characteristic of Wylton's question.

Finally, in case (5) the abbreviation of T makes the resulting passage less clear because earlier the term *propositio* was never used in connection with the claim at stake (*si extrema sint idem, medium est idem*).

There is also a major case of expansion in T. It occurs in an argument by Wylton against the opinion which ascribes to Averroes the view that the agent intellect is the form of the possible intellect:

> Para. 42: Praeterea, non est de intentione Commentatoris nec alicuius alterius quod in nobis sit duplex potentia cognoscitiva abstracta. Sed si intellectus agens esset forma intellectus materialis, sequeretur *hoc*. Nam intellectus materialis certum est quod est potentia cognoscitiva abstracta. Similiter intellectus agens . . .
>
> T: Praeterea, non est de intentione Commentatoris nec alicuius quod in nobis sit duplex potentia cognoscitiva abstracta. Sed si intellectus agens esset forma, sequeretur *quod in anima nostra esset duplex potentia cognoscitiva abstracta*. Nam intellectus materialis certum est quod est potentia cognoscitiva. Similiter intellectus agens . . .

This passage occurs in the portion of the text where all three witnesses are available, but P is of no help in this case because it omits (by quasi-homoeoteleuton) the passage *si intellectus agens . . . similiter* in which the expansion occurs. Note that unlike the major additions in T discussed above, this case is a purely linguistic expansion, which leaves the content of the argument unchanged. This makes it difficult to choose between the contracted version *hoc* of O and the expanded version *quod in anima nostra . . . abstracta* of T. We have chosen the contracted version, taking into account that O is generally more reliable than T and because

of some external evidence found in Jandun. In q. 6 he reports Wylton's argument as follows:

> Item, ipsi arguunt sic: non est de intentione Commentatoris quod in nobis sit duplex potentia cognoscitiva abstracta; sed si intellectus agens esset forma intellectus possibilis, *hoc* sequeretur secundum illam positionem, quia uterque illorum intellectuum est potentia abstracta cognoscitiva secundum Commentatorem. (q. 6, col. 252)

Jandun reiterates the same argument later on, in a section of q. 25 in which he follows very closely and essentially copies the section of Wylton's question containing the arguments against the opinion which attributes to Averroes the view that the agent intellect is the form of the possible intellect:

> Item, non est intentio Commentatoris quod in nobis sit duplex potentia cognoscitiva abstracta; sed *hoc* contingeret secundum istam positionem quia certum est quod intellectus agens est potentia cognoscitiva abstracta, ut patet ex isto tertio; quare etc. (q. 25, col. 368)

In both passages from Jandun one finds the *hoc* of O rather than the expansion of T, although neither of the two passages follows the argument in Wylton completely *ad litteram*. There is, however, also an aspect of O that may be interpreted as evidence in favour of the expansion of T. After the first occurrence of *abstracta*, O first writes *nam intellectus materialis semper* (where *semper* is a mistaken reading of O for *certum*), i.e. the beginning of the sentence starting after *hoc*, and then cancels it. Now if the model of O had the expanded version present in T, then the fact that O starts writing the sentence *nam intellectus materialis . . .* could easily be explained as an omission by homoeoteleuton of the intervening sentence *Sed si intellectus materialis . . . abstracta*, made by the scribe of O and immediately corrected by him, not however by reproducing the sentence present in his model in full but by abbreviating the final part of it. So the contracted version in O would turn out to be a modification that the scribe of O introduces with respect to his model. Although this hypothesis is attractive, we consider it rather too speculative and prefer to accept the contracted version of O supported by the evidence in Jandun.

Some simple (i.e. one-word) substitutions in T are also of some interest. In his polemical remarks against the Catholic view of the soul, while comparing the way in which Averroes, on the one hand, and Catholics, on the other, could explain the union between the intellectual soul and the human body, Wylton claims:

> Para. 124: Dicant ergo catholici quo modo ex intellectiva—non obstante quod sit subsistens—et corpore humano fit unum, et similem modum et etiam *veriorem/apparentiorem* modum unitatis poterit Commentator assignare. Et dico *'veriorem'/'apparentiorem'* quoniam . . .

The reading *veriorem* is that of P, and the reading *apparentiorem* is that of T.

Clearly, here the variant of T is a deliberate attempt to mitigate the force of Wylton's remarks against the Catholic view, by saying that it is not less true but only less evident.

Similar concerns seem to lie behind the omission in T of the rather personal remark *sed sola fide teneo* in para. 179. The idea that the Catholic view is held solely by faith and the implication that the view is bereft of supporting reasons would offend not only adherents of the Thomistic view of the human soul as the form of man but also more Augustinian thinkers such as traditional Franciscans. Presumably it is safe to assume that no particular intention lies behind the substitutions in T of *opinio* for *fides* in paras. 116 and 124, since P and T share the same reading of *opinio catholica* and *opinio fidei* in several other places (e.g. paras. 85, 95, 155, 198).

2.3. *Criteria of the edition*

The study of variants has shown that of the two complete copies of the text, P is more correct and more reliable than T. Accordingly, we have chosen the readings of P as the basis for our edition, using T and O essentially to correct the errors of P. In the first part of the text, however, taking into account the slight evidence for a pairing OP, when there is a reading of OT against P our policy is to choose the reading of OT. Thus, in short, these are the general criteria of our edition: to choose the reading of P except when it is obviously mistaken or greatly inferior or when OT together go against P. However, we have not applied these general criteria with absolute regularity. For the sake of clarity, elegance, and consistency of the text, we have in some cases preferred the reading of T or O to that of P, or the reading of P to that of OT.

3. Senko's edition

Wylton's *Quaestio de anima intellectiva* was published by Senko in *Studia mediewistyczne*, 5 (1964), on the basis of the two manuscripts O and P, the Tortosa manuscript T being unknown to him. So for the first third of the text (paras. 1–74) the edition of Senko is based on O and P and for the remainder on P alone. The policy of Senko's edition seems to be to follow as closely as possible the text transmitted by P, using O to correct it. This is a sound procedure, given the fragmentary nature of O and the fact that O and P are essentially of the same value. However, Senko's edition is of very poor quality. In many cases he follows the text of P even when it is evidently mistaken and could have been emended rather easily, either using O or more frequently on the basis of sense or context (as in quotations from Averroes' commentary). In other cases Senko's text does not in fact correspond to P or O: that is, there are reading errors. Other mistakes originate from ambiguous abbreviations that the editor fails to expand in the way required by sense or context. Finally, there are cases of mistaken punctuation. In what follows we shall present some of the errors in Senko's edition in the order in which they appear in the text. Examples (1) to (7) are taken from the first part of the text, where both O and P were available, the remainder from the second part, where Senko had access to P alone. We use 'Ed.' to refer to his edition, with parenthetical references to the paragraph numbers in our edition. In the passages quoted from Senko we print the relevant parts in italics.

> (1) Ed., 76. 11–17 (para. 7): Circa secundum principale *secundum* intentionem Averrois in ista materia sic procedam: primo recitabo . . . secundo recitabo opinionem suam quantum ad conclusionem, quam tenuit, cum motivis suis et *modo suo*; tertio reducam rationes tam suam quam aliorum, quae videntur mihi esse ponderis contra opinionem suam; quarto discurram per *alias* rationes inquirendo, si aliqua istarum convincat evidenter suam opinionem esse falsam.

The reading *secundum* is that of P but it is mistaken. The correct reading is *scilicet*, as can be gathered from the plan of the question given by Wylton in a preceding passage:

> Ed., 75. 18–19 (para. 5): Circa hanc quaestionem sic procedam: primo exponam duos terminos positos in quaestione; *secundo recitabo opinionem Averrois* . . .

Furthermore, O does have the correct reading *scilicet* but this is not recorded in the critical apparatus.

According to Senko, the reading *modo suo* is that of P. This is not the case; the reading of P is *modo suo possibili*, although *possibili* is in fact a mistake. In this case too, however, O has the correct reading *modo suo ponendi*, which is recorded by Senko in the critical apparatus. Furthermore, there is internal evidence that the correct reading is that of O. In the second article of the question, the *secundum principale*, the section presenting the *modus* of Averroes starts:

> Ed., 94. 5 (para. 95): Modus autem ponendi suus fuit iste . . .

The reading *alias* is that of P but it is mistaken. O has the correct reading *illas*, which is recorded by Senko in the critical apparatus. Again, a look at the actual content of the question is enough to show that the correct reading is that of O.

> (2) Ed., 77. 9–13 (para. 11): Istum autem intellectum materialem posuit aeternum esse ut patet ex quinto commento et multis aliis commentis *eiusdem* tertii libri. Istum tamen intellectum non dixit esse materialem quia *immixtum*, ut ipsemet dicit contra Alexandrum 25° commento . . .

According to Senko, *eiusdem* is the reading of P whereas O has *illius*. In fact this is not the case: P also reads *illius*.

immixtum is taken by Senko to be the common reading of O and P, but it seems to us that O reads *mixtum*. P originally had this reading too, but the scribe subsequently altered it to *immixtum*, erroneously. Indeed, the passage from Averroes' comment 25 on book 3 of *De anima* shows that the correct reading here is *mixtum*.

> (3) Ed., 78. 6–10 (para. 18): nam si intellectus materialis, ut distinguitur contra agentem, sit sola potentia passiva non video quod *pro temperie pro qua* album et nigrum praesentantur, *sensum et intellectum* in illa approximatione, qua nata sunt tam potentiam sensitivam quam intellectivam distincte et sub propriis rationibus movere, possibile sit eundem intellectum *formaliter hanc propositionem* ⟨*formare*⟩ "album *esse* nigrum" . . .

pro temperie pro qua does not make sense and is not the reading of P or O. Both manuscripts have the good reading *pro tempore pro quo*.

sensum et intellectum is the reading of P but does not make grammatical sense. O has the correct reading *sensui et intellectui*, which is not noticed by Senko.

In both manuscripts one can easily read *formare* instead of Senko's reading *formaliter*, and this makes the further insertion of *formare* superfluous.

esse is the reading of P but is less correct than the reading *est* of O, recorded by Senko in the apparatus.

> (4) Ed., 81. 15–18 (paras. 34–5): Item *secundo* commento dicit, quod intellectus materialis perficitur per agentem. Item eodem commento *secundo* dicit parum ante finem, quod intellectus, qui est in nobis, componitur ex intellectu agente et materiali.

Senko presents both occurrences of *secundo* as common to both O and P. This is not the case. As for the first occurrence, P has *secundo* (abbreviated as '2°') but O has *20*. As for the second occurrence, both O and P have *20* (not *secundo*), which is indeed the correct reading. In this case too a look at Averroes' commentary would have been enough to identify the correct reading.

> (5) Ed., 85. 22 (para. 59): Nam secundum *opinionem Averrois* in prologo 8 Physicorum

opinionem Averrois is given by Senko as the common reading of OP, but is found in neither. P actually reads *commentatorem Averrois*, which is mistaken, and O reads *commentatorem Averroem*, which is correct.

> (6) Ed., 85. 29–34 (para. 60): Alia fiunt in nobis voluntarie quae vel per doctrinam vel inveniendo per inquisitionem, quorum notitia deducitur ex notitia principiorum, ita quod notitia talium dependet tamquam ex causa totali ex primis propositionibus seu verius ex intellectu materiali habituato *vel* primis propositionibus et intellectu agente; *solum* autem *causa* illarum propositionum ⟨*et*⟩ intellectus agentis est intellectus materialis, sicut tam lux quam species coloris habent diaphanum pro subiecto aliquo. . . .

vel and *solum* are the readings of P but they are both copy-mistakes. O has the correct readings *illis* and *subiectum*, respectively, but these are not noticed by Senko.

causa is Senko's expansion of an ambiguous abbreviation that could also be expanded as *tam*, which is the correct reading.

Senko's insertion of *et* is intended to correct the erroneous reading *qua* of P and O. In fact O has *quam*, which is correct.

> (7) Ed., 86. 24–7 (para. 62): et videtur inniti *ratione* Themistii per locum a maiori, quae est ista: virtus immaterialis, quae comprehendere potest minus perfectum, potest comprehendere *maius* perfectum, licet non e converso; ideo intellectus materialis, cum sit virtus *abstracta*, potest comprehendere materialia dignius *etiam quam* immaterialia.

The passage presents an argument which Averroes uses to prove that our intellect can know separate substances, which are immaterial things. The argument is based on the principle that if an immaterial power (our intellect, in the application of the argument to our case) can know less perfect things (material things in our case), it can also know more perfect things (immaterial things or separate substances in our case). So since the intellect can know material things, it follows from that principle that it can also know immaterial things. The sense of the argument, however, is lost in Senko's text. According to it, the 'application' of the principle to the case of the intellect is that since the material intellect is an abstract power it can understand material things in a more 'dignified' way than the immaterial things, which is clearly not an application of the principle in question. One reason for Senko's mistaken interpretation of the argument is that he follows P in omitting *et* after *abstracta*, without noticing that O does have *et* and that *et* makes very good sense. Similarly, *etiam quam*, or rather *est quam*, is a mistaken reading of P, but O has the correct reading *quod et*, which Senko mistakenly reads as *quoque*.

In two other cases in this passage Senko follows the mistaken readings of P, relegating the correct readings of O to the critical apparatus: *ratione* instead of *rationi* (without noticing that the scribe of P did in fact alter *ratione* to *rationi*) and *maius* instead of *magis*.

> (8) 90. 27–9 (para. 77): sed secundum intentionem suam in 12° ipsemet intellectus materialis iam denudatus a potentia est intelligens *et intellectus et etiam forma repraesentans alias substantias separatas*. Istae autem duae Sententiae non concordant, ut videtur.

The part printed in italics is present in P but omitted in Senko's text.

> (9) 96. 3–5 (para. 111): nec alia substantia aliqua aeterna est causa huiusmodi copulationis, quoniam haec copulatio est nova et ab aeterno et immutabilis, *a tali autem substantia immutabili* non procedit actus novus secundum eum.

The part printed in italics is a marginal addition of the scribe of P, accepted by Senko. As we have explained above,[53] however, this addition must be rejected because it ruins the sense of the passage.

[53] p. xix.

(10) 96. 12–21 (para. 112): Ad primum respondet Commentator, quod intellectus speculativus constituitur per duo *intellecta*, a quorum uno habet esse verum et per illud *solum* intelligit *rem; extra* quae est obiectum motivum eius sub lumine intellectus agentis; res enim extra est causa agens una cum intellectu agente intellecta speculativa. Et quia eo, quod res est vel non est, est oratio vera vel falsa, veritas etiam est adaequatio rei et *intellectus. Ideo* dicit, quod intentiones intellectae habent suam veritatem ab isto subiecto, puta a re *existendo solum* ad obiectum. Aliud subiectum habent intellecta speculativa, *a quo quod* sunt unum entium in mundo videlicet quod sunt universalia in actu distincta contra particularia et ut sic non sunt in rebus secundum ipsum, sed in intellectu *solummodo, licet* subiectum secundo modo dictum sit incorruptibile, subiectum tamen primo modo dictum est *incorruptibile*.

The passage as given is pretty unintelligible, although a look at Averroes' actual reply, to which the text refers, would have been enough to make sense of it. Let us see some of the details.

intellecta is Senko's misreading for *subiecta* in P, which is the correct reading.

solum is a copy-mistake of P, reproduced by Senko. The correct reading is *subiectum*.

The semicolon between *rem* and *extra* is mistaken. *Extra* qualifies *rem* here as also immediately below (*res enim extra* . . .).

Similarly the full point between *intellectus* and *Ideo* is mistaken, since the clause starting with *ideo* is that which is explained by the causal clause *Et quia eo, quod* . . .

As for *existendo solum*, the correct reading is *extendendo subiectum*. Now, the copy-mistake *solum* for *subiectum* is present in P but *extendendo* can be read in P, rather than *existendo*.

a quo quod suggests that something is missing. Indeed, P omits *habent* after *quo*, as one gathers from the corresponding passage in T. But even without T, the text of P could have been emended by deleting *quod*.

A full point rather than a comma is required between *solummodo* and *licet*.

Finally, *incorruptibile* at the very end of the passage does not make sense of the contrast between the two subjects. The correct reading is *corruptibile*. In fact, although the first reading of P is *incorruptibile*, this is corrected to *corruptibile* by the scribe. The correction is overlooked by Senko.

(11) 98. 35–99. 3 (para. 124): Dicant ergo catholici, quo modo ex intellectiva, non obstante, quod sit subsistens, et corpore humano fit unum. Et similem modum et etiam veriorem modum unitatis poterit Commentator assignare; et dico veriorem, quoniam, cum ad unitatem compositi requirantur inclinatio, dependentia et ordo naturalis inter formam et materiam, intellectus materialis plus dependet a suo primo perfectibili quam anima mea, quae ⟨*non*⟩ potest subsistere sine aliquo perfectibili et aeternaliter *subsistere*, postquam esset separata, nisi accideret novum *miraculum. Et valde magnum ad hoc, quod uniatur non sic, diceret* Averroes de intellectu materiali respectu sui primi perfectibilis, quod posset esse, si natura humana non esset . . .

The insertion of *non* spoils the sense of this important passage. The point that Wylton wants to make here is that in Averroes' view the material intellect is more dependent on its first *perfectibile*, which is human nature in general, according to Wylton's interpretation (see the very end of the passage), than the intellectual soul depends on its first *perfectibile*, which is each individual man, according to the Catholic view. This point is proved by remarking that Averroes would deny that the material intellect could exist if human nature did not exist, while for Catholics my soul can exist without me. The point would not be proved if one accepts the insertion of *non*. The reading *subsistere* is Senko's correction for *subsisteret* in P, but the rationale for this correction is not clear. Finally, Senko's punctuation in the part printed in italics at the end of the passage is mistaken. The correct punctuation is: 'novum miraculum et valde magnum, ad hoc quod uniatur. Non sic diceret Averroes . . .'

> (12) 104. 5–12 (para. 141): Et ita sunt *gloriandae* auctoritates Philosophi, cum dicit, quod nullius corporis est actus et habitus, secundum intentionem Commentatoris . . . et ideo dixit Aristoteles in definitione animae, ut ipse dicit ibidem, quod quae est *prima perfectio* naturali*s, organica non est, dum medium utrumque* per omnes virtutes perficitur corpus eodem modo, aut est ex eis ⟨*et*⟩ *per consequentiam* corpus non perficitur, aut si perficitur, erit alio modo.

gloriandae is Senko's mistaken expansion of an ambiguous abbreviation in P, also capable of expansion as *glossandae*, which is indeed the correct reading, as is pretty obvious from the context.

The text from *et ideo* until the end of the passage is unintelligible in Senko's version. It is, however, a quotation *ad litteram* from Averroes' commentary, and could easily have been emended by checking Averroes' text. But even a careful transcription of the text of P would have been enough to make sense of most of the passage. Instead of *organica non est dum medium utrumque* P reads: *organici non est dum manifestum utrum*, which makes sense of the passage if one adds *corporis* after *perfectio*. Instead of Senko's insertion ⟨*et*⟩ the correct insertion is ⟨*aliqua*⟩, as is clear from Averroes. Finally, *per consequentiam* is Senko's mistaken reading of *per quam* in P, which is correct.

> (13) 104. 35 (para. 145): Sed quod haec ⟨*est*⟩ opinio Aristotelis, probo.

Senko is aware that something is missing from the text of P, and adds *est*. This restores the syntax of the sentence but not the sense. It is obvious from the context that what Wylton actually proves is that the opinion at stake is not the opinion of Aristotle. So the most economical emendation of P's text is ⟨*non est*⟩.

> (14) 105. 21–4 (para. 148): Contra istam responsionem, primo sic: *Philosophus* in *magno suo volumine* dicit, quod *rationalis* se habet ut forma respectu consonantis, et

hoc non *absolute* vult Philosophus, quod quia *dissolvitur* ab invicem B et A in hac syllaba BA, B et A possunt manere separata. Propter hoc oportet ponere aliud et aliud principium formale in hac syllaba; ergo eodem modo in proposito non obstante, quod in homine anima sit actus et materia *et* potentia.

The first occurrence of *Philosophus* is Senko's mistaken reading for 'Priscianus' in P.

magno is a copy-mistake of P, which would have been very easy to emend to *maiori* if Senko had realized that the author in question is not Aristotle but Priscian.

Instead of *suo volumine* P has the inversion *volumine suo*.

rationalis is Senko's mistaken reading for *vocalis* in P.

absolute is a copy-mistake of P, but again the correction to *obstante* is discoverable through careful examination of what follows in the argument (see the last sentence of the passage, in which P has the correct reading *obstante*).

dissolvitur is Senko's mistaken reading of *dissolutis* in P, and this misreading has led the editor to a mistake in the punctuation: we need a comma, not a full point, after *separata*, since *propter hoc oportet* provides the main clause following the causal clause beginning *quia*.

Finally, inclusion of *et* before *potentia* at the end of the passage is a mistake in P, not eliminated by Senko.

4. Presentation of the text

Latin Text. With regard to orthography, we have chosen to normalize the spelling in this edition according to the conventions of classical Latin because we believe that this results in increased clarity, something highly desirable in the case of a text as complex—both conceptually and linguistically—as Wylton's question. On the other hand, our practice will not deprive those who are interested in medieval spelling of access to original examples. All medieval spellings in our manuscripts are standard.

Similarly, capitalization and punctuation have been freely employed to assist the reader. Italicization has been used for titles of works. Citations of the actual words of an author have been enclosed in single quotation marks, which are also used for terms in material supposition (e.g.: 'homo' in suo intellectu primo includit substantiam corpoream).

Angle brackets (⟨ ⟩) have been used for editorial additions and square brackets ([ ]) for editorial deletions. These editorial interventions have also been reported in the apparatus criticus.

Arabic numerals have been used for the comments of Averroes' works and for chapters. They have also been used for books of the works of Aristotle (except for *Metaphysics*), Averroes, and other authors only when the title of the work is explicitly mentioned (e.g.: '2 *De anima*, commento 57'); otherwise we have written out the number (e.g.: 'commento 18 illius tertii').

To facilitate reference, paragraphs have been numbered consecutively. All internal references are by paragraph numbers.

To help the reader follow the structure of Wylton's question, we have introduced headings (in capitals and within angle brackets) both for the major sections (the five articles) and for further relevant subdivisions of them. The list of these headings is given in the *Conspectus Quaestionis* at the start of the edition.

English translation. This is not an easy text to translate because of the very dense philosophical content, the highly technical terminology, and the frequent quotations from the Latin translation of Averroes' Arabic commentary on the *De anima*. We have made some effort to produce an English translation which is at the same time literal, so that it captures the exact sense of the Latin text, and intelligible, so that it reads smoothly and makes apparent the structure of the argumentation.

Apparatus criticus. We have recorded all the variant readings of all three witnesses (including corrections and marginal additions) except the following trivial ones:

ergo/igitur
aliqua/alia etc.
iste/ille etc.
econtra/econverso
huius/huiusmodi
cuius/cuiusmodi
cum/tamen
videlicet/scilicet
infra/intra

We have used the following abbreviations:

add.	*addidit/addiderunt*
corr.	*correxit/correxerunt*
del.	*delevit/deleverunt*
fin.	*finit*
hom.	*per homoeoteleuton*
i.m.	*in margine*
inv.	*invertit/inverterunt*
iter.	*iteravit/iteraverunt*
om.	*omisit/omiserunt*

scrips.   *scripsit/scripserunt*
suppl.   *supplevit/suppleverunt*
s.l.   *supra lineam*

Apparatus fontium. We have identified Wylton's acknowledged sources and internal references in footnotes cued by arabic numerals. References are to the editions listed in the Index Auctorum.

5. The main doctrinal points of Thomas Wylton's *Quaestio de anima intellectiva*

In his question on the intellectual soul Wylton investigates the problem whether it is possible to demonstrate by natural and necessary reasoning that the intellectual soul is the form of the human body. Although all the initial arguments *pro* and *contra* are based on Aristotelian authorities,[54] the question contrasts the Aristotelian view as interpreted by the Commentator, Averroes, with the Catholic view of the intellectual soul. The main assumptions of the latter view are that the intellectual soul is a subsisting form, as opposed to an inherent form; that it is created but incorruptible; and that it is numerically distinct in differing human beings. Finally, the Catholic opinion stipulates that the intellectual soul conceived of in this manner is the form of the human body.

Wylton concedes that the Catholic opinion should be accepted as true. He is, however, deeply sceptical of the possibility that its truth can be proved by natural reasoning. As he explains, its truth rests on faith alone, and he openly confesses his inability to come up with naturally accessible and necessary arguments in its favour.

The immediately apparent problem which besets the Catholic conception is that of the unity of body and soul. The intellectual soul does not seem to be linked to the human body in such an intimate and close manner as would seem to be required by its status as the substantial form of the human being. Wylton's approach to and understanding of this well-known problem are quite original. For him, the problem of accounting for the unity of body and soul in man does not arise because the intellectual soul is assumed to be a subsisting thing and not simply an inhering form in the human body. The problem arises because of the additional properties which Catholics ascribe to the human soul, viz. that it is numerically distinct in different human beings and that it survives the individual human being whose form it is supposed to be.

Wylton confronts this problem by way of a detailed and careful presentation of Averroes' view on the intellect and by contrasting the Commentator's conception

[54] See paras. 1–4.

with that of the Catholics. During this investigation he comes across as a resolute advocate of the reasonableness of Averroes' view. Wylton is in no doubt that the material intellect of Averroes, unlike the intellectual soul of the Catholics, is one for all men and that it is not only incorruptible but ingenerable, i.e. eternal. On the other hand, he rejects the current interpretation of Averroes according to which the material intellect is a substance separate from man. To Wylton it is clear that Averroes' material intellect, like the intellectual soul of the Catholics, is the substantial form of man and, accordingly, that it is something intrinsic to man. Moreover, in a straightforward assault on the Catholics' reading of the Commentator, Wylton develops an elaborate argumentation in order to demonstrate that Averroes offers a theory of the union between intellect and body which, in terms of rationality, is far superior to that of the Catholics. In this connection Wylton's key point is that while the intellectual soul, according to the Catholic view, is separable from the human body, this does not obtain within the framework of Averroes' understanding. Wylton also argues that in accepting the unity and the eternity of the intellect Averroes is a faithful interpreter of Aristotle.

Though Wylton recognizes the superiority of Averroes' psychology in explaining the unity between the human body and the human soul, he openly concedes that the Catholic view is true and should be sustained. In particular, Wylton rejects the Averroistic assumption of the unity of the intellect and he accepts that each human being possesses a proper individual intellect. To Wylton this does not entail a total *sacrificium intellectus*, since by accepting the plurality and individuality of intellectual souls it is possible to gain significant advantages in epistemology. It is routinely accepted that the first object of intellectual cognition is the universal, whereas the particular is known only secondarily and indirectly. For Wylton, this opinion is at best problematic since the multiplicity of the intellect makes it very difficult to explain how the particular intellect can be the immediate and proper subject of what is universal. Granted the multiplicity of intellectual souls, a much more plausible view is available, according to which it is possible to claim that the first and direct object of intellectual cognition is the single thing, while cognition of what is universal is based on the cognizing of singulars. The immediate advantage of such an epistemological theory is that there will be close congruence between the intellect as subject and the objects of intellection.

5.1. *The structure of Wylton's question*

Wylton's question is divided into five articles. The first (para. 6) is a very short preliminary section devoted to the definition of the two relevant terms in the title of the question, namely, 'intellectual soul' and 'form of the body'.

Article 2 (paras. 7–141) contains Wylton's presentation of Averroes' view.

This article occupies approximately two-thirds of the question and is fundamental to Wylton's argument. It is divided into four main parts.

In the first part (paras. 8–83) Wylton expounds the meanings of the various expressions used by Averroes in describing the intellect. The terms under scrutiny are 'possible intellect' (paras. 9–23), 'agent intellect' (paras. 24–54), 'speculative intellect' (paras. 55–8), 'intellect in habit' (paras. 59–60), 'accomplished intellect' (paras. 61–82), and 'passive intellect' (para. 83). In his explanation Wylton closely follows Averroes' texts, quoting many of them verbatim, so that the structure of this part is almost that of a commentary on the relevant parts of Averroes' commentary on the third book of the *De anima*. In commenting on Averroes, however, Wylton does not only provide a literal exposition of the Commentator's texts but takes a stance on some of the controversial points raised by Averroes' exposition. For example, he considers and rejects the view that the possible intellect is something purely potential; in opposition to this he maintains that the possible intellect is an act and that it is precisely the proper actuality of the intellect that allows it to be in potency with respect to acts of intellection and to concepts. This first part also contains a lengthy digression on Averroes' explanations of the cognition of separate substances as set out in his commentaries on *De anima* 3 and on *Metaphysics* 12 (paras. 62–81).

In the second part (paras. 84–95) Wylton addresses the main topic of the debate by way of a presentation of Averroes' answer to the question whether the intellectual soul is the form of the human body. Drawing on his definitions of 'intellectual soul' and 'form of the body' presented in the first article and on his clarification of Averroes' terminology in connection with the intellect in the first part of the second article, Wylton establishes that, in Averroes' psychology, the possible intellect is the entity that satisfies the definition of 'intellectual soul'. He concludes that for Averroes, as for Catholic thinkers, the possible intellect or the intellectual soul is the form of the human body (para. 84).

Accordingly, the opposition between Averroes and the Catholic party does not concern the issue of whether the intellectual soul is the form of the human body. What separates Catholics from Averroes is their differing perceptions of two other properties of the intellectual soul (paras. 85–6). In the first place, for Averroes the material intellect is both incorruptible and ingenerable, whereas the intellectual soul, according to the Catholics, is incorruptible but has a beginning in time inasmuch as it is said to begin to exist by divine creation and together with the conception of an individual human being whose form it is said to be. Secondly, according to Averroes the material intellect is a single entity and common to all human beings, whereas Catholics think that the intellectual soul is multiplied so that different human beings are each endowed with their own numerically distinct intellectual soul. Wylton reiterates and expounds Averroes' arguments in favour of the unity of the intellect (paras. 87–94), and he explains how the material intellect is related to distinct individual human beings (para. 95).

In the third part of the second article (paras. 96–111) Wylton draws up three series of arguments against Averroes' opinion: (i) those of Averroes himself (paras. 96–103); (ii) those of Albert the Great (paras. 104–7); (iii) those of an anonymous opinion (paras. 108–11). The majority of the arguments in the three series challenge the unity of the material intellect and attempt to show that this unity makes it impossible for the material intellect to be an intrinsic component of individual human beings.

In the fourth part (paras. 112–41) Wylton replies to the arguments directed against Averroes' opinion which had been set forth in the third part. It is in this section of the question that Wylton's sympathy with Averroes' psychology appears most clearly. From the doctrinal point of view, the characteristic feature of Wylton's defence of Averroes is his reliance on a realist assumption regarding universal natures. As Wylton remarks, the arguments which strive to locate an incompatibility between the unity of the intellect and its being an intrinsic perfection of man are based on the assumption that the intrinsic components of individual human beings must by nature be divided and single. In Wylton's view, however, this assumption is clearly mistaken. An individual human being is also a bearer of a universal component, namely human nature, which is something common to all human individuals. It is precisely this common component that makes it possible for the material intellect to be an intrinsic perfection of individual human beings (paras. 115, 120, 121, 122, 123). Another original aspect of Wylton's defence is his firm rejection of the interpretation of Averroes current at the time; according to this reading of the Commentator, the material intellect is a substance separate from man, united with man only through the operation of intellection (paras. 124, 135–8). Equally striking is Wylton's refutation of the anonymous arguments against Averroes (paras. 124–34). In replying to these Wylton transforms his defence of Averroes' view into an attack on the Catholic view which forms the background to this criticism. He argues that the material intellect of Averroes satisfies the conditions for being the form of the human body much better than the intellectual soul of the Catholics. In this sense, Averroes is able to offer an account of the union between the human body and the human soul which is 'truer' than that of the Catholic party.

In the third article (paras. 142–76) Wylton compares Aristotle and Averroes with respect to their perception of the two disputed properties of the material intellect: its eternity and its numerical unity. Wylton maintains that Aristotle and Averroes agree in ascribing both properties to the material intellect. Concerning the eternity of the intellect, Wylton appeals to the Aristotelian principle that the eternal into the future (*a parte post*) and incorruptible must also be eternal into the past (*a parte ante*), and hence ingenerable (para. 175). As regards the unity of the intellect, Wylton attributes to Aristotle the view that it is generally true of immaterial forms that there is only one individual for any given species (para. 176).

The main part of the article, however, is taken up by a treatment of two opinions which perceive a disagreement between Aristotle and Averroes. The first is in agreement with the anonymous arguments which appeared in the third and fourth parts of the second article. This opinion claims that Aristotle denied both the eternity of the intellect and its numerical unity: rather, Aristotle maintained, according to the interpretation of this opinion, that the human intellect is incorruptible but begins to exist simultaneously with the human body of which it is the form, and that there are as many human souls as there are human bodies (paras. 142–4). To Wylton it is clear that this opinion expounds Aristotle in agreement with the proper conception of Catholics. The main component of Wylton's refutation of this interpretation of Aristotle's opinion consists in showing that it clashes with an argument of Aristotle's in *Metaphysics* 7, which seems to imply that it cannot be the case that a composite ceases to be at the same time as all of its components remain (paras. 145–56). Wylton reproduces numerous attempts to counter Aristotle's argument, and by so doing indicates that at the time this argument was considered to be a major obstacle to reconciling Aristotle's view with that of the Catholics.

The second opinion agrees with the first in so far as it maintains that Aristotle supported the multiplicity of intellects. It departs, however, both from the first opinion and from Averroes' conception on the subject of the corruptibility or incorruptibility of the intellect. This opinion claims that Aristotle believed that the intellect is corruptible and that it ceases to be together with the human composite to which it belongs (paras. 162–6). Wylton argues forcefully against this opinion by showing that such a view entails the unacceptable consequence that, according to Aristotle, the intellect would be nothing more than a material and organic power (paras. 167–73).

In the fourth article (paras. 177–9) Wylton presents his considered opinion on the question at issue, viz. whether it can be established by evident and necessary reasoning that the intellectual soul, in the sense of the Catholics' conception, is the form of the human body. He openly admits that he is unable to identify any convincing arguments in favour of an affirmative answer and declares that he accepts the Catholic view solely by faith. As Wylton emphasizes, the main difficulty in producing such arguments derives from the dual affirmation of the Catholics, viz. that the intellectual soul has a beginning in time and that it survives the individual human being whose form it is supposed to be.

The fifth article (paras. 180–208) contains Wylton's reply to the arguments advanced by Averroes (paras. 181–205) and by Aristotle (paras. 206–8) against the conception of the Catholics. The relevant arguments of Averroes are those in favour of the unity of the material intellect, and these had already been listed in the second part of the second article (paras. 87–94). According to Wylton, the main reason which induced Averroes and Aristotle to support the unity of the intellect was their concern to safeguard universal cognition, since only an undivided intellect is capable of cognizing universal natures. Accordingly, in replying to Averroes' arguments Wylton discusses the question of how knowledge of universals may accrue to an individual intellect, as stipulated by the Catholic view. He considers the standard way of answering this question, which consists in distinguishing the mode of being of an intelligible species from its mode of representation, but this he finds totally unconvincing. On the other hand, Wylton draws attention to a distinct advantage of abandoning Averroes' view on the unity of the intellectual soul. According to Wylton's appraisal, upholding the individuality of the intellectual soul makes it possible to defend the much more reasonable stance that singulars are the first objects of intellectual cognition.

5.2. *The nature of the material intellect and the role of the agent intellect*

Wylton stresses that Averroes' use of the adjective 'material' as a characterization of the intellect should not be taken to imply that this kind of intellect is joined to or contains matter. The reason why an intellect of this sort may be called 'material' is that by nature it is in potency with respect to entities which are its formal perfections. These formal entities are the concepts (*intentiones*) of material natures (e.g. concepts of inanimate and animate substances and their properties), which are the end products of the process of cognition. This kind of intellect is what Latin philosophers term 'possible intellect' (paras. 11, 9).

While Averroes explicitly distinguishes the material intellect from prime matter (para. 10), his descriptions of it emphasize its potentiality. For example, he claims that the only nature of the material intellect *qua* material is potentiality (*possibilitas*), and that it is not a being before it understands, i.e. before it receives concepts (para. 9).[55]

Averroes' strong emphasis on the potentiality of the material intellect might induce the inattentive reader to assume that Averroes—and by implication Wylton— endorses the view that the material intellect is not an act at all but pure potentiality. According to this reading of Averroes, it is not only the case that the material intellect is by nature in potency to concepts but also that it does not have any

[55] It is clear that the term 'potential intellect' could be perceived to support the view that this kind of intellect is pure potentiality. In order to forestall an argument along these lines, Wylton points out that the expression is only conventional terminology or 'naming' ('quasi appellatione') and should not be mistaken for an essential description.

actuality of its own apart from that which is conferred on it by its received concepts (para. 12).[56]

However, Wylton emphatically rejects this understanding of the material intellect, and he proceeds to show that it conflicts with Averroes' stated opinion. First of all, Averroes classifies the material intellect as an immaterial substance which subsists by itself. Secondly, Averroes views the material intellect as the first perfection of man, which is to say, the substantial form of man (paras. 13, 14). Thirdly, Wylton demonstrates that this 'minimalistic' reading of Averroes is in fact erroneous. The conception that the material intellect should be regarded as pure potentiality and that this pure potentiality is first actualized by acts of intellection and concepts clashes squarely with the Aristotelian principle that accidental forms cannot be the first actuality of something purely potential since accidents presuppose a substantial form in the thing which they modify. Concepts, on the other hand, are accidental forms and thus they depend on the intellect as an entity endowed with a substantial form (para. 15).

Furthermore, if the material intellect were purely potential, it would be a solely passive cognitive power. Wylton presents two short arguments to show that the cognitive role of the intellect cannot simply be that of a totally passive recipient of concepts. Both arguments are based on man's inner experience of cognitive acts. Wylton outlines two situations which reveal the inadequacy of a purely passive material intellect. In the first scenario he posits that someone has a clear and distinct grasp of a white thing and a black thing; none the less, it is still possible for the intellect to form the (admittedly false) proposition 'white is black' (para. 18). The second instance highlights the huge difference which everyone experiences between scientific knowledge of some thing and the immediate grasp of the same object; the first requires study and attention, while the second does not (para. 19). The first situation reveals the active role of the intellect by highlighting the ability of the intellect to form propositions which are contrary to the input of the sensory and intellectual faculties. The second example underlines the ability of the intellect to reach a degree of cognition which is more perfect than the one achieved by a predominantly passive reception. Apparently Wylton's two 'cognitive' arguments influenced the debates concerning the nature of the material intellect which took place in Paris at the time. Wylton's contemporary, the Carmelite master Guy Terreni, who regarded the material intellect as a purely potential and passive potency, considered that Wylton had produced very strong arguments against his position.[57]

---

[56] Peter Auriol was a well-known champion of this opinion, which he defendend both in his commentary on *Sentences* 2 and in his *Quodlibet*; see Nielsen, 'The *Quodlibet* of Peter Auriol'. There is no indication that Auriol is the particular target of Wylton's criticism of this conception.

[57] See Guy Terreni, *Quodlibet* 3, q. 6 ('Utrum intelligere sit de genere actionis'), edition in Nielsen and Trifogli, 'Guido Terreni and his Debate with Thomas Wylton', §§ 4.3.1, 4.3.3, 646, and introduction, 577–8.

For Wylton it is clear that the material intellect, according to Averroes' view, is in act by itself, even prior to cognition of any kind. Furthermore, as he explains, the potentiality of the material intellect is not like that of prime matter but rather like that of a surface which is not actually white but can become white (*dealbabilis*): the surface is in itself an actuality at the same time as it is in potentiality to whiteness. In much the same way the material intellect is in itself an actuality even if it is in potentiality to concepts (para. 21).

Since the material intellect is by nature in potency to concepts, there must be another cognitive power which is responsible for actualizing the potentiality of the material intellect. As Wylton sees it, this is the argument which Averroes used to show why it is necessary to posit the so-called 'agent intellect' (para. 24). Like the material intellect, the agent intellect is immaterial, but in contradistinction to the material intellect the agent intellect does not contain any potentiality because it is without contact with and knowledge of objects in the changeable and material world (paras. 29–30).

As Wylton makes clear, the agent intellect is not a sufficient cause of the actualization of the material intellect. The reason for this is that, once the material intellect is actualized in the proper sense, it can perform acts of intellection. Moreover, for Aristotle and Averroes, acts of intellection also depend on the presence of sensible images (*phantasmata*). Accordingly, the sufficient cause of the actualization of the material intellect consists of both the agent intellect and sensible images. In order to describe the action of the agent intellect, Wylton reiterates and expands on Averroes' analogous case of the vision of colours. Colours become visible in the transparent medium because of the presence of light; this basic structure is mirrored in the case of the intellect's acquisition of concepts since it is the presence of the agent intellect which causes sensible images to become intelligible and universal in the material intellect (para. 27). In itself this analogy does not throw much light on the process of abstraction which leads to the formation of universals, or on the precise role played by the agent intellect in this process. In this context Wylton is apparently not concerned with developing a more informative account. Presumably the reason for this parsimony is his strong reservations vis-à-vis the theory of abstraction, which was current at the time and was generally attributed to Aristotle and Averroes. Wylton presents his reasons for repudiating this theory in a question which treats of the intellectual cognition of singulars, and there will be occasion to return to this question below.

In the present context it is incumbent on Wylton to consider the question whether the material intellect and the agent intellect are substances in their own right or are simply the material and formal components of the human intellectual soul. Some supporters of the idea that the material intellect is pure potentiality opt for the latter alternative. They maintain that the agent intellect actualizes the material intellect by being a form inhering in it in much the same way as a material form actualizes its corresponding matter. Arguing along these lines, they attempt to explain how a purely potential intellect can be actualized by accidental forms, i.e. by its concepts: the material intellect is first actualized by the agent intellect as a substantial form and subsequently by acts of intellection and concepts (para. 16). It is highly likely that the particular champion of this view whom Wylton targets in this context is Guy Terreni.[58]

There are several passages in Averroes' commentary which seem to suggest the view that the agent intellect is the form of the material intellect. This could be perceived to be the point of Averroes' analogy between the transparent medium and light in the process of vision, on the one hand, and, on the other, the material intellect and the agent intellect (para. 33).[59] Wylton is, however, convinced that Averroes did not think along these lines. On the contrary, according to Wylton, the common view among Aristotelian commentators, supported by Aristotle himself, is that the agent intellect is a substance by itself and, accordingly, separate from the material intellect (paras. 40–4). When Averroes suggests that the agent intellect is the form and perfection of the material intellect, this should not be taken to imply that the agent intellect is a form which inheres in the material intellect as in corresponding matter. What Averroes wished to convey is that the agent intellect is an 'assisting' form, i.e. something which by its presence and assistance enables the material intellect to cognize the natures of material things (paras. 45–7).

While Wylton insists that the agent intellect is not the form of the material intellect, so long as one is talking about the material intellect's gradual acquisition of cognition, he does nothing to conceal the fact that Averroes' view includes something more. For the Commentator, the agent intellect is not always simply an external agent with respect to the material intellect. At the final stage, when the material intellect has acquired all cognition and shed all potentiality, the agent intellect becomes united with the material intellect as a proper form. The material intellect in this final stage is called by Averroes the 'accomplished intellect' (*intellectus adeptus*). At precisely this stage of 'accomplishment' the material intellect attains knowledge of the higher separate substances. Wylton makes a good exegetical effort to clarify this rather opaque aspect of Averroes' thought (paras. 61–82). However, this aspect of the Commentator's exposition is not central to the main theme of Wylton's question. What does emerge with lucidity from Wylton's exposition is that Averroes' version of the agent intellect is not a suitable candidate

---

[58] See Guy Terreni, *Quodlibet* 3, q. 3 ('Utrum alicui possit convenire ratio agentis et non possit agere'), edition in Nielsen and Trifogli, 'Guido Terreni and his Debate with Thomas Wylton', 612–36.
[59] See also paras. 34–9.

for being the form of human beings, since it comes into contact with man only in the final stage of the development of the material intellect.[60]

5.3. *The material intellect as the form of the human body*

For Wylton, the material intellect, according to Averroes' understanding, satisfies the definition of the intellectual soul as the formal principle by virtue of which man cognizes the natures of material things, i.e. the principle of universal cognition (paras. 6, 84). The definition of 'intellectual soul' used by Wylton is totally traditional inasmuch as it builds on Aristotle, who characterizes the rational soul as that by which we understand (*illud quo intelligimus*).[61] Accordingly, the definition would be accepted, though explained differently, both by unitarians, who posit only one substantial form in man, and by pluralists, who claim that the substantial form of man is composed of several forms.[62] Wylton's claim, however, that only the material intellect satisfies this definition is controversial. It would not be accepted by those who maintain that the material intellect is something purely potential and that the agent intellect is its form so that the intellectual soul is composed of both the material and the agent intellects as material and formal components.[63]

More controversial is Wylton's claim that the ontological status of the material intellect, according to Averroes' understanding, is essentially the same as that of the intellectual soul according to the perception of Catholic thinkers. As Wylton explains it, Averroes views the intellectual soul as the substantial form of the human body in precisely the same sense as Catholic thinkers (para. 84). With regard to the intellectual soul, the differences which separate Averroes and the Catholics lie elsewhere. To Averroes the material intellect is eternal both into the past and into the future (*a parte ante et a parte post*), whereas Catholics view the intellectual soul as incorruptible and eternal into the future (*a parte post*) but created in time. To Averroes, the material intellect is one for all men whereas the Catholic party regards the intellectual soul as numerically distinct in differing human beings (paras. 85–6).

When Wylton claims that for Averroes the material intellect is the form of the human body in the same way as the intellectual soul is the form of man for

---

[60] For Averroes' view of the conjunction of the human intellect with the agent intellect see H. A. Davidson, *Alfarabi, Avicenna, and Averroes on Intellect: Their Cosmologies, Theories of the Active Intellect, and Theories of Human Intellect* (Oxford, 1992), 321 ff.

[61] Arist. *DA* 3. 4, 429^{a}10–11.

[62] The controversy between pluralists and unitarians is not directly relevant to Wylton's discussion in this question. Wylton refers explicitly to the difference between the pluralist and the unitarian views on only one occasion, in connection with his discussion of Aristotle's argument in *Metaphysics* 7 about the permanence of the components of a composite, but he makes it clear that his discussion is not affected by the difference between the two views. See para. 145.

[63] See above, pp. xlvi–xlvii.

Catholics, he is careful to employ the expression 'form of the human body' in a univocal sense. The distinction between inhering forms and subsisting forms, i.e. forms which inhere in matter and forms which have being without being enmeshed in matter, is something Wylton elaborates on. To him it is beyond doubt that both the intellectual soul of Catholics and the material intellect of Averroes are subsisting forms. It is also clear to him that a subsisting form, in the same way as an inhering form, *informs* its corresponding matter. This implies two things: firstly, that the composite thing which results from the union of a subsisting form and matter is something essentially one (*per se unum*); secondly, that the specific being of this composite thing is determined by the form. For Wylton the difference between the two kinds of form is that an inhering form informs matter by inhering in it, whereas a subsisting form informs its matter by having a natural inclination towards and dependence on that matter (para. 6).

It is well worth noticing that Wylton does not elaborate on the particular properties or features which are supposedly implied by his notion that a form may have a natural inclination towards and dependence on its corresponding matter. Later in the question Wylton again employs this complex notion in his evaluation of the varying ways in which the union between body and soul is explained both by the Catholics and by Averroes.[64] It is clear, however, that Wylton's notion of subsisting form is not particularly original. In the main, it mirrors the ideas employed by Thomas Aquinas in his explanation of how the intellectual soul is something subsisting as well as the substantial form of the body rather than just a substance in its own right.[65] What is original with Wylton is his claim that the material intellect, as Averroes sees it, is not a substance separate from man, but rather the subsisting and substantial form of the human body, and that in this respect there is agreement between Averroes and Catholics. According to Wylton's definition of subsisting form, this implies that the material intellect, in Averroes' case, or the intellectual soul, in the case of the Catholics, is an intrinsic component of man and provides man with his specific being, so that man is a composite of the human body and the material intellect or the intellectual soul. In both cases this holds good without requiring that the material intellect or intellectual soul should also inhere in the human body.

In support of his interpretation Wylton manages to identify some passages in Averroes' commentary. For example, in his commentary on the third book of the *De anima* Averroes assumes that the material intellect is the first perfection of man and that man differs from all other living beings by virtue of the material intellect. In *De substantia orbis* he claims that, unlike the heavens, man is intelligent by

---
[64] See § 5.5 below.
[65] See e.g. Thomas Aquinas, *Quaestiones disputatae de anima*, q. 1 ('Utrum anima humana possit esse forma et hoc aliquid'), ed. Leonina, 24, ed. B.-C. Bazan (Rome, 1996), 3–12.

virtue of a part existing in him, which Wylton takes to imply that the material intellect, which is the form by virtue of which man is intelligent, is an intrinsic part of man (para. 85).[66]

Wylton is keenly aware that his interpretation of Averroes is not universally accepted, in spite of the fact that it is not without textual support. He adduces an alternative interpretation, according to which the material intellect is not an intrinsic formal component of man but is extrinsic to man in the sense that it is a substance separate from man. For Averroes, at least according to this interpretation, the only intrinsic components of man are the body and the sensitive soul. Man understands or is intelligent by virtue of the union (*copulatio*) of the material intellect with man, and this union is brought about by way of the phantasms present in the sensitive soul of man (para. 178). This alternative interpretation reflects the current view, the *opinio communis*, of Averroes' position, and it was endorsed by, for example, Thomas Aquinas and John Duns Scotus.[67]

This alternative opinion and its broad support in the community of scholarship do not rattle Wylton. He rejects the interpretation as fallacious since it amounts to nothing more than rendering Averroes' conception self-defeating. For Wylton it is a plain contradiction that some thing should be intelligent and that the intellect, the principle by virtue of which the thing is intelligent, should be neither identical with the thing nor an intrinsic part of it. A separate and distinct supposit cannot make another thing intelligent. Wylton's justification for drawing this inference is that an act of intellection is an immanent act which belongs to the agent. Therefore the principle which originates the act of intellection and that in which this act is primarily received must be intrinsic to the agent. In other words, the agent of an act of intellection and the principle of that act must be one and the same supposit (para. 178).

It is worthy of note that the argument by which Wylton defends his alternative interpretation of Averroes is the same as that which Aquinas and Scotus, among others, had employed in order to reject Averroes' view. In this question Wylton attributes this argument to none other than Averroes himself (para. 97). The essential ingredient of the argument is the inference 'man is intelligent [*homo intelligit*]; therefore, the intellect is intrinsic to man'. Aquinas and Scotus, on the one hand, and Wylton, on the other, consider this inference as necessarily true and readily accept the truth of the antecedent 'man is intelligent'. Accordingly, Aquinas, Scotus, and Wylton all agree that the conclusion that the intellect is intrinsic to man is necessarily true. Where they differ is in their assessment of Averroes' position

[66] See para. 141 for Wylton's explanation of some passages in Averroes that apparently imply that the material intellect is separate from the human body.

[67] See Thomas Aquinas, *De unitate intellectus contra Averroistas*, 3, ed. Leonina, 43 (Rome, 1976), 303; John Duns Scotus, *Opus Oxoniense*, 4, dist. 43, q. 2 ('Utrum possit esse notum per rationem naturalem resurrectionem generalem hominum esse futuram'), ed. Vivès, 20 (Paris, 1894), 37.

with respect to this conclusion. Aquinas and Scotus believe that the conclusion is not true for Averroes and, consequently, they reject his view. Wylton, on the other hand, believes that Averroes recognized the truth of this conclusion.[68]

At precisely this juncture in his question, Wylton seems to have in mind a particular contemporary defender of the *opinio communis*, viz. Guy Terreni, who determined a quodlibetal question on 'whether it can be shown with evidence that the rational soul is the form of man informing the body', the very topic of Wylton's question. Terreni's discussion is much less elaborated than that of Wylton. It is clear, however, that the two thinkers sharply disagree both on the main problem of the question and on the assessment of Averroes' view. Terreni believes that it can be convincingly argued that the intellectual soul is the form of man and that Aristotle and Averroes can be shown to have been fundamentally mistaken. Terreni's main conceptual tool in his defence of the Catholic view, and in his onslaught on Averroes in particular, is exactly the inference 'man is intelligent; therefore, the intellect is a formal principle intrinsic to man'.[69]

In agreement with his main assumption that the material intellect, according to Averroes, is the substantial form of man and that which distinguishes man from all other species, Wylton further affirms that for Averroes the material intellect is joined to a human being at its first instant of being. The first perfection of man is the material intellect and, for this reason, a human being cannot start to exist unless the material intellect is joined to a human being as an intrinsic formal principle. Wylton characterizes this union of the material intellect and man as a 'union in being' (*secundum esse*) and he distinguishes it sharply from a union in operation— the sole union between the material intellect and man which the *opinio communis* perceives in Averroes' exposition (para. 136).

5.4. *The realist assumption in Wylton's interpretation*

According to Wylton, Averroes' characteristic thesis on the unity of the material intellect agrees squarely with his basic assumptions in metaphysics. The Commentator does not think that matter or extension is a principle of individuation, that is, as the principle which causes the multiplying of individuals within the same species. None the less, Averroes is persuaded that the existence of several individuals within a species is possible only in the case of material entities, i.e. entities that are composed of matter and inhering forms. Since the material intellect is not a material substance or a material form, but a subsisting form (para. 88), it is clearly the case that there can be only one material intellect. As Wylton explains, using

---

[68] See Aquinas, *De unitate intellectus*, 3, 303–4; Scotus, *Opus Oxoniense*, 4, dist. 43, q. 2, 37–8.
[69] See Guy Terreni, *Quodlibet* 6, q. 6 ('Utrum evidenter possit ostendi quod anima rationalis sit forma hominis informans corpus'), edition in Nielsen and Trifogli, 'Guido Terreni and his Debate with Thomas Wylton', §§ 1.4.1–2.9.5, 652–9, and introduction, 575–81.

the terminology of the Scotists, this single material intellect is individual, but in contradistinction to a material individual its hecceity or personal property is the same as its quiddity.

Moreover, this perception of the unity and individuality of the material intellect does not go against Averroes' claim that the material intellect is the form of man. As Wylton carefully explains, Averroes' understanding of the manner in which the single intellect relates to human beings is not fundamentally different from the way in which Catholics are used to regarding this relationship. According to Catholic opinion, the single substantial soul of an individual human being informs the whole of the particular individual's body as its first and principal perfectible thing. With Averroes the parallel situation obtains in so far as the material intellect is first and foremost the perfection of human nature and only secondarily of the several human supposits or individual human beings. Furthermore, according to the Catholic theory, the individual human soul is not dependent on informing this or that single part of the particular human body, e.g. this finger or that foot; at any rate, the loss of a limb does not necessarily spell the end of a human being. In just the same way, Wylton explains, the material intellect, according to Averroes' theory, does not depend on informing this or that individual human being since it is human nature as such that is first and foremost perfected by the material intellect (para. 95).

In spite of this evident structural isomorphism between Catholic theory and Averroes' understanding, the latter's view is not without its adversaries, and, as Wylton underscores, the Commentator's thesis on the unity of the material intellect gives rise to numerous objections. Even Averroes was not blind to its difficulties. Among others, he presents the following argument against the idea of the unity of the intellect: if Plato and Socrates are men by virtue of the material intellect, and the material intellect is one in number, it follows that Socrates and Plato are numerically one and the same man, but this is clearly not the case (para. 98).

In arguing against the unity of the intellect Albert the Great presents an even more explicit formulation of Averroes' argument. He specifies that a man, e.g. Socrates, is *hoc aliquid*, i.e. an individual substance of a given species, by virtue of his substantial form. Therefore, the substantial form of Socrates, being the principle by virtue of which Socrates is a particular human being, must be as individual as Socrates (para. 104).

Averroes' argument, as well as the version presented by Albert, rests squarely on the assumption that the substantial form of an individual substance is itself individual, and that it cannot be shared by other individuals of the same species. This assumption is taken to be a particular case of the more general claim that the intrinsic principles of particulars are themselves particular—a claim which Albert the Great finds in Aristotle and which he uses against Averroes (para. 105).

Albert's assumption is not, however, simple and uncontroversial since it reflects an anti-realist ontology with regard to universals, and it implies a denial of the existence of universal things as 'components' of individuals. At any rate, it is not a rule which could be accepted without reservations by a realist. Since Wylton is a realist in ontology, it is not surprising that he feels at liberty to deny this premiss in Averroes' and Albert's argument and to reject their reasoning as fallacious. In replying to the argument Wylton refuses to accept that an individual human being is both man and a particular being by virtue of the same ontological principle, viz. the intellectual soul or the substantial form. In the individual human being there is, according to his appraisal, a real distinction between two main principles. In the first place, there is that by virtue of which the human being is man, and this is human nature. Secondly, there is that by virtue of which the particular human being is an individual man, and this is the principle of individuation or, in Wylton's terminology, the hecceity.[70] Distinct individual men have distinct hecceities, but they are all men and hence human nature is a component shared by all individual men and a universal thing. Inasmuch as the substantial form of human beings is the ultimate formal principle by virtue of which human beings belong to the species of man, it is not a principle of individuation. It is precisely this strong distinction between human nature and hecceity as the individuating principle which allows Wylton to uphold the unity of the material intellect and at the same time to maintain its role as the substantial form of man. The substantial form of man is what defines human nature, and human nature, unlike the hecceity, is essentially one in all men (paras. 115, 121).

Although Averroes does not explicitly reply to the objection against the unity of the intellect reproduced above and to other objections to the same effect, Wylton believes that his realist solution reflects the *imaginatio* and the *intentio* of the Commentator. To Wylton it is clear that by positing only one material intellect for all men, Averroes would be willing to grant that there is only one human nature in all men. In this manner, the material intellect is primarily the highest perfection of human nature and only secondarily of this or that individual human being; or, seen from the perspective of the individual human being, it is the highest component without being limited by the principle of individuality. In Wylton's words, the first perfectible of the material intellect, i.e. the first thing of which the material

---

[70] Wylton's use of the Scotistic 'hecceity' does not indicate that he subscribes wholeheartedly to Scotus' view on the principle of individuation. He claims that the 'hecceity' of man is *ratione corporis* (para. 115) and that the individual difference is derived *ex parte materiae hominis* (para. 121). On the other hand, in these particular contexts the words 'matter' and 'body' refer to something which is formed, and, as Wylton later explains, individuation depends on both matter and form inasmuch as individual intentions are added to the species and received in matter (para. 176). Presumably this is also what Wylton alluded to in his question on the formal distinction; see Nielsen, Noone, and Trifogli, 'Thomas Wylton's Question on the Formal Distinction as Applied to the Divine', § 2.2.3, 353.

intellect is a perfection, is not Socrates or Plato but human nature, which includes Socrates and Plato among its supposits (paras. 95, 120).

Wylton's realist assumption regarding human nature does not suffice to solve the one–many problem which is inherent in Averroes' conception. The reason for this is that the unity of the material intellect is not adequately the same as that of human nature. Wylton assumes that a universal nature is numerically distinguished by its supposits which, in their turn, are multiplied by the principle of individuation (para. 120).[71] Accordingly, there is an incongruity between the material intellect, which exists as numerically one in distinct human beings, and human nature, which is numerically multiplied in distinct human supposits. In other words, Socrates' material intellect is numerically the same as that of Plato, but human nature as it exists in Socrates is numerically distinct from human nature as it exists in Plato.

One of Albert the Great's arguments against Averroes points out this discrepancy. The standard division of human nature is into animality and rationality. In order to make the individuation of human nature in Socrates congruent with the unity of the material intellect, it would, according to Albert, be necessary to stipulate that animality, which does not involve the intellect, is individuated in Socrates, whereas rationality, which is the essential property of the intellect, remains undivided. Accordingly, the specific nature of man would, on the basis of Averroes' principles, be composed of an individuated component, i.e. the nature of the genus, and an undivided and non-individuated component, i.e. the nature of the specific difference. To Albert this is clearly absurd (para. 107).

Wylton, on the other hand, does not find this irrational. To him it is clear that Averroes was required to allow such heterogeneous principles in the composition of man. The reason for this is that this composite of diverse principles is implied by the unbroken chain of being in the universe. The order of the universe implies that there is a continuous transition from the realm of immaterial substances to that of material substances. This continuity is safeguarded by the existence of a nature in which the two realms meet in such a way that this particular nature contains immaterial principles, which cannot be numerically divided and, by implication, become several within the same species, as well as material principles which are numerically many in distinct individuals. It is precisely human nature that holds this special place in the order of the universe (para. 123).

Wylton's appeal to the cosmological principle of the unbroken chain of being does not do away with all the problems inherent in his position. It does not address the fundamental question of how it is at all possible that the same form or nature can preserve its numerical identity while existing in numerically distinct indivi-

---

[71] In Wylton's treatment there is a noticeable lack of clarity in the definition and distribution of singularity, numerical diversity, and individuality. See also para. 199.

duals. Some of Averroes' opponents focus on exactly this problem and question whether it is at all possible for the material intellect to be united with several individual human beings; they claim that Averroes' conception fits only the divine nature which because of its infinity remains one at the same time as it is three persons (para. 110).

In replying to this objection Wylton relies on his general distinction between primary and secondary perfectibles. As he explains, a limited nature cannot exist as numerically one in distinct supposits of that nature, if these subjects are its first perfectibles. On the other hand, if the several supposits are its secondary perfectibles, the unity of the nature in question is not under threat. In the present context the force of Wylton's distinction between first and secondary perfectibles is that the being (*esse*) of a nature depends on its first perfectible whereas it does not rely on its secondary perfectibles. Applied to the case at hand, this implies that human nature cannot exist as numerically one in distinct human beings since individual human beings are the first perfectibles of human nature, and the being of human nature depends on these several supposits. On the other hand, the material intellect can exist as undivided and numerically one in distinct human beings, since individual human beings are not its first perfectibles; the first perfectible of the material intellect is human nature, and the material intellect is dependent on human nature as such (para. 133).

Wylton's response is clearly in need of further clarification, but unfortunately in his question he fails to give any supplementary explanation of the distinction. One obvious problem implied by his reply is that it does not seem to address the fundamental issue. If the being of the material intellect is said to depend on human nature and human nature depends on individual human beings, then, by implication, the material intellect would also seem to depend on individual human beings. It is remarkable that Wylton does not consider this possible countermove against his reply. Perhaps he would consider refuting this objection by positing that common natures possess proper being prior to their supposits and that the material intellect depends on precisely this ideal being of human nature.[72] At any rate, Wylton's question does not rule out an argument along these lines.

5.5. *Averroes' view and the Catholic view*

The attack on Averroes by several Catholic philosophers forms the immediate background to Wylton's critical appraisal of the Catholic opinion on the intellectual soul as the substantial form of man and the assumed rationality of this view. Wylton does not name these Catholic philosophers but it is said that they are

---

[72] Perhaps this is what Wylton alludes to in para. 120 when he attributes 'weak singularity' to human nature seen in isolation from its several supposits.

doctores, i.e. theologians; that they have commented on Aristotle's *De anima*; and that they attribute the standard Catholic view of the intellectual soul to Aristotle. These opponents are convinced that for Aristotle the intellectual soul is numerically distinct in distinct human beings; that the soul survives the individual human being whose form it is; and that the soul is brought into being by creation in time and at the time of the generation of the human individual. Moreover, they follow Thomas Aquinas in maintaining that the intellectual soul is the only substantial form in man, so that man is composed of prime matter and the intellectual soul, which is the principle of intellectual acts as well as of vegetative and sensitive operations.[73]

In their attack on Averroes these theologians maintain that most of what Averroes believed about the intellectual soul is *fictitious*, i.e. without rational foundation. In particular, they are convinced that it is irrational to claim that the material intellect is the perfection or act of man; to them it is folly to maintain that an entity which is a subsisting and separate thing can be the perfection of man, since man is another thing which is one by itself (para. 108).

In replying to this onslaught on Averroes, Wylton admits that 'it is difficult to understand in what manner one thing comes to be from a form that is non-inhering, but subsisting, and from matter' (para. 124). He is not slow to point out, however, that this problem concerns not only Averroes but also Catholics, since the intellectual soul of the Catholics is a subsisting and not an inhering form, just like Averroes' material intellect (para. 124).

Furthermore, Wylton claims that it is more difficult to understand the union between body and soul if talk is of the intellectual soul of the Catholics than it is to understand it in the case of Averroes' material intellect (para. 124). According to Wylton, the reason for this lack of intellectual transparency on the side of Catholic opinion is that the unity of a composite thing which includes a subsisting form and corresponding matter requires that the subsisting form has a natural dependence on matter.[74] While the material intellect of Averroes is inextricably dependent on its corresponding perfectible thing, this does not seem to be true of the Catholics' intellectual soul. According to the Catholics, the intellectual soul can be separated from its body without undergoing substantial change or loss of identity, whereas this does not hold good of Averroes' material intellect. To Wylton this difference between Averroes and the Catholics is crucial.

It is equally important, according to Wylton, to understand that the inextricable connection between the material intellect and human nature does not in any way

---

[73] Their arguments against Averroes are listed in paras. 108–11. References to them as *doctores* and as commentators on the *De anima* together with their interpretation of Aristotle's view are found in paras. 142–4. Their unitarian position on the substantial form of man is mentioned in para. 145.

[74] See above, § 5.3, for Wylton's definition of a subsisting form.

jeopardize the eternity of the material intellect. Since the first perfectible of the material intellect is human nature and not individual human beings, and since human nature is eternal, the material intellect will never be deprived of primary or secondary perfectibles.

As far as Wylton is concerned, the question concerning the separability of Averroes' material intellect consists in deciding whether the material intellect is separable from human nature and, more specifically, whether it may be separated from its counterpart in human nature, i.e. the human body with its sensitive powers. In identifying Averroes' stance Wylton accepts a traditional criterion of separability which was suggested by Aristotle and explicitly used by Thomas Aquinas. This rule lays down that separability in operation entails or is equivalent to separability in being.[75] For this reason, the question regarding the separability of the material intellect must be decided by considering whether for Averroes the proper operation of the material intellect, viz. intellectual cognition, can take place without involving the human body and its sensitive powers. Wylton claims that Averroes did not allow separation of the material intellect from human nature. According to Wylton's reading of Averroes—and also of Aristotle—there can be no doubt that intellectual cognition necessarily depends on the human body. This is true in the sense that *intelligere* is not properly an operation of the intellect alone but of the composite of intellect and body. The necessary contribution of the body to intellectual cognition is, roughly speaking, that the body provides the phantasms, the sensible images, which are necessary both for the acquisition of concepts and for their use. In this connection Wylton repeats the standard claim that our intellect understands nothing without conversion to phantasms (paras. 124–5). Catholics, on their side, are also willing to accept this claim as true but only in a qualified sense, so that it holds good as long as the intellect is joined to the body. With Averroes, however, this claim is true without any qualifications at all, and consequently he is much more consistent in his view of the inseparability of the material intellect.

This principle of dependence in being and in operation is also employed by Wylton in order to explain why the agent intellect, unlike the material intellect, is not an intrinsic formal principle of man. The proper operation of the agent intellect is the intellection of God and of the separate substances superior to it; this kind of intellection is in no way dependent on the human body (paras. 126, 128).[76] Accordingly, it is incontestable that the agent intellect is not dependent on human nature or human beings with regard to its being.

---

[75] Arist. *DA* 1. 1, 403ª10–12; Thomas Aquinas, *Summa theologiae*, pars 1, q. 75, a. 2, ed. Leonina, 5 (Rome, 1889), 196.

[76] By a similar chain of reasoning Wylton demonstrates that the intelligence which moves a celestial sphere cannot be an intrinsic formal principle of the heavens. See paras. 127, 131.

Wylton's exposition of Averroes' view on the material intellect and its salient features is beset with numerous problems. One of the immediately apparent questions is how the inseparability of the material intellect relates to human beings as individuals. Wylton underscores that the material intellect is inseparable from human nature and is tied to human nature for its being. Equally, he states that the operation of the material intellect, viz. intellection, is dependent on phantasms. It is, however, obvious that phantasms belong to human beings as supposits and not to human nature as such; phantasms are generated and corrupted in individual human beings, who consist of intellectual soul and individual human bodies which are endowed with the powers of sense. Consequently, in being the material intellect is inseparable from human nature, but in operation it is inextricably linked to the operations of the several individual human beings. To all appearances, Wylton ends up with the same disappointment as before: the distinction between primary and secondary perfectible things does not extricate the material intellect from being dependent on what is individual and contingent.

Wylton addresses this particular problem in his discussion of Averroes' understanding of the so-called 'speculative intellect', i.e. the composite which consists of the material intellect together with universal intentions as its perfections (para. 57). In this connection he makes the point that, according to Averroes, the material intellect possesses from eternity abstract intentions of ordinary objects in the material world. However, the material intellect does not always possess these intentions as abstracted from the phantasms of this or that particular human being, but solely for the duration of its being joined to these particular individual human beings. Consequently, for the functioning of the material intellect it is sufficient that there are phantasms belonging to some human beings, but, as far as the material intellect is concerned, it is without importance whether these phantasms belong to one individual human being rather than another.

While defending Averroes' stance on the material intellect Wylton introduces some conceptual innovations into the discussion of the status of the human soul. In previous treatments of this topic the subsistence of the soul had been seen as a necessary and sufficient condition for its separability.[77] Wylton, however, denies this strict linking of subsistence and separability. As he sees it, Averroes' material intellect is a subsisting thing but it cannot be said to be separable. Furthermore, with most authors of the Christian persuasion the difficulty of proving that the intellectual soul is the form of man is rooted in the fact that the soul is considered to be a subsisting thing. Inversely, for Wylton, who disconnects subsistence from separability, the difficulty of viewing the intellectual soul as the form of man is prompted by the fact that it requires ascribing separability to the soul. This shift in emphasis is also made clear by the way in which he justifies his scepticism

---

[77] See e.g. Thomas Aquinas, *Summa theologiae*, pars 1, q. 75, a. 2, 196–7.

with regard to the Catholics' way of addressing this problem. It is precisely the Catholics' claim that the intellectual soul survives the individual human being whose form it is that makes it so hard to understand how it may be a form (para. 179). As Wylton underscores, this is true even if the term 'form' is used in a very broad sense so as to encompass both inhering and subsisting forms (para. 177).

5.6. *Cognition of universals and cognition of singulars*

Despite his reservations with regard to the possibility of finding convincing rational arguments in favour of the Catholic opinion, Wylton accepts that the Christian opinion is true and that Averroes was mistaken in positing only one intellect for all men. According to Wylton's interpretation of both Aristotle and Averroes, individuality is simply incompatible with immateriality and for this reason there cannot be many individuals of the same immaterial species. This does not imply, however, that Wylton is reluctant to accept that, in actual fact, individuality and immateriality are compatible and that the intellect is both an immaterial cognitive power and an individual. Where he does spot a problem is in explaining how the individuality of the intellect is compatible with universal cognition, which is the very hallmark of the intellect. As Wylton observes, the main motive which prompted Aristotle and Averroes to claim that there is only one intellect was precisely their concern to preserve the intellect's ability to attain cognition of universals (para. 187). Being something undivided and non-individual is, as Averroes argued, what distinguishes the intellect from the senses. If the intellect were individual and multiplied with its human supposits, it would enjoy the same type of cognition as the senses, i.e. cognition of singulars (para. 91).

Wylton is strongly impressed with this argument of Averroes', which he discusses at length. In elaborating on it, he appeals to the general principle that 'the thing received is received according to the way of the receiver', which applied to the case at hand leads to the conclusion that every intention will be singular if the intellect itself is singular. Moreover, an intention in an individual intellect will be singular in two ways: both as regards its being and with respect to representation (para. 91). This means that the intention of, for example, a horse received in the intellect of some individual human being is not only itself a single entity, which is numerically distinct from the intention of a horse received in another intellect: it is also singular in the sense that it represents only some particular horse, whereas it does not represent the universal nature of the horse. Accordingly, it is the singularity in representation that prevents the individual human being from reaching universal cognition and obliterates the distinction between sensory and intellectual cognition.[78]

As Wylton explains, ordinarily the Catholics respond to this argument by admitting the singularity in being of an intellectual intention; on the other hand, they deny that the intellectual intention is singular in representation and claim that it is universal in representation. In order to justify this claim, they adduce the fact that an intention is singular in representation not because of the singularity of the cognitive faculty in which it is received, but because of its materiality. Consequently, a sensible intention is singular not only in being but also in representation, since the senses are both singular and corporeal. On the other hand, an intellectual intention is singular in being but universal in representation because of the immateriality of intellect (para. 185). Seen from the stance of the Catholics, Averroes' counter-argument is based on the unwarranted assumption that an individual intellect must by necessity be material.

As Wylton sees it, this attempt to save the universal cognition of an individual intellect is unsuccessful. He assumes that the intellect and the senses share the property of being singular, and that the difference between the intellect and the senses is that the senses are organic and corporeal whereas the intellect is immaterial. This makes materiality the obvious candidate for explaining why the senses yield intentions which are singular both in being and in representation—that is, why the senses know only singulars. However, Wylton does not accept this easy answer. According to him, materiality as such is not incompatible with universality; materiality is incompatible only with immateriality (para. 186). For this reason, the materiality of the senses precludes only sensible cognition of immaterial substances, but not that of universal natures of material things. What makes impossible sensible cognition of universals must be the singularity of the senses (para. 187). But this is precisely the property which the senses have in common with the intellect.

Wylton attempts to solve this conundrum by very careful reasoning. He accepts that intellectual species are caused by the corresponding phantasms together with the agent intellect which acts on the phantasms. It is also clear that phantasms and the agent intellect are incapable of producing an intention which is universal in representation. The phantasms in the imagination are singular both in being and in representation, since they are sensible images. The agent intellect is also singular and, accordingly, its act of illuminating the phantasms is singular as well (paras. 194–5). In the final analysis Wylton admits to being unable to come up with the 'golden' solution to the problem of how the intellect attains cognition of universal natures. On the basis of the idea that the material or possible intellect is

---

[78] For the problem of the infinite regress in abstraction created by the individuality in being and the relatively easy solution to it, see paras. 92, 200–3.

individuated together with its human supposits and that the universal is the proper object of the intellect, Wylton suggests a rather ambiguous answer. He proposes that one might say that the agent intellect is singular in being but universal in its acts of illuminating the phantasms. Together with the immateriality of the recipient of the act of intellection, i.e. the possible intellect, this might account for the formation of concepts which are universal in representation. On the other hand, Wylton finds the reason why the species in the sensible soul are singular, both in being and in representation, in the combination of materiality and singularity which is characteristic of the sensible soul. However, he is not at all convinced of the validity of reasoning along these lines (para. 196).

For this reason it is not surprising that Wylton proposes a radical modification to the theory of intellectual cognition. Following in the footsteps of Aristotle and Averroes, it is generally assumed that the primary and direct object of intellectual cognition is the universal, whereas the singular is known only indirectly; the intellect is assumed to be receptive of only universal intentions or species so that there cannot be intelligible species of singulars. This is the reason why the intellect enjoys direct knowledge of the nature of, for example, the horse, while its only possibility of perceiving a particular horse goes by the indirect linking or 'joining' of the universal intention of the horse with the phantasms of a particular horse. As Wylton stresses, it is necessary to assume the primacy of universals as objects of intellectual cognition within the framework of Aristotle's and Averroes' epistemology, but this does not hold good in the kind of epistemology that is opened up by the Catholics' stipulation of individual intellectual souls. According to Aristotle and Averroes, the material intellect is not singular, and there is no congruity between the intellect and the species of a singular thing; accordingly, this kind of intellect can harbour only universal species. Given the Catholic belief in the singular intellectual soul, all this is changed. The single intellect is the congenial recipient of species of single objects. This means that the primacy of universal cognition will have to be redefined if the basic assumptions of the Catholic position are sustained.

What Wylton envisages is, firstly, that the intellect has direct cognition of singulars. This is fitting since the intellectual soul is the form of the human body and in this indirect manner it is a 'material' thing. Secondly, Wylton is ready to accept that singulars are the first objects of intellectual cognition in the sense that the cognition of singulars comes first in time. According to him, this entails that the intellect receives singular species, viz. intentions which are singular both in being and in representation, and that intelligible objects of this kind are first in the process of cognition. Thirdly, he is not willing to give up the idea that universals are the proper objects of the intellect. With him, however, this merely implies that what is universal can be known only by the intellect and falls outside the scope of the senses (para. 198). Wylton is also totally clear as to how the intellect achieves universal cognition. This requires the presence of the agent intellect, which enables the possible intellect to gain insight into the universal by a process of 'abstraction'. In other words, the intellect has direct cognition of singulars and achieves cognition of the corresponding universals precisely on the basis of the cognition of singulars which are necessarily required elements in the process (para. 197). Wylton does not develop his new theory of cognition in the question on the intellectual soul. Here he merely sketches the outline of what he has in mind, and additionally he refers the reader to another of his questions, which deals with the problem of whether the intellect forms concepts of what is singular.

This question is part of Wylton's so-called *Quodlibet*, and here he focuses exclusively on the nature of intellectual cognition. It transpires from this question that Wylton's innovation concerns not only the intellectual cognition of singulars but also the nature of abstraction, i.e. the formation of universal concepts. Whereas abstraction is normally placed in the lower imaginative or phantasmatical part of the sensitive soul, Wylton transports it to the level of the intellect. The reason for this is that he fails to see how abstraction from the singular phantasms in the sensible part of the soul could engender anything in the intellect. Irrespective of how phantasms are illuminated by the agent intellect, they still exist in the sensible part of the soul, and here they can represent only particular things (*ut hic et nunc*). However, the results of abstraction are supposed to reside in the intellect and be universal.[79] Furthermore, Wylton argues, even if this two-tier type of abstraction were granted, it would preclude intellectual cognition of singulars, and even the indirect cognition which is commonly allowed.[80]

According to Wylton's alternative account, abstraction is a process which belongs on the level of the intellect. The starting-point of abstraction is not phantasms but the intellectual species or intentions of singulars. These intentions of singulars are the primary results of the cognitive process, and they are the presupposition of intellectual cognition of universals. The process of abstraction on the basis of the intentions of singulars Wylton explains as follows:

> How the intellect arrives at cognition of the universal I understand along the following lines. This takes place by means of the power of the agent intellect, since the agent intellect illuminates the species existing in the possible intellect, which is the subject and recipient of this light—in contradistinction to the imaginative power, which has no spiritual light. By means of this light the intellect as actuated by the said species can consider the thing which is presented under the 'here and now' conditions as detached

[79] Thomas Wylton, *Quodlibet*, qq. 7–8 ('An intellectus noster possit de duobus singularibus formare duo verba'), ed. Senko, 'Tomasza Wiltona Quaestio', 120. 26–32. Wylton's theory of abstraction is diametrically opposed to the theory defended by Guy Terreni; see Nielsen and Trifogli, 'Guido Terreni and his Debate with Thomas Wylton', 581–5.
[80] Ed. Senko, 117. 33–42.

from the 'here and now', and this is the same as abstracting the quiddity from the individual conditions of the single thing. But this whole process of abstraction presupposes that there is a species of the single thing in the intellect from which abstraction can take place.[81]

In the question on the intellectual soul Wylton appears to suggest that his innovative account of the formation of universal concepts, which was elaborated in the quodlibetal question, presents a reply to the objections which had previously been raised against the possibility of universal cognition in a singular intellect (para. 197). As already mentioned, the crucial problem consists in identifying the manner in which a singular intellect produces or contains species which are universal in representation. It is not immediately clear that Wylton can be said to have provided a solution to this problem by basing the formation of universal concepts or species on the intentions, species, or concepts of singular objects. Possibly he would be willing to consider a theory according to which the possible or material intellect obtains cognition of individual intentions or properties. In that case the process of abstraction as described above would seem to be possible even in the case that the intellect had access to only a single species of some individual thing. However, Wylton's account would still leave the role played by the agent intellect somewhat in the dark. At any rate, he does not explore this subject further in the present question.

[81] Ibid. 119. 28–35.

THOMAS WYLTON

QUAESTIO DE ANIMA INTELLECTIVA

CONSPECTUS QUAESTIONIS

INTRODUCTIO (1–5)
RATIONES PRO (1–3)
RATIO CONTRA (4)
PROCESSUS CIRCA QUAESTIONEM (5)

ARTICULUS 1: DEFINITIO ANIMAE INTELLECTIVAE ET
    FORMAE CORPORIS (6)

ARTICULUS 2: DE INTENTIONE AVERROIS (7–141)
PUNCTUS 1 ARTICULI 2: DISTINCTIO INTELLECTUS (8–83)
  DE INTELLECTU MATERIALI (9–23)
    OPINIO AVERROIS (9–11)
    OPINIO ALIORUM 1: INTELLECTUS MATERIALIS
      EST PURUM POSSIBILE (12)
    CONTRA OPINIONEM ALIORUM 1 (13–15)
    OPINIO ALIORUM 2: INTELLECTUS AGENS EST
      FORMA INTELLECTUS MATERIALIS (16)
    CONTRA OPINIONEM ALIORUM 2 (17–19)
    CONTRA OPINIONEM ALIORUM 1—RESUMPTIO (20)
    AD RATIONES PRO OPINIONE ALIORUM 1 (21–3)
  DE INTELLECTU AGENTE (24–54)
    DUBITATIO 1: DE SEPARABILITATE INTELLECTUS
      AGENTIS (32–44)
    AD ARGUMENTA OPINIONIS CONTRARIAE (45–9)
    DUBITATIO 2: DE COMMUNITATE INTELLECTUS
      AGENTIS ET MATERIALIS (50–4)
  DE INTELLECTU SPECULATIVO (55–8)
  DE INTELLECTU IN HABITO (59–60)
  DE INTELLECTU ADEPTO (61–82)
    OPINIO AVERROIS DE COGNITIONE
      SUBSTANTIARUM SEPARATARUM IN 3
      DE ANIMA (62–8)

OVERVIEW OF THE QUESTION

INTRODUCTION	(1–5)
ARGUMENTS FOR AN AFFIRMATIVE ANSWER	(1–3)
ARGUMENT AGAINST AN AFFIRMATIVE ANSWER	(4)
PROCEDURE FOR DEALING WITH THE QUESTION	(5)
ARTICLE 1: DEFINITION OF THE INTELLECTUAL SOUL AND THE FORM OF THE BODY	(6)
ARTICLE 2: ON AVERROES' CONCEPTION	(7–141)
POINT 1 OF ARTICLE 2: THE DIVISION OF THE INTELLECT	(8–83)
ON THE MATERIAL INTELLECT	(9–23)
THE OPINION OF AVERROES	(9–11)
OPINION OF OTHERS 1: THE MATERIAL INTELLECT IS SOMETHING PURELY POSSIBLE	(12)
AGAINST THE OPINION OF OTHERS 1	(13–15)
OPINION OF OTHERS 2: THE AGENT INTELLECT IS THE FORM OF THE MATERIAL INTELLECT	(16)
AGAINST THE OPINION OF OTHERS 2	(17–19)
AGAINST THE OPINION OF OTHERS 1—RESUMED	(20)
IN ANSWER TO THE ARGUMENTS FOR THE OPINION OF OTHERS 1	(21–3)
ON THE AGENT INTELLECT	(24–54)
DOUBT 1: ON THE SEPARABILITY OF THE AGENT INTELLECT	(32–44)
IN ANSWER TO THE ARGUMENTS FOR THE OPPOSITE OPINION	(45–9)
DOUBT 2: ON THE COMMUNITY OF THE AGENT AND MATERIAL INTELLECTS	(50–4)
ON THE SPECULATIVE INTELLECT	(55–8)
ON THE INTELLECT IN HABIT	(59–60)
ON THE ACCOMPLISHED INTELLECT	(61–82)
OPINION OF AVERROES CONCERNING THE COGNITION OF SEPARATE SUBSTANCES IN *ON THE SOUL* 3	(62–8)

OPINIO AVERROIS DE COGNITIONE
    SUBSTANTIARUM SEPARATARUM IN 12
    METAPHYSICAE (69–76)
CONTRADICTIO AVERROIS (77–78)
AD RATIONES PROBANTES CONTRADICTIONEM
    AVERROIS (79–81)
QUADRUPLEX STATUS INTELLECTUS HOMINIS (82)
DE INTELLECTU PASSIVO (83)
PUNCTUS 2 ARTICULI 2: SENTENTIA AVERROIS (84–95)
    CONCORDIA ET DISCORDIA AVERROIS CUM FIDE
        CATHOLICA (85–6)
    RATIONES AVERROIS PRO UNITATE INTELLECTUS
        MATERIALIS (87–94)
    MODUS PONENDI AVERROIS (95)
PUNCTUS 3 ARTICULI 2: RATIONES CONTRA AVERROEM (96–111)
    RATIONES AVERROIS (96–103)
    RATIONES ALBERTI (104–7)
    RATIONES ALIORUM (108–11)
PUNCTUS 4 ARTICULI 2: AD RATIONES CONTRA
    AVERROEM (112–41)
    AD RATIONES AVERROIS (112–20)
    AD RATIONES ALBERTI (121–3)
    AD RATIONES ALIORUM (124–34)
    DE COPULATIONE INTELLECTUS CUM INDIVIDUO (135–8)
    AD RATIONES PRINCIPALES (139–41)

ARTICULUS 3: DE CONCORDIA ET DISCORDIA
    AVERROIS CUM ARISTOTELE (142–76)

ARTICULUS 4: OPINIO THOMAE WYLTON (177–9)

ARTICULUS 5: AD RATIONES PHILOSOPHORUM
    ADVERSUS VERITATEM FIDEI (180–208)

OPINION OF AVERROES CONCERNING THE
  COGNITION OF SEPARATE SUBSTANCES IN
  METAPHYSICS 12   (69–76)
CONTRADICTION OF AVERROES   (77–78)
IN ANSWER TO THE ARGUMENTS PROVING THE
  CONTRADICTION OF AVERROES   (79–81)
THE FOURFOLD STATE OF THE INTELLECT OF
  MAN   (82)
ON THE PASSIVE INTELLECT   (83)
POINT 2 OF ARTICLE 2: THE STATED OPINION OF
  AVERROES   (84–95)
AGREEMENT AND DISAGREEMENT OF AVERROES
  WITH THE CATHOLIC FAITH   (85–6)
AVERROES' ARGUMENTS FOR THE UNITY OF THE
  MATERIAL INTELLECT   (87–94)
AVERROES' WAY OF UPHOLDING   (95)
POINT 3 OF ARTICLE 2: ARGUMENTS AGAINST
  AVERROES   (96–111)
AVERROES' ARGUMENTS   (96–103)
ALBERT'S ARGUMENTS   (104–7)
ARGUMENTS OF OTHERS   (108–11)
POINT 4 OF ARTICLE 2: IN ANSWER TO THE
  ARGUMENTS AGAINST AVERROES   (112–41)
IN ANSWER TO AVERROES' ARGUMENTS   (112–20)
IN ANSWER TO ALBERT'S ARGUMENTS   (121–3)
IN ANSWER TO THE ARGUMENTS OF OTHERS   (124–34)
ON THE CONJOINING OF THE INTELLECT WITH AN
  INDIVIDUAL   (135–8)
IN ANSWER TO THE PRINCIPAL ARGUMENTS   (139–41)

ARTICLE 3: ON THE AGREEMENT AND DISAGREEMENT
  OF AVERROES WITH ARISTOTLE   (142–76)

ARTICLE 4: OPINION OF THOMAS WYLTON   (177–9)

ARTICLE 5: IN ANSWER TO THE ARGUMENTS OF THE
  PHILOSOPHERS IN OPPOSITION TO THE TRUTH
  OF FAITH   (180–208)

AN INTELLECTIVAM ESSE FORMAM HUMANI CORPORIS POSSIT RATIONE NECESSARIA ET EVIDENTI CONVINCI

⟨INTRODUCTIO⟩

⟨RATIONES PRO⟩

1. Quod sic probatur quia homo experitur se intelligere. Actus autem intelligendi est actus immanens intelligenti ex 9 *Metaphysicae*.[1] Igitur vel intellectus, qui est pura potentia receptiva actus intelligendi, est homo totus vel pars hominis. Non est homo totus, quia 'homo' in suo intellectu primo includit substantiam corpoream, 'intellectus' non. Igitur intellectus est pars hominis. Non materialis, quia distinguit hominem specifice a quacumque alia specie. Ergo pars formalis.

2. Confirmatur haec ratio per intentionem Philosophi, 2 *De anima*,[2] dicentis quod illud quo vivimus, sentimus et intelligimus est actus corporis. Anima intellectiva est huiusmodi. Igitur etc.

3. Secundo ad idem arguitur: 'rationale' secundum intentionem Philosophi et omnium philosophorum definientium hominem est differentia specifica hominis. Igitur forma a qua homo dicitur 'rationalis' est formale in compositione hominis.

⟨RATIO CONTRA⟩

4. Contra. Aristoteles, qui inter philosophos maxime viguit ratione naturali, hoc non sensit, ut Averroes eum exponens sibi imponit, qui tamen inter expositores eius eum melius intellexit et magis circa istam materiam laboravit.

⟨PROCESSUS CIRCA QUAESTIONEM⟩

5. Circa hanc quaestionem sic procedam: primo exponam duos terminos positos in quaestione;[3] secundo recitabo opinionem Averrois;[4] tertio inquiram an

---

1–3 AN . . . CONVINCI] An intellectivam esse formam corporis humani possit ratione necessaria probari et convinci evidenter O; Utrum possit convinci evidenti ratione animam intellectivam esse formam corporis T   6 Quod . . . probatur] quod sic O; Et arguitur quod sic T   7 intelligenti] in intellectu T || vel *om.* T   8 pura potentia] *inv.* O; potentia T || intelligendi] vel *add.* T || vel] aut O; est *add.* P   9 est *om.* T || homo *om.* P || quia] quoniam P   10 hominis] sed *add.* T   11 hominem specifice] *inv.* P || quacumque . . . specie] quocumque non homine O || Ergo] est *add.* T || pars *om.* T || formalis] et *add.* T   13 corporis] sed *add.* O.   13–14 intellectiva *om.* O   14 Igitur etc. *om.* P   15 ad . . . arguitur] arguitur ad idem T || Philosophi] Aristotelis T   16 specifica hominis] eius specifica O   17 qua] quo OP || 'rationalis'] rationale T   20 ut] vel nec *add. i.m.* T || sibi imponit] *inv.* T   21 eius *om.* T || magis] *iter. et corr.* P   23 sic procedam *om.* T

WHETHER IT CAN BE ESTABLISHED BY NECESSARY AND EVIDENT REASONING THAT THE INTELLECTUAL SOUL IS THE FORM OF THE HUMAN BODY

⟨INTRODUCTION⟩

⟨ARGUMENTS FOR AN AFFIRMATIVE ANSWER⟩

1. That this is the case is proved by the fact that man experiences himself as understanding. But the act of understanding is an act immanent to the thing that understands (from *Metaphysics* 9).[1] Therefore the intellect, which is the pure receptive potency of the act of understanding, is either the whole man or it is a part of man. It is not the whole man, since 'man' in its primary sense includes bodily substance, whereas 'intellect' does not. Therefore the intellect is a part of man. It is not a material part, since it specifically distinguishes man from any other species. Therefore it is a formal part.

2. This argument is confirmed by the conception of the Philosopher in *On the Soul* 2,[2] where he states that that by which we live, sense, and understand is an act of body. The intellectual soul is such a thing. Therefore etc.

3. Secondly, the same conclusion can be argued for in the following way: 'rational', according to the conception of the Philosopher, and of all philosophers who define man, is the specific difference of man. Therefore the form on account of which man is called 'rational' is a formal principle in the composition of man.

⟨ARGUMENT AGAINST AN AFFIRMATIVE ANSWER⟩

4. To the contrary. Aristotle, who among philosophers most excelled in natural reasoning, did not think so, as Averroes maintains in his interpretation of Aristotle, and after all, among Aristotle's interpreters he understood him best and worked the most on this matter.

⟨PROCEDURE FOR DEALING WITH THE QUESTION⟩

5. In dealing with this question I shall proceed in the following way: firstly I shall expound the two terms used in the question;[3] secondly I shall set out the opinion of Averroes;[4] thirdly I shall investigate whether his opinion accords with

---

[1] Arist. *Metaph.* 9. 8, 1050^{a}34–6.
[2] Arist. *DA* 2. 2, 414^{a}12–14.
[3] See below, para. 6.
[4] See below, paras. 7–141.

opinio sua concordet opinioni Aristotelis;[5] quarto dicam quid mihi videtur esse dicendum ad quaestionem;[6] quinto dicam ad argumenta quae contra partem videntur facere quam tenebo.[7]

⟨ARTICULUS 1: DEFINITIO ANIMAE INTELLECTIVAE
ET FORMAE CORPORIS ⟩

6. De primo primo exponam quid intelligam per animam intellectivam; secundo, quid intelligam per formam corporis. Per animam intellectivam intelligo formam quae est homini principium cognoscendi quidditates rerum abstractas, per quam cognitionem homo in cognoscendo excellit bruta. Per formam, quae multipliciter dicitur in usu philosophorum, intelligo formam informantem corpus humanum vel eius materiam non-inhaerentem—ut inhaerere est proprietas opposita per se esse vel subsistere per naturam. Nam licet haec sit conditio aliarum formarum omnium quae educuntur de potentia materiae, tam substantialium quam accidentalium, licet aliter et aliter, tamen omnes in hoc conveniunt—et sancti et alii—de intellectiva, quae ponitur forma hominis, quod non est forma sic informans. Sed intelligo in proposito per formam informantem formam habentem inclinationem naturalem, ordinem et dependentiam ad aliud, ita quod ex alio et ipsa natum sit fieri unum compositum, quod per ipsam distinguitur specifice a quocumque alio.

⟨ARTICULUS 2: DE INTENTIONE AVERROIS⟩

7. Circa secundum principale, scilicet intentionem Averrois in ista materia, sic procedam: primo recitabo quandam distinctionem de intellectu qua ipse in diversis commentis 3 *De anima* utitur, et membra illius distinctionis exponam, | ut eius intentio clarius innotescat.[8] Secundo recitabo opinionem suam quantum ad conclusionem quam tenuit, cum motivis suis et modo suo ponendi.[9] Tertio reducam rationes, tam suas quam aliorum, quae videntur mihi esse ponderis contra opinionem suam.[10] Quarto discurram per illas rationes inquirendo si aliqua illarum convincat evidenter suam opinionem esse falsam.[11]

---

1 concordet opinioni] contendet opinionem T || dicam *om.* T || quid] quod O **1–2** esse dicendum] *inv.* T **2** ad² *om.* T **2–3** contra... facere] videntur facere contra partem T || **2** partem] *corr. ex* partes O **6** De primo] quantum ad primum O || primo exponam] *inv.* T; primo ponam P **6–7** secundo] secundum O **8** abstractas] abstracta O **9** excellit] excedit OT **10–11** corpus humanum] *illegibile* T **11** vel] et T || inhaerentem] inhaerenter O; inhaerens T || inhaerere est] est inhaerens T **12** vel] et T || per naturam *om.* OT || Nam licet] licet enim P **14** licet... aliter² *om.* P || et²] etiam O **15** forma sic] *inv.* T **16** formam² *om.* P **17** naturalem, ordinem] *inv.* O || et²] ex *add.* O || natum sit] *inv.* O **20** scilicet] secundum P **21** quandam *om.* P **24** conclusionem] *iter. et corr.* P || ponendi] possibili P **25** tam... quam] suas et etiam T || mihi esse *om.* O **26** illas rationes] *inv.* O; alias rationes P || inquirendo *om.* T || illarum] istarum *suppl. i.m.* P **27** convincat] *corr. ex* evincat O; devincat T

the opinion of Aristotle;[5] fourthly I shall say what seems to me necessary to be said in reply to the question;[6] fifthly I shall address the arguments which seem to militate against the position that I shall maintain.[7]

⟨ARTICLE 1: DEFINITION OF THE INTELLECTUAL SOUL AND THE FORM OF THE BODY⟩

6. As to the first point, I shall first explain what I understand by intellectual soul; secondly, what I understand by bodily form. By intellectual soul I understand the form which serves man as the principle of cognizing the abstract quiddities of things, by which cognition man surpasses brutes in cognizing. By form, a word which is used equivocally by philosophers, I understand the form that informs the human body or its matter without inhering—in so far as inhering is a property opposed to being by itself or subsisting by nature. For although this is the condition of all other forms which are elicited from the potency of matter, both substantial forms and accidental forms, although in differing ways, still all people—both saints and others—agree on this: that the intellectual soul, which is claimed to be the form of man, is not a form that informs him in this way. In the proposed case, however, I understand by an informing form a form having a natural inclination, an order, and a dependence towards something else, in such a way that from itself and something else one composite is apt by nature to come to be, which by virtue of such a form is specifically distinguished from every other thing.

⟨ARTICLE 2: ON AVERROES' CONCEPTION⟩

7. Concerning the second principal point, namely Averroes' conception of this matter, I shall proceed in the following way: firstly I shall set out a distinction concerning the intellect which he himself uses in several of his comments on *On the Soul* 3, and I shall expound the elements of this distinction, so that his conception may become more clearly known.[8] Secondly I shall set out his opinion regarding the conclusion which he held, with his motives and his way of upholding it.[9] Thirdly I shall repeat the arguments, both his own and those of others, which seem to me to have weight against his opinion.[10] Fourthly I shall run through those arguments and investigate whether any one of them establishes with evidence that his opinion is false.[11]

---

[5] See below, paras. 142–76.
[6] See below, paras. 177–9.
[7] See below, paras. 180–208.
[8] See below, paras. 8–83.
[9] See below, paras. 84–95.
[10] See below, paras. 96–111.
[11] See below, paras. 112–41.

⟨PUNCTUS 1 ARTICULI 2: DISTINCTIO INTELLECTUS⟩

8. Circa primum sciendum quod Commentator, 3 *De anima*, in diversis commentis, utitur nomine 'intellectus' secundum diversas acceptiones, quas exponit determinando ipsum per diversas determinationes. Loquitur enim de intellectu materiali, de intellectu agente, de intellectu speculativo, de intellectu in habitu, de intellectu adepto et de intellectu passibili seu passivo.

⟨DE INTELLECTU MATERIALI⟩

⟨OPINIO AVERROIS⟩

9. Intellectum materialem vel intellectum quem nos vocamus quasi appellatione 'intellectum possibilem' ipse describit in principio 5 commenti dicens quod 'nullam naturam aut essentiam habet qua constituatur secundum quod materialis, nisi naturam possibilitatis, cum denudetur'[12] etc. Postea ibi dicit quod definitio eius est 'quod est in potentia omnes intentiones formarum materialium'.[13] Postea etiam ibi dicit quod 'non est aliquod entium antequam intelligat'.[14]

10. Et postea ibidem dat duplicem differentiam inter intellectum materialem et materiam primam. Prima est quod intellectus materialis est in potentia omnes intentiones formarum universalium; materia autem singularium formarum, quarum conclusio in materia est terminatio materiae in eis; non sic intellectus.[15] Secunda differentia est quod materia non cognoscit res; intellectus autem materialis distinguit et cognoscit.[16] Tertiam differentiam ponit 14 et 28 commento istius tertii, et est quod materia non est causa cuiuscumque receptionis, sed receptionis transmutabilis; intellectus autem absque transmutatione, id est absque abiectione perfectionis, recipit.[17] Propter quod in 14 commento assimilat ipsum intellectum tabulae nudae, quae, cum de novo depingitur, perficitur, sed non transmutatur, eo quod nulla perfectio abicitur.[18] Hanc autem passionem intellectus vocat Commentator, 2 *De anima*, commento 57, 'evasionem',[19] et hoc sive procedat intellectus ab ignorantia in scientiam, sive ab habitu in actum secundum. Utroque modo patitur intellectus,

---

3 acceptiones] exceptiones T   **4** determinationes] acceptiones T; *fortasse scribendum* adjectiones   **6** et ... passivo *om.* T; et de intellectu passivo O   **9** Intellectum materialem] intellectus autem materialis natura est O; intellectus autem materialis P ‖ vel intellectum *om.* OP ‖ quem] quam O ‖ nos *om.* T   **9–10** quasi appellatione *om.* OP   **10** possibilem] quem *add.* O ‖ ipse] sic *add.* O ‖ **11** constituatur] constituitur O   **12** Postea] post P ‖ ibi *om.* O   **13** est[1] *om.* O ‖ Postea] post P   **15** Et *om.* O ‖ duplicem] *fortasse scribendum* triplicem   **16** est[1] *om.* T *et differentia add.* ‖ in *om.* O ‖ omnes] formas *add. et del.* O   **17** formarum[1] *om.* O ‖ autem] vero T ‖ singularium formarum] *inv.* O   **18** in materia] *suppl. i.m.* P ‖ in[2]] *corr. i.m. ex* et P ‖ non] nec O   **19** autem *om.* OT ‖ materialis *om.* O   **19–20** distinguit ... cognoscit] cognoscit et distinguit O *et res add.*   **20** istius tertii] libri tertii De anima T ‖ et est] etc. P   **22** id est] et T   **23** in] *om.* T ‖ assimilat ... intellectum] ipsum intellectum assimilat O; ipsum assimilat T   **26** commento 57] *inv.* O   **27** scientiam] scientia O ‖ sive] procedat *add.* P ‖ secundum *om.* O   **27–12.1** Utroque ... perfectionem *om.* T

⟨POINT 1 OF ARTICLE 2: THE DIVISION OF THE INTELLECT⟩

8. Concerning the first point, it must be realized that the Commentator, in several of his comments on *On the Soul* 3, uses the noun 'intellect' according to several different meanings, which he explains by limiting it with different determinations. For he speaks of the material intellect, of the agent intellect, of the speculative intellect, of the intellect in habit, of the accomplished intellect, and of the passible or passive intellect.

⟨ON THE MATERIAL INTELLECT⟩

⟨THE OPINION OF AVERROES⟩

9. At the beginning of his comment 5 he describes the material intellect, or the intellect which by naming we call 'possible intellect', saying that 'it has no nature or essence by which it could be constituted in so far as it is material, except the nature of possibility, when it is stripped bare'[12] etc. Later he says there that its definition is that 'it is in potency all intentions of material forms'.[13] Later again he says there that it 'is not even one among beings before it understands'.[14]

10. And later, in the same place, he provides a double difference between the material intellect and prime matter. The first is that the material intellect is in potency all intentions of universal forms; but matter belongs to singular forms, whose inclusion in matter is also the delimitation of matter in them; the intellect is not like this.[15] The second difference is that matter does not cognize things; the material intellect, however, distinguishes and cognizes.[16] He posits a third difference in comments 14 and 28 on the third book, and it is that matter is not the cause of just any reception, but of a transmutable reception; the intellect, however, receives without transmutation, that is without the casting away of perfection.[17] Because of this, in comment 14 he assimilates the intellect itself to a blank tablet, which, when it is painted anew, is perfected, but is not transmuted, since no perfection is cast away.[18] However, the Commentator (*On the Soul* 2, comment 57) calls this passion of the intellect a 'going out',[19] and this is the case whether the intellect proceeds from ignorance to knowledge, or from habit to second act. In either way the intellect is passive, inasmuch as it receives its perfection passively,

---

[12] Aver. *In DA* 3, t. c. 5, 387. 12–15.
[13] Ibid. 387. 23–5.
[14] Ibid. 387. 25–6.
[15] Ibid. 387. 27–388. 31.
[16] Ibid. 388. 31–7.
[17] Ibid., t. c. 14, 429. 20–34; t. c. 28, 466. 15–467. 47.
[18] Ibid., t. c. 14, 430. 50–65.
[19] Ibid. 2, t. c. 57, 216. 14–217. 39.

pro quanto recipit passive suam perfectionem, sed neutro modo patitur passione qua aliqua eius perfectio ab ipso abiciatur.

11. Istum autem intellectum materialem posuit aeternum esse, ut patet ex commento[20] et multis aliis commentis illius tertii libri.[21] Istum tamen intellectum non dixit esse materialem quia mixtum, ut ipsemet dicit contra Alexandrum, 25 commento,[22] sed quia quandoque est in potentia ad suam perfectionem, saltem secundum quod huic vel illi singulari individuo copulatur.

⟨OPINIO ALIORUM 1: INTELLECTUS MATERIALIS EST PURUM POSSIBILE⟩

12. Propter descriptionem naturae intellectus materialis supra positam dicunt quidam esse de | intentione Commentatoris et etiam dicunt verum esse quod intellectus noster materialis seu possibilis nec est actus in se nec aliquem actum habens ante intelligere, sed est purum possibile quoddam | sicut materia prima, licet a materia prima distinguatur triplici differentia supra dicta.[23]

⟨CONTRA OPINIONEM ALIORUM 1⟩

13. Contra: primo quod non sit de intentione Commentatoris, quoniam 19 commento tertii libri dicit quod intellectus materialis est ultimus in ordine intellectuum abstractorum.[24] Igitur secundum eum est una substantia abstracta et separata, et per consequens per se subsistens in actu, quod puro possibili repugnat secundum naturam.

14. Praeterea, nullum purum possibile est prima perfectio hominis, quoniam cum homo sit ens in actu, sua prima perfectio est actus. Sed Commentator, 5 commento 3 *De anima* in secunda quaestione quam movet contra se ipsum, supponit quod intellectus materialis sit prima perfectio hominis.[25] Similiter in 1 commento illius tertii dicit hominem per intellectum ab aliis distingui.[26] Igitur iste intellectus non est purum possibile secundum mentem Commentatoris.

15. Ad idem, nullum purum possibile actuatur et perficitur immediate et primo per aliquam formam accidentalem, quoniam ex ordine essentiali forma acciden-

1–2 passione qua] passive ita quod O   2 ab ipso *om.* T; ab eo O   3 posuit] ponit OT   4 tamen] autem T   5 esse *om.* OT || mixtum] *lectio incerta* O; *corr. s.l. in* immixtum P || ipsemet] ipse T || contra] contingit (*lectio incerta*) O   6 saltem] *suppl. i.m.* P   7 singulari individuo] *inv.* O   10 materialis] materialem P   11 etiam *om.* T || dicunt . . . esse] asserunt verum esse O; verum esse dicunt T   12 noster materialis] *inv.* T || seu possibilis *om.* O; sive possibilis T || aliquem] est P   13 sicut] sed P   14 licet] sed O || a . . . prima *om.* O || distinguatur] distinguitur O || dicta] posita T; sed *add.* O   16 quoniam] Commentator O || 19] 14 (*lectio incerta*) P   19 puro] potentiae P   22 in *om.* T || est actus] *inv.* P   25 illius] eiusdem T || tertii] libri *add.* T   25–26 iste . . . Commentatoris] secundum mentem Commentatoris iste intellectus non est purum possibile T; non est de intentione Commentatoris etc. O   27 Ad idem] praeterea O; item T || et[1]] vel T || immediate et *om.* T   28 aliquam *om.* T || forma] formae P

but in neither way is it passive by a passion by which some perfection belonging to it is cast away from it.

11. However, he maintained that this material intellect is eternal, as is obvious from comment 5[20] and many other comments on the third book.[21] But he did not say that this intellect is material because it is mixed, as he himself says against Alexander, comment 25,[22] but because it is, at some point, in potency to its own perfection, at least in so far as it is conjoined with this or that singular individual.

⟨OPINION OF OTHERS 1: THE MATERIAL INTELLECT IS SOMETHING PURELY POSSIBLE⟩

12. Because of the description of the nature of the material intellect given above, some people say that it is the conception of the Commentator—and they also claim it to be true—that our material or possible intellect is neither an act in itself nor does it have an act before it understands, but it is something purely possible like prime matter, although it is distinguished from prime matter by the triple difference mentioned above.[23]

⟨AGAINST THE OPINION OF OTHERS 1⟩

13. To the contrary. My first objection is that this is not the conception of the Commentator, since in comment 19 on the third book he says that the material intellect is the last in the order of abstract intellects.[24] Therefore, according to him, it is one substance, abstract and separate, and consequently it is something that subsists by itself in act, which is incompatible with pure possibility according to nature.

14. Moreover, nothing that is purely possible is the first perfection of man, since man's first perfection is act inasmuch as man is a being in act. But the Commentator, in comment 5 on *On the Soul* 3, in the second question which he raises against himself, takes it for granted that the material intellect is the first perfection of man.[25] Likewise, in comment 1 of this third book he says that man is distinguished from other things by the intellect.[26] Therefore this intellect is not something purely possible according to the mind of the Commentator.

15. To the same effect, nothing that is purely possible is actuated and perfected immediately and first by an accidental form, since in the essential order an acci-

---

[20] Ibid. 3, t. c. 5, 389. 57–70.
[21] Ibid., t. c. 4, 385. 56–8; t. c. 18, 439. 71–6; t. c. 20, 450. 198–202; t. c. 36, 482. 90–2, 499. 559.
[22] Ibid., t. c. 25, 463. 51–3.
[23] See above, para. 10.
[24] Aver. *In DA* 3, t. c. 19, 442. 62–4.
[25] Ibid., t. c. 5, 392. 158–60.
[26] Ibid., t. c. 1, 379. 18–23.

talis praesupponit formam substantialem in materia quam perficit. Sed intellectus materialis primo et immediate recipit intentiones intelligibiles, quae sunt accidentia. Igitur non est purum possibile.

⟨OPINIO ALIORUM 2: INTELLECTUS AGENS EST FORMA INTELLECTUS MATERIALIS⟩

16. Nec video quod istae rationes possent solvi nisi ponendo quod anima intellectiva nostra componatur ex intellectu materiali ut ex materia et intellectu agente ut forma, quod dicunt aliqui esse de intentione Commentatoris. Et secundum hoc posset dici quod intellectus materialis primo perficitur per intellectum agentem tamquam per formam substantialem, et tunc actuatus per intellectum agentem recipit formas intelligibiles.

⟨CONTRA OPINIONEM ALIORUM 2⟩

17. Sed istud non est de intentione Commentatoris, ut inferius in articulo sequente de intellectu agente videbitur.[27]

18. Item, istud non solvit difficultates. Nam si intellectus materialis, ut distinguitur contra agentem, sit sola potentia passiva, non video quod, pro tempore pro quo album et nigrum praesentantur sensui et intellectui in illa approximatione qua nata sunt tam potentiam sensitivam quam intellectivam distincte et sub propriis rationibus movere, possibile sit eundem intellectum formare hanc propositionem 'album est nigrum', cuius contrarium quilibet experitur | in se ipso.

19. Similiter non video, obiectis praesentatis modo praedicto potentiae sensitivae et intellectivae alicuius intelligentis, quin aequaliter acquireret scientiam de aliquo aeque perfecte absque omni sollicitudine et studio, sicut si cum maxima attentione studeret, cuius contrarium quilibet experitur in se.

⟨CONTRA OPINIONEM ALIORUM 1—RESUMPTIO⟩

20. Praeterea, illi qui dicunt quod intellectus materialis est una potentia animae, et tamen quod est purum possibile, in dicto suo implicant contradictionem,

2 intentiones] accidentales sive intentiones *add.* T 2–3 accidentia] quaedam *add.* T 3 est *om.* O || possibile] etc. O 7 nostra *om.* O || componatur] componitur OP || intellectu materiali] *inv.* T || ut] tamquam T || et] ex *add.* O 8 ut] tamquam T || quod] *lectio incerta* O 13–14 sequente *om.* T; sequenti O 15 si *om.* T 16 contra] intellectum *add.* T || agentem] si *add.* T || sola] pura T || pro² *om.* T 17 sensui] sensum P || intellectui] intellectum P 20 album] non *add.* T || est] esse P 21 video] quod *add.* T || potentiae] potentiis T 21–22 sensitivae et *om.* P 22 alicuius intelligentis] alicui intellectui O; alicuius T || scientiam *om.* T 23 studio] ex parte intelligentis *add.* OP || sicut] sed P || si *om.* T 24 attentione] cura T || studeret] studendi T || contrarium] etiam *add.* O 26 illi qui] quod alii P 27 tamen] cum hoc T || in . . . suo *om.* T

dental form presupposes a substantial form in the matter which it perfects. But the material intellect first and immediately receives intelligible intentions, which are accidents. Therefore it is not something purely possible.

⟨OPINION OF OTHERS 2: THE AGENT INTELLECT IS THE FORM OF THE MATERIAL INTELLECT⟩

16. And I do not see that these arguments could be refuted, except by positing that our intellectual soul is composed from the material intellect as from matter and from the agent intellect as from form, as some say is the conception of the Commentator. And in accordance with this it could be said that the material intellect is first perfected by the agent intellect just as if by a substantial form, and that then, actuated by the agent intellect, it receives intelligible forms.

⟨AGAINST THE OPINION OF OTHERS 2⟩

17. But this is not the conception of the Commentator, as will be seen below in a following article concerning the agent intellect.[27]

18. Again, this does not resolve the difficulties. For if the material intellect, as it is distinguished from the agent intellect, were only passive potency, I do not see that it would be possible, at a given point in time at which white and black are presented to the sense and to the intellect in that approximation in which they are apt by nature to move both the sensitive power and the intellectual soul distinctly and according to their own proper essences, for the same intellect to form the proposition 'white is black'; however, everyone experiences the opposite of this in himself.

19. Similarly, I do not see how, when objects are presented in the way described above to the sensitive power and to the intellectual soul of some intelligent being, it would not equally acquire knowledge of something equally perfectly and without any worry or effort, as if it were studying with the greatest attention; however, everyone experiences the opposite of this in himself.

⟨AGAINST THE OPINION OF OTHERS 1–RESUMED⟩

20. Moreover, those who say that the material intellect is one power of the soul, and nevertheless that it is something purely possible, imply a contradiction

---

[27] See below, paras. 24–54.

quia necessario habent dicere quod sit ipsa anima vel aliquod accidens fundatum in
T 25rb anima, sicut ponunt aliqui quod est potentia naturalis de genere | qualitatis. Si detur
primum, cum anima per essentiam sit actus, sequitur quod intellectus materialis
sit actus et non purum possibile, cuius contrarium dicunt. Si detur secundum, cum
quodlibet accidens sit forma quaedam et per consequens actus, adhuc sequitur 5
idem, scilicet quod intellectus materialis in se sit actus, licet sit in potentia ad
intentiones intelligibiles, sicut superficies in se est actus, licet sit in potentia ad
colores.

⟨AD RATIONES PRO OPINIONE ALIORUM 1⟩

21. Ad motiva eorum respondeo. Ad primam auctoritatem, cum dicit quod 10
'nullam naturam habet qua constituatur etc. nisi naturam possibilitatis',[28] dico
quod hoc non dicit absolute, sed addit 'secundum quod materialis'. Et hoc concedo.
Sicut enim superficies secundum quod dealbabilis est solum dicit potentiam
ad albedinem, tamen in se est quidam actus, et necessario requiritur quod sit actus,
aliter non esset immediatum receptivum albedinis, sic dico quod intellectus mate- 15
rialis secundum quod materialis solum dicit potentiam et ordinem ad universales
intentiones rerum materialium, in se tamen est quidam actus, aliter non esset immediatum
receptivum illarum intentionum, quoniam illis intentionibus repugnat,
cum sint accidentia, in puro possibili immediate recipi.

22. Ad aliam auctoritatem, cum dicit quod 'est in potentia omnes intentiones 20
formarum materialium universalium', et quod haec est definitio eius,[29] dico quod
ex hoc solum sequitur quod non est aliquod de numero rerum materialium, quarum
intentiones recipit. Cum hoc tamen bene stat quod sit quaedam actualitas in se.
Iuxta quod intelligendum quod haec definitio intellectus materialis est definitio
naturalis quae datur per notiora nobis, non simpliciter, cuiusmodi definitio est 25
haec 'natura est principium motus'[30] etc.

23. Ad tertiam auctoritatem, quae plus inter alias ponderatur, cum dicit quod
intellectus materialis 'non est aliquod entium ante intelligere',[31] et eandem

2 anima] ea T ‖ sicut] sed P ‖ Si] enim *add*. T   3 per ... sit] sit per essentiam sit O; sit per essentiam suam T   5 sequitur] illud *add*. T; ad *add. et del*. P   6 intellectus] noster *add*. O ‖ materialis] possibilis OP *et sit add*. O ‖ in² *om*. P   7 intentiones] formas O ‖ sicut] sed P ‖ est *om*. P   8 colores] et sicut potentia visiva in se est quidam actus, licet sit in potentia ad actum visionis *add*. T   10 eorum] ipsorum T ‖ respondeo *om*. P; responsio O; ‖ quod *om*. T   11 qua ... etc. *om*. O; qua constituitur etc. P ‖ possibilitatis] etc. O ‖ dico] dicitur P   13 Sicut] sed P ‖ dealbabilis] dealbata T ‖ solum *om*. T ‖ dicit] puram *add*. T   14 quidam actus] *inv*. O   16–17 universales intentiones] intentiones intelligibiles O   17 rerum] naturalium *add. et del*. P ‖ in ... tamen] tamen in se T   18 illarum] talium T ‖ quoniam ... intentionibus] quia eis O   18–19 repugnat ... accidentia] cum sint accidentia repugnat T   19 possibili] possibile O   21 universalium *om*. T   23 recipit] requirit O ‖ hoc] quo O ‖ tamen bene *om*. O ‖ se] sed *add. et del*. P   26 etc. *om*. P; et illa anima est actus corporis organici etc. *add*. T   27 quae ... ponderatur *om*. T   28 intelligere] intellectum P

by their claim, since necessarily they have to say that it is the soul itself or that it is some accident founded in the soul, just as some posit that it is a natural power in the category of quality. If the first alternative is granted, since the soul is act essentially, it follows that the material intellect is act and not purely possible; however, they state the opposite of this. If the second is granted, since every accident is a form and consequently an act, the same conclusion still follows, that is that the material intellect is in itself act, although it is in potency to intelligible intentions, just as a surface is an act in itself, although it is in potency to colours.

⟨IN ANSWER TO THE ARGUMENTS FOR THE OPINION OF OTHERS 1⟩

21. I respond to their motives. In answer to the first authority, when he says that 'it has no nature by which it could be constituted etc. except the nature of possibility',[28] I reply that he does not say this absolutely, but adds 'in so far as it is material'. And this I concede. For just as a surface, in so far as it is able to be made white, implies only a potency for whiteness, but nevertheless is an act in itself, and it is necessarily required that it is act, otherwise it would not be an immediate recipient of whiteness, so I say that the material intellect in so far as it is material implies only a potency and aptitude for universal intentions of material things, but nevertheless is an act in itself, otherwise it would not be an immediate recipient of those intentions, since it is incompatible with the nature of those intentions, since they are accidents, to be immediately received in something purely possible.

22. In answer to another authority, when he says that 'it is in potency all intentions of universal material forms', and that this is its definition,[29] I reply that from this it follows only that it is not any of the material things whose intentions it receives. With this, nevertheless, it is certainly compatible that it is an actuality in itself. In accordance with this, it is to be understood that this definition of the material intellect is a natural definition which is given through what is better known to us, not in the absolute sense; of this sort is the following definition, 'nature is the principle of motion'[30] etc.

23. In answer to the third authority, which has more weight compared with the others, when he says that the material intellect 'is not one among beings before it understands',[31] and the text of the Philosopher offers the same stated opinion ac-

---

[28] See above, para. 9.
[29] See above, para. 9.
[30] Arist. *Phys.* 2. 1, 192^{b}21–3.
[31] See above, para. 9.

sententiam praetendit textus Philosophi secundum omnem translationem,³² dico quod illud scribit tam Commentator quam Philosophus inpingendo in opinionem Empedoclis,³³ qui propter hoc quod omnis cognitio secundum philosophos omnes quasi fit per assimilationem cognoscentis ad cognitum, posuit, cum anima intelligat omnia, quod propter hoc ex omnibus componeretur realiter, ita quod 5 quodam esse reali anima in se comprehenderet omnia entia et sic quodam modo esset omnia entia. Philosophus autem et Commentator ponunt intellectum nostrum omnino immixtum et simpliciter simplicem; nec ponunt aliquam assimilationem inter ipsum et res materiales nisi per intentiones abstractas a rebus materialibus mediante intellectu agente. Dicit igitur contra opinionem Empedoclis quod intel- 10 lectus 'non est aliquod entium', scilicet aliorum a se, 'antequam intelligat', id est antequam receperit intentionem obiecti, per quam assimilatur obiecto. Tunc enim fit omnia entia, puta intentionaliter. Unde Philosophus dicit in 3 *De anima* quod anima est quodam modo omnia,³⁴ quod intelligendum est intentionaliter, | non realiter, ut posuit Empedocles. Hanc puto esse intentionem | Commentatoris de 15 intellectu materiali.

T 25ᵛᵃ
P 218ʳᵇ

⟨DE INTELLECTU AGENTE⟩

24. De intellectu agente primo ponit eius necessitatem, 17 commento,³⁵ et vis rationis suae est ista: in omni genere rerum naturalium, ubi aliquid est quandoque in potentia essentiali ad aliquem actum, aliquando in actu, necesse est in eodem 20 genere ponere aliquod agens quod ipsum possit reducere ad actum, quod agens realiter ab ipso distinguitur. Haec est per se manifesta. Nam nihil ducit se de potentia essentiali ad actum. Sed intellectus materialis est in potentia essentiali quantum est ex se respectu cuiuscumque intentionis seu formae intelligibilis quam recipit, ut patet ex praedictis.³⁶ Igitur etc. 25

25. Postea eodem commento in fine incipit declarare eius naturam exemplariter, dicens quod se habet respectu intellectus materialis sicut ars ad materiam.³⁷ Dicit etiam 19 commento quod se habet ad intellectum materialem sicut principium movens ad materiam.³⁸ Ista enim duo bene concordant. Ars enim in mente

1 Philosophi *om.* O ‖ omnem] novam T   2 tam . . . Philosophus] Commentator et Philosophus O ‖ inpingendo in] impugnando O   3 qui . . . hoc] *iter.* O   3–4 secundum . . . quasi] quasi secundum omnes philosophos T   5 hoc] anima *add.* T ‖ ex . . . componeretur] componeretur ex omnibus T   6 comprehenderet] comprehendat P   6–7 et . . . entia *om. hom.* PT   7 omnia] *iter. et corr.* O   8 simpliciter] *scripsimus; om.* T; similiter (*fortasse legendum* simpliciter) O; substantiam P   10–13 quod . . . intentionaliter] illa verba T   12 assimilatur obiecto] ei assimilatur O ‖ enim] dum P   13 Philosophus . . . *De anima*] in 3 De anima dicit Philosophus T   15 Hanc . . . Commentatoris] hic (*fortasse legendum* haec) T   18 intellectu] vero *add.* T ‖ 17] 27 T   19 est quandoque] *inv.* T   20 aliquando] quandoque O; vero est *add.* T   22 Haec . . . manifesta] hoc est per se manifestum O   23 ad] in P   24 intentionis] intellectionis T ‖ seu] vel T   25 ut . . . etc.] Igitur etc. Minor autem patet ex supra dictis T   26 eius] enim T   28 19 commento] *inv.* T

cording to every translation,[32] I reply that both the Commentator and the Philosopher write this to refute the opinion of Empedocles,[33] who because of the fact that every cognition, according to all philosophers, occurs as if by assimilation of the knower to the known thing, claimed that, since the soul understands everything, it is because of this composed of all things in a real sense, so that in real being the soul would encompass all beings within itself and so, in a way, would be all beings. The Philosopher, however, and the Commentator claim that our intellect is entirely unmixed and absolutely simple; and they do not posit any assimilation between it and material things except through intentions abstracted from material things, by means of the agent intellect. Therefore he declares against the opinion of Empedocles that the intellect 'is not one among beings', that is those beings that are other than itself, 'before it understands', that is before it has received the intention of an object, through which it is assimilated to the object. For then it becomes all beings, intentionally, that is. From this the Philosopher says in *On the Soul* 3 that the soul is in a way all things,[34] which is to be understood intentionally, not in a real sense, as Empedocles claimed. This, I think, is the conception of the Commentator on the material intellect.

⟨ON THE AGENT INTELLECT⟩

24. Concerning the agent intellect, he first posits its necessity (comment 17)[35] and the force of his argument is this: in every genus of natural thing, where something is sometimes in essential potency to some act, at other times in act, it is necessary to posit in the same genus some agent which can reduce it to act, which agent is really distinguished from it. This is immediately manifest. For nothing leads itself from essential potency to act. But, in its own right, the material intellect is in essential potency with respect to whatever intention or intelligible form it receives, as is obvious from what was said earlier.[36] Therefore etc.

25. Later in the same comment, at the end, he begins to describe its nature using examples, saying that it relates to the material intellect as art to matter.[37] He also says in comment 19 that it relates to the material intellect as the moving principle to matter.[38] For these two points accord well with each other. For art in the mind of

---

[32] Arist. *DA* 3. 4, 429ᵃ22–4.
[33] Ibid. 1. 2, 404ᵇ8–15.
[34] Ibid. 3. 8, 431ᵇ21.
[35] Aver. *In DA* 3, t. c. 17, 436. 8–19.
[36] See above, paras. 9–10.
[37] Aver. *In DA* 3, t. c. 17, 437. 23–7.
[38] Ibid., t. c. 19, 442. 58–62.

artificis est principium productivum efficiens formae artificialis in materia extra, ut patet ex intentione Commentatoris, 7 *Metaphysicae*,[39] et 12 *Metaphysicae*, commento 36, ubi dicit quod balneum in anima est agens motum.[40] Sic intellectus agens causat intentiones universales in intellectu materiali tamquam in materia sibi correspondente, quae intentiones quantum ad immaterialitatem assimilantur intellectui agenti, a quo effective illa immaterialitas causatur, sicut forma domus in materia assimilatur arti.

26. Sciendum tamen, ut dicit Commentator, commento 18 illius tertii,[41] quod intellectus agens non sufficit per se ad reducendum intellectum materialem de potentia ad actum, quoniam tunc posset intellectus noster intelligere absque conversione ad phantasmata, quod negat Philosophus.[42] Similiter non sufficiunt phantasmata ut potentiam intellectus materialis reducant ad actum, quoniam solum sunt intelligibilia in potentia; intellectus autem materialis solum recipit intentiones actu intellectas, scilicet abstractas et universales. Ex quibus sequitur quod intellectus agens cum phantasmate est una causa totalis sufficiens qua intellectus materialis reducitur de potentia ad actum.

27. Sciendum etiam quod Commentator in 5 commento illius tertii circa medium, et etiam 18 commento dicit intellectum agentem se habere ad intellectum materialem sicut lux ad visum, pro quanto visus non immutatur a colore nisi praesente lumine, sic nec intellectus materialis res intelligit nisi in lumine intellectus agentis.[43] Similiter parum ante finem 5 commenti ponit aliam comparationem, ubi vult quod intellectus agens se habet ad intellectum materialem sicut lux ad diaphanum et se habet ad phantasmata sicut lumen ad colores.[44] Et | esset valde simile, si diaphanum esset potentia cognoscitiva colorum, et cum hoc intellectus agens esset forma informans intellectum materialem sicut lumen informat diaphanum, et simul cum his colores non haberent actum in se per quem immutant visum, sicut nec phantasmata per quem immutant intellectum. Cuius contrarium dicit Commentator, 2 *De anima*, commento 67, ubi dicit cum Philosopho[45] quod color est per se visibilis, nec requiritur lumen propter colorem, sed propter medium, cuius est dispositio necessaria ad hoc quod aliquid videatur.[46]

1 ut] *om*. T   2 *Metaphysicae*¹] *om*. T ‖   12] 2 T   3 agens] movens T ‖   motum] accusative *add*. O ‖   Sic] sicut T   4 intentiones] intellectiones T   5 immaterialitatem] materialitatem P   6 sicut] sed P   9 per] pro T   10 ad] in T   11–12 quod ... phantasmata] *suppl. i.m.* P   11 non] etiam *add*. P   14 et *om*. T   15 una causa] *inv*. P ‖   materialis] noster *add*. O   16 reducitur] reducatur T   17 in *om*. O   18 etiam] in *add*. O ‖   intellectum¹] *corr. i.m. ex* medium P   19 visus *om*. OP   20 nec ... materialis] intellectus possibilis non T ‖   res *om*. T; dis *add. et del*. P   21 parum ... finem] ante finem parum P ‖   ponit ... ubi *om*. T   22 intellectum *om*. T; sicut *add. et del*. O   23 et *om*. T ‖   lumen] lux O   24 diaphanum] est *add. et del*. P ‖   cognoscitiva] cognitiva T ‖   colorum] calorum P; coloris T ‖   et *om*. P   25 materialem] possibilem T   26 immutant] immutarent T   27 sicut ... intellectum *om*. T ‖   sicut] sed P   27–28 Cuius ... Philosopho] licet contrarium communiter teneant scilicet T   28 2] 3 O   29 requiritur] requirit (*lectio incerta*) O ‖   lumen] *suppl. i.m.* O ‖   colorem] colores T   30 est ... necessaria] dispositio necessaria est O ‖   aliquid] color O ‖   videatur] videtur O

the artist is the efficient productive principle of artificial form in external matter, as is obvious from the conception of the Commentator in *Metaphysics* 7,[39] and *Metaphysics* 12, comment 36, where he says that a bath in the soul is the agent of motion.[40] So the agent intellect causes universal intentions in the material intellect just as if in the matter corresponding to it, which intentions as to their immateriality are assimilated to the agent intellect, by which that immateriality is effectively caused, just as the form of a house in matter is assimilated to art.

26. It must be realized, however, as the Commentator says in comment 18 of the third book,[41] that the agent intellect does not suffice by itself to reduce the material intellect from potency to act, since then our intellect would be able to understand without turning towards phantasms, which the Philosopher denies.[42] Likewise phantasms do not suffice to reduce the potency of the material intellect to act, since they are intelligible only in potency; but the material intellect receives only intentions that are actually understood, that is abstract and universal intentions. Accordingly it follows that the agent intellect together with a phantasm is the one total and sufficient cause by which the material intellect is reduced from potency to act.

27. It must also be realized that the Commentator says around the middle of comment 5 of the third book, and also in comment 18, that the agent intellect relates to the material intellect as light to sight, inasmuch as sight is not altered by colour except when light is present, and in the same manner the material intellect does not understand things except in the light of the agent intellect.[43] Likewise just before the end of comment 5 he posits another comparison, where he wants it to be the case that the agent intellect relates to the material intellect as light to the transparent medium, and relates to phantasms as light to colours.[44] And it would be very similar, if the transparent medium were a cognitive power of colours, and in addition to this the agent intellect were the form informing the material intellect as light informs the transparent medium, and together with these conditions colours did not in themselves have an act through which they altered sight, just as phantasms do not have one through which they alter the intellect. The Commentator says the opposite of this in comment 67 on *On the Soul* 2, where he agrees with the Philosopher[45] that colour is by its own nature visible, and that light is not required because of colour, but because of the medium, of which light is a disposition necessary for something to be seen.[46]

---

[39] Aver. *In Metaph.* 7, t. c. 23, fol. 173^{rb}F–^{vb}L.
[40] Ibid. 12, t. c. 36, fol. 318^{va}I–^{vb}K.
[41] Aver. *In DA* 3, t. c. 18, 438. 36–46.
[42] Arist. *DA* 3. 7, 431^{a}16–17.
[43] Aver. *In DA* 3, t. c. 5, 401. 400–18; t. c. 18, 439. 58–71.
[44] Ibid., t. c. 5, 410. 688–411. 702.
[45] Arist. *DA* 2. 7, 418^{a}29–^{b}1
[46] Aver. *In DA* 2, t. c. 67, 233. 74–94.

28. Post, 18 commento, declarat naturam actus intellectus agentis, dicens quod 'abstrahere nihil aliud est quam facere intentiones imaginatas actu intellectas, postquam erant in potentia'. Et magis exponens se addit quod hoc est 'transferre idem in suo esse de ordine in ordinem', hoc est de singularitate in universalitatem.[47]

29. Post, 19 commento, comparat intellectum agentem materiali secundum convenientiam et differentiam. Et primo secundum convenientiam in tribus, scilicet in separabilitate, impassibilitate et immiscibilitate, quas conditiones dicit posse demonstrari de intellectu agente per eas rationes per quas superius probatae sunt de intellectu materiali[48]—quae rationes ponentur inferius.[49]

30. Post, eodem commento 19, comparat intellectum agentem ad materialem secundum duplicem differentiam, quarum prima est quod intellectus agens est substantia actu ens.[50] Quod exponens Commentator dicit: 'id est non est in potentia ad aliquid' sicut intellectus materialis. 'Nihil enim—ut dicit—intelligit de his quae sunt hic', sed 'intellectus materialis est utrumque', id est et in actu et in potentia. Et quia, ut dicit, intellectus agens se habet respectu materialis sicut principium movens quodam modo ad materiam motam, cum agens | sit perfectius patiente, sequitur quod intellectus agens sit perfectior intellectu materiali. Ubi notandum quod haec propositio 'agens est perfectius passo' habet intelligi de agente principali, comparando etiam agens ad patiens secundum principia activa et passiva. Aliter bene capit instantiam.

31. Secunda differentia est quam ponit inter intellectum materialem et agentem secundum expositionem Commentatoris[51] quod in intellectu agente hoc est proprium, ut scientia in actu sit eadem cum scito, quod tamen dicit non esse verum in intellectu materiali. Et causam reddit quia intellectus materialis intelligit res extra se, quae non sunt intellectus. Hanc puto esse sententiam Commentatoris de intellectu agente.

⟨DUBITATIO 1: DE SEPARABILITATE INTELLECTUS AGENTIS⟩

32. Sed hic sunt duae dubitationes. Una est utrum intellectus agens et materialis sint duae substantiae per se subsistentes vel sint duo principia ad modum

---

1 Post] postea T   4 idem] illud T || in¹] de T || de¹] in *add. et del.* T || in²] ad O || in³] ad O   4–5 universalitatem] Item *add.* T   6 commento *om.* P   7 Et *om.* T || convenientiam²] tripliciter vel *add.* T   7–8 scilicet *om.* T   8 separabilitate] in *add.* T || impassibilitate] passibilitate P || et] in *add.* T   9 demonstrari *om.* O   10 inferius] Item *add.* T   12–13 substantia] sicut T   13 ens] est O || Commentator] ipse *add.* T || dicit] primo *add. et del.* O   14 sicut] sed P || enim] *corr. s.l. ex illegibili* P || ut . . . intelligit] intelligit T; intelligit ut dicit O   15 hic *om.* T || id est] scilicet T   17 movens *om.* T   19 passo] etc. O   20 patiens] ut *add. et del.* O   21 Aliter] autem *add.* O || bene] propositio T   22 materialem . . . agentem] agentem et possibilem T   24 ut] quod T *et* in intellectu agente quod *add.*   25 in] de T   26 non] *suppl. i.m.* O || puto] credo T || esse *om.* T   29 duae dubitationes] *inv.* O || Una est *om.* O   29–30 materialis] possibilis T   30 sint²] sunt O

28. Later, in comment 18, he describes the nature of the act of the agent intellect, saying that 'to abstract is nothing else than to make imagined intentions actually understood, after they were in potency'. And, explaining himself further, he adds that that is 'to transfer the same thing in its being from one order to another', that is from singularity to universality.[47]

29. Later, in comment 19, he compares the agent intellect with the material according to what they agree in and where they differ. And first according to what they agree in in three respects, that is in separability, in impassibility, and in immiscibility, which conditions, he says, can be demonstrated for the agent intellect by those arguments by which they are proved above for the material intellect[48]—which arguments are stated below.[49]

30. Later, again in comment 19, he compares the agent intellect to the material according to two differences, of which the first is that the agent intellect is a substance existing in act.[50] Interpreting this, the Commentator says: 'that is, it is not in potency to anything' as the material intellect is. 'For nothing', as he says, 'does it understand of these things which are here', but 'the material intellect is both', that is both in act and in potency. And because, as he says, the agent intellect relates to the material as what is in a way the moving principle does to the moved matter, since the agent is more perfect than the patient, it follows that the agent intellect is more perfect than the material intellect. At this point it must be noted that this proposition, 'the agent is more perfect than that which is acted upon', has to be understood of the principal agent, also in comparing the agent and the patient according to the active and passive principles. Otherwise one easily finds a counter-example.

31. The second difference which he posits between the material intellect and the agent intellect according to the exposition of the Commentator[51] is that in the agent intellect the following is proper to it, that knowledge in act is the same as the known thing, which however he says is not true in the material intellect. And he gives the reason for this that the material intellect understands things outside itself, which are not the intellect. This, I think, is the stated opinion of the Commentator concerning the agent intellect.

⟨DOUBT 1: ON THE SEPARABILITY OF THE AGENT INTELLECT⟩

32. But here there are two doubts. One is whether the agent and material intellects are two substances subsisting in themselves or whether they are two

---
[47] Ibid. 3, t. c. 18, 439. 76–80.
[48] Ibid., t. c. 19, 440. 8–10.
[49] Ibid. 441. 16–442. 1.
[50] Ibid. 442. 53–62.
[51] Ibid. 443. 85–90.

materiae et formae componentia animam intellectivam nostram, secundum quem modum | ponit Commentator 5 commento 3 libri *De anima* quod omnis substantia abstracta citra primum est composita ex aliquo simili materiae et aliquo simili formae.[52]

33. Quod intellectus agens sit forma intellectus materialis probatio. Dicit enim in 5 commento quod 'quemadmodum lux est perfectio diaphani, sic intellectus agens est perfectio intellectus materialis'.[53]

34. Item, 20 commento dicit quod intellectus materialis perficitur per agentem.[54]

35. Item, eodem commento 20 dicit parum ante finem quod intellectus qui est in nobis componitur ex intellectu agente et materiali.[55]

36. Item, 36 commento dicit quod intellectus agens est forma in nobis.[56] Dicit etiam ibidem quod intellectus in nobis est compositus ex intellectis speculativis et intellectu agente, et quod intellectus materialis est subiectum utriusque.[57]

37. Ex quibus omnibus sequitur | quod intellectus agens et materialis non sunt duae substantiae subsistentes, sed principia unius substantiae.

38. Praeterea, ex modo loquendi Commentatoris probatur idem, quoniam in 5 commento dicit quod in anima sunt duae virtutes, activa et passiva.[58]

39. Similiter 20 commento dicit quod in intellectu continuato nobis sunt duae virtutes, activae et passivae.[59] Sed non diceret istas duas virtutes esse in anima vel in intellectu singulariter, nisi istae duae virtutes congregarentur ad constituendum unam animam seu unum intellectum. Ergo etc.

40. Contra. Quod sint duae substantiae subsistentes probo ex intentione Commentatoris. Primo quia 36 commento dicit parum ante finem quod intellectus agens non est in nobis forma in actu in principio, sed solum in fine, quando completur motus intellectus in habitu.[60] Vult etiam in eodem commento prius quod ante generationem intellectus speculativi in nobis non unitur nobis intellectus agens ut forma nisi in potentia.[61] Sed in primo instanti productionis hominis intellectus materialis nobis coniungitur ut forma et perfectio nostra in actu, ut patet per Commentatorem, 1 commento 3 *De anima*, qui dicit nos per illum intellectum ab aliis speciebus distingui.[62] Et in 5 commento dicit quod est prima perfectio hominis.[63]

---

1 componentia] componibilia ad invicem et integrantia T   2 Commentator] in *add.* P || libri *om.* O   3 abstracta *om.* T || citra] *corr. i.m. ex illegibili* P   4 formae] ita *add.* O   5 Quod] autem *add.* T   6 quemadmodum] quaedam (*lectio incerta*) *et corr. i.m. in* sicut P   8 20] 2 P; 10 T   10 commento 20] *inv.* T   12 commento *om.* T   16 substantiae[1]] per se *add.* T   17 probatur] hoc *add.* O; ponitur P || quoniam] quia O   18 in] *suppl. s.l.* O || virtutes] scilicet *add.* T   20 activae] scilicet *add.* T || esse *om.* T   21 in *om.* P || virtutes *om.* T || congregarentur] congregantur P || ad constituendum] constituendo OP   22 intellectum] medium T   23 substantiae] per se *add.* T   23–24 Commentatoris] *scripsimus*; commenti OPT   24 Primo] probo O || quia *om.* O || 36] dicit *add. et del.* O   26 etiam] Philosophus *add.* T || prius *om.* T   29 nobis coniungitur] unitur nobis T   30 1 commento] *inv.* T   30–31 qui ... distingui *om.* T

principles after the manner of matter and form composing our intellectual soul, according to which manner the Commentator posits in comment 5 of book 3 of *On the Soul* that every abstract substance apart from the first is composed from something similar to matter and something similar to form.[52]

33. The proof that the agent intellect is the form of the material intellect. For he says in comment 5 that 'in the same way as light is the perfection of the transparent medium, so the agent intellect is the perfection of the material intellect'.[53]

34. Again, in comment 20 he says that the material intellect is perfected by the agent intellect.[54]

35. Again, in the same comment 20 he says just before the end that the intellect which is in us is composed of the agent and the material intellects.[55]

36. Again, in comment 36 he says that the agent intellect is a form in us.[56] He also says in the same place that the intellect in us is composed of speculative understood things and the agent intellect, and that the material intellect is the subject of both of these.[57]

37. From all these remarks it follows that the agent and material intellects are not two subsisting substances, but principles of one substance.

38. Moreover, from the Commentator's manner of speaking the same thing is proved, since in comment 5 he says that in the soul there are two powers, an active and a passive.[58]

39. Likewise in comment 20 he says that in the intellect that is continuous with us there are two powers, active and passive ones.[59] But he would not say that these two powers were in the soul or in the intellect in the singular, unless these two powers were grouped together in order to constitute one soul or one intellect. Therefore etc.

40. To the contrary. I prove from the conception of the Commentator that they are two subsisting substances. First because in comment 36 he says just before the end that the agent intellect is not in us a form in act from the beginning, but only at the end, when the motion of the intellect in habit is fulfilled.[60] Earlier in the same comment he also wants it to be the case that before the generation of the speculative intellect in us the agent intellect is not united with us as a form, except in potency.[61] But in the first instant of the production of a man the material intellect is conjoined with us as a form and as our perfection in act, as is obvious from the Commentator, who says, in comment 1 on *On the Soul* 3, that we are distinguished from other species by means of this intellect.[62] And in comment 5 he says that it is the first perfection of man.[63] Therefore according to the conception

---

[52] Ibid. 3, t. c. 5, 409. 657–410. 667.
[53] Ibid. 411. 691–3.
[54] Ibid., t. c. 20, 450. 205–8.
[55] Ibid. 453. 278–80.
[56] Ibid., t. c. 36, 484. 129–34.
[57] Ibid. 499. 502–4, 581–5.
[58] Ibid., t. c. 5, 406. 556–9.
[59] Ibid., t. c. 20, 451. 219–22.
[60] Ibid., t. c. 36, 500. 607–501. 616.
[61] Ibid. 500. 599–605.
[62] Ibid., t. c. 1, 379. 21–3.
[63] Ibid., t. c. 5, 392. 159.

Igitur secundum intentionem Commentatoris intellectus agens et possibilis non constituunt unam substantiam incorruptibilem, quia si sic, intellectus agens a principio uniretur nobis ut forma in actu sicut intellectus materialis et verius.

41. Praeterea, 12 *Metaphysicae*, commento 17, repetit dicta sua in 3 *De anima* de intellectu agente, et corrigens se dicit quod intellectus in potentia est quasi locus istius intellectus, scilicet intellectus agentis, non quasi materia.[64]

42. Praeterea, non est de intentione Commentatoris nec alicuius alterius quod in nobis sit duplex potentia cognoscitiva abstracta. Sed si intellectus agens esset forma intellectus materialis, sequeretur hoc. Nam | intellectus materialis certum est quod est potentia cognoscitiva abstracta. Similiter intellectus agens secundum Commentatorem est potentia cognoscitiva, ut patet superius,[65] ubi dat duplicem differentiam inter intellectum agentem et possibilem. Ibi enim vult quod in intellectu agente scientia et scitum sint idem, et per consequens intellectus agens est virtus cognoscitiva.

43. Item, nulla forma informans aliquam materiam agit in propriam materiam quam informat, ex qua et ipsa fit per se unum reducens ipsam de potentia essentiali in actum, ut patet inductive. Unde forma ignis non agit in materiam propriam, sed in materiam alterius suppositi. Similiter nec lumen in medio agit in medium, sed sol illud lumen agit, causando ipsum in medio. Et hoc dicit Commentator, 8 *Physicorum*, quod agens et patiens sunt ad invicem contigua, non continua.[66] Igitur cum intellectus agens se habeat ad materialem sicut principium movens ad materiam motam, ut dicit Commentator,[67] et per consequens ut agens ad patiens, sequitur quod intellectus agens non est forma perficiens intellectum materialem, ita quod ex his fiat una substantia quae dicatur 'anima rationalis'.

44. Dico igitur quod de intentione Commentatoris fuit—et Avicennae et quasi omnium Peripateticorum—quod intellectus agens est quaedam substantia per se subsistens. Et credo quod ista sit intentio Aristotelis, qui ita commendat istam veritatem.

---

2 quia *om.* O   **2–3** a principio *om.* T   **4** 12] 2 O ‖ **17**] *scripsimus*; 18 OPT ‖ dicta sua] ea quae dixit T   **6** intellectus² *om.* O   **7** alterius *om.* OT   **8** abstracta] nam intellectus materialis semper *add. et del.* O   **8–10** si . . . Similiter *om.* P   **9** intellectus materialis¹] *om.* T ‖ hoc] quod in anima nostra esset duplex potentia cognoscitiva abstracta T ‖ certum] semper O   **10** quod est *om.* O ‖ abstracta *om.* T   **11** potentia] *corr. s.l. ex* sed P ‖ cognoscitiva] cognitiva P; abstracta *add.* T ‖ ubi] ut O ‖ duplicem *om.* O   **12** intellectum *om.* O   **13** sint] sunt T ‖ per consequens] pro quasi (*lectio incerta*) O   **14** virtus] potentia T ‖ cognoscitiva] cognitiva P   **15** aliquam] a materia P   **16** per . . . ipsam] unum per se ipsum reducens T ‖ ipsam] ipsum P   **17** inductive] inducendo P ‖ materiam propriam] *inv.* T   **18** materiam] materia P ‖ in³] ipsum *add.* T   **19** illud . . . agit] agit ipsum lumen O ‖ ipsum *om.* O   **21** habeat] habet OP ‖ sicut] sic P ‖ movens] se habet *add.* T   **24** dicatur] vocetur T ‖ anima *om.* O   **25** fuit . . . Avicennae] et Avicennae fuit T   **27** ista *om.* OP ‖ sit] fuerit O   **28** veritatem] virtutem O

of the Commentator the agent and the possible intellects do not constitute one incorruptible substance, because if this were the case, the agent intellect would be united with us from the beginning as a form in act, just as the material intellect is, and more truly so.

41. Moreover, in *Metaphysics* 12, comment 17, he repeats what he said in *On the Soul* 3 about the agent intellect, and, correcting himself, he says that the intellect in potency serves as a sort of place for this intellect (that is, the agent intellect) and not a sort of matter.[64]

42. Moreover, it is not the conception of the Commentator, nor of anyone else, that there should be a double abstract cognitive power in us. But if the agent intellect were the form of the material intellect, this would follow. For as to the material intellect, it is certain that it is an abstract cognitive power. Likewise the agent intellect, according to the Commentator, is a cognitive power, as is obvious above,[65] where he gives the double difference between the agent and the possible intellects. For there he wants it to be the case that in the agent intellect knowledge and the known thing are the same, and consequently the agent intellect is a cognitive power.

43. Again, no form informing any matter acts on its own matter which it informs, from which and itself something that is one thing by itself comes to be, by reducing it from essential potency into act, as is obvious by induction. Because of this, the form of fire does not act on its own matter, but on the matter of some other supposit. Likewise, neither does light in a medium act on the medium, but the sun brings forth that light, by causing it in the medium. And the Commentator says this, on *Physics* 8, that the agent and the patient are contiguous to one another, not continuous.[66] Therefore since the agent intellect relates to the material as the moving principle does to the matter moved, as the Commentator says,[67] and consequently as the agent does to patient, it follows that the agent intellect is not the form perfecting the material intellect, so that from these two there might come to be one substance which would be called the 'rational soul'.

44. I say therefore that it was the conception of the Commentator—and of Avicenna and of almost all the Peripatetics—that the agent intellect is a substance subsisting by itself. And I believe that this is the conception of Aristotle, who thus supports this truth.

---

[64] Aver. *In Metaph.* 12, t. c. 17, fol. 303[ra]B.
[65] See above, para. 31.
[66] Aver. *In Phys.* 8, t. c. 30, fol. 367[va]H–I.
[67] See above, para. 25.

⟨AD ARGUMENTA OPINIONIS CONTRARIAE⟩

45. Ad auctoritates in contrarium[68] respondeo quod pro tanto dicit Commentator quod intellectus agens est perfectio intellectus materialis sicut lux diaphani pro quanto sicut colores non videntur per diaphanum nisi praesente lumine, ita nec intellectus materialis intelligit res materiales nisi praesente lumine intellectus agentis, quod lumen est ipse intellectus agens. In alio tamen est dissimile quoniam lumen est forma inhaerens ipsi diaphano, intellectus autem agens est lumen solum assistens intellectui materiali, nec quantum ad hoc attenditur similitudo hinc inde.

46. Per idem ad aliud,[69] intellectus agens est perfectio intellectus materialis pro tanto quia solum per eius praesentiam vel assistentiam natus est immutari a suo obiecto, sicut visus per praesentiam lucis natus est videre colorem.

47. Ad tertium[70] dicendum quod illa compositio non est sicut ex forma informante et materia, sed tamquam ex forma assistente, sicut si diceretur quod color non per se videtur, sed compositum ex colore et lumine, pro quanto lumen requiritur ad hoc quod color videatur, ipsi colori assistens, licet non inhaereat colori, sed medio.

48. Intelligendum etiam est secundum usum loquendi Commentatoris quod aliquid potest dici perfectio alicuius, licet ipsum non informet. Nam commento 14 3 *De anima* dicit quod formae abstractae perficiuntur per se invicem, scilicet inferior per superiorem.[71] Similiter, 12 *Metaphysicae*, commento 44, dicit quod perfectio uniuscuiusque moventium unumquemque orbium perficitur per primum motorem.[72] | Sed certum est quod nec primum nec aliqua substantia separata est perfectio informans aliam. Et ideo non sequitur quod intellectus agens sit perfectio informans intellectum materialem. Quo modo autem sit forma et perfectio intellectus materialis et non solum agens respectu eius, et etiam forma informans eum dicetur inferius in articulo | de intellectu adepto.[73]

49. Ad alias duas auctoritates[74] primo dico quod ille modus loquendi suus in singulari non est ponderandus, quando dicit quod in anima singulariter sunt duae virtutes. Nam aliquando etiam utitur modo contrario. Nam parum ante finem 18 commenti dicit quod agens et recipiens sunt substantiae aeternae,[75] et intelligit per agentem et recipientem intellectum agentem et materialem. Dico igi-

---

2 contrarium] oppositum T   3 materialis] possibilis T   4 quanto] quod *add. s.l.* P   5 nec . . . materialis] intellectus materialis non T   6 quod . . . agens *om.* T || ipse *om.* O || tamen] bene *add.* O   9 aliud] illud P   10 praesentiam vel *om.* O; praesentiam et T   12 dicendum] est *add.* O || sicut] sed P   13 sicut] sed P   15 ad . . . quod] ut T || non . . . colori] sibi non inhaereat T || inhaereat] adhaereat O   17 etiam est] *inv.* T   20 superiorem] *lectio incerta* P   22 substantia] forma T || est²] forma vel *add.* T   24 forma et *om.* T   24–25 intellectus . . . eum *om.* T   25 et²] *scripsimus*; nec OP || eum] cum P   26 inferius *om.* T || articulo] capitulo T   27 primo *om.* T || loquendi suus] *inv.* O   28 singulari] sognis P *et corr. i.m. in* singulis || anima] alia T   29 Nam¹] et *add.* T   30 substantiae] duae *add.* T   30–31 intelligit] intendit T   31 recipientem] *lectio incerta* O || materialem] possibilem T

⟨IN ANSWER TO THE ARGUMENTS FOR THE OPPOSITE OPINION⟩

45. To the authorities for the opposite opinion[68] I respond that the Commentator says that the agent intellect is the perfection of the material intellect just as light is that of the transparent medium only to the extent that as colours are not seen by means of the transparent medium except in the presence of light, so neither does the material intellect understand material things except in the presence of the light of the agent intellect, which light is the agent intellect itself. In another respect, however, it is dissimilar, since light is a form inhering in the transparent medium itself, but the agent intellect is a light only assisting the material intellect, and the similarity between one and the other does not extend to this aspect.

46. By the same reasoning one can reply to the other argument:[69] the agent intellect is the perfection of the material intellect to the extent that only by its presence or assistance is the material intellect apt by nature to be altered by its object, just as sight by the presence of light is apt by nature to see colour.

47. In answer to the third argument,[70] it must be said that that composition is not like that of the informing form and matter, but just like that of the form that assists, just as if it were said that it is not colour by itself that is seen, but the composite of colour and light, to the extent that light is required, assisting the colour itself, in order that colour can be seen, although light does not inhere in the colour, but in the medium.

48. It must also be understood that, according to the Commentator's usage, something can be said to be the perfection of something else, although it does not inform it. For in comment 14 on *On the Soul* 3 he says that abstract forms are perfected by themselves in turn: that is, the lower by the higher.[71] Likewise, in *Metaphysics* 12, comment 44, he says that the perfection of every single mover of every single sphere is perfected by the first mover.[72] But it is certain that neither the first mover nor any separate substance is a perfection informing another. And therefore it does not follow that the agent intellect is a perfection informing the material intellect. But in what way it is the form and perfection of the material intellect and not only the agent in relation to it, and also the form informing it, will be stated below in the article concerning the accomplished intellect.[73]

49. In answer to the other two authorities[74] I say first that that manner of speaking of his in the singular is not to be given much weight, when he says that in the soul, in the singular, there are two powers. For sometimes he also uses the opposite manner. For just before the end of comment 18 he says that the agent and the recipient are eternal substances,[75] and he understands by the agent and recipient the agent intellect and the material intellect respectively. I say therefore

---

[68] See above, para. 33.
[69] See above, para. 34.
[70] See above, paras. 35–7.
[71] Aver. *In DA* 3, t. c. 14, 429. 36–7.
[72] Aver. *In Metaph.* 12, t. c. 44, fol. 327^{vb}L.
[73] See below, para. 61.
[74] See above, paras. 38–9.
[75] Aver. *In DA* 3, t. c. 18, 439. 73–4.

tur ad illas auctoritates quod pro tanto loquitur singulariter, cum dicit quod in anima nostra vel in intellectu nostro sunt duae virtutes, quia intellectus agens aliquo modo est forma respectu intellectus materialis, licet non sit forma informans. Et tali modo loquendi utitur Commentator 1 *De caelo et mundo*,[76] ubi vult quod caelum est corpus animatum, et quod intelligentia movens est anima et forma caeli, cum tamen illa intelligentia solum uniatur caelo ut movens caelum appropriatum. Sed in proposito intellectus agens non solum unitur intellectui materiali ut agens, sed etiam aliquo modo ut forma, ut infra patebit.[77]

⟨DUBITATIO 2: DE COMMUNITATE INTELLECTUS AGENTIS ET MATERIALIS⟩

P 218vb   **50.** Alia | dubitatio est de intellectu agente de ratione Philosophi per quam probat quod est ponere intellectum agentem.[78] Videtur enim velle quod in omni genere in quo est potentia receptiva alicuius actus [quod] in eodem genere oportet ponere potentiam activam reducentem illam potentiam ad actum. Nam si intelligat de genere physico, hoc est falsum. Nam sol agit in ista inferiora reducendo materiam de potentia ad actum, cum tamen sol sit incorruptibilis, et ista inferiora generabilia et corruptibilia sunt. Corruptibile autem et incorruptibile differunt genere physico ex 10 *Metaphysicae*.[79]

51. Nec valet si dicatur quod materia istorum inferiorum est incorruptibilis sicut sol, et ideo activum et passivum primum sunt eiusdem generis physici, quoniam secundum hoc ignis non posset agere in aquam, cum principium agendi ignis et patiendi aquae differant sicut corruptibile et incorruptibile, et per consequens genere physico.

52. Praeterea, nec oportet quod agens et patiens sint in eodem genere logico, quoniam primus motor ut Deus movet primum mobile. Primum autem mobile est in genere corporum. Primum autem movens omnino in nullo genere est.

53. Dicendum quod non oportet agens secundum suam substantiam esse in eodem genere cum patiente nec physico nec logico, ut probat ista ratio, sed sufficit

---

1 cum dicit *om.* T   **2** in *om.* OT   **3** respectu *om.* T   **4** tali] hoc T ‖ loquendi *om.* T ‖ De... mundo] Caeli et mundi O   **5** anima ... forma] forma et anima T   **6** illa *om.* T ‖ caelo *om.* OP ‖ caelum] saltem OP   **7** non ... materiali] unitur intellectui materiali non solum T ‖ agens] movens T   **8** etiam *om.* OP ‖ infra patebit] inferius videbitur O; infra videtur P   **12** quod¹ *om.* P   **13** quod] *delevimus*; *scrips.* OPT ‖ oportet] de ratione Philosophi *add. et del.* P   **16** incorruptibilis] incorruptibile OT ‖ et ista] ista P; ista autem O   **16–17** generabilia ... sunt] generabilia et corruptibilia O; sunt generabilia et corruptibilia T   **17** autem *om.* O   **18** ex *om.* T ‖ 10] 8 T ‖ Metaphysicae] na *add. et del.* P   **20** sicut] sed et P ‖ passivum primum] *inv.* T   **21** ignis²] in igne T   **22** aquae] in aqua T   **24** nec] non O   **25** Primum autem] sed primum T   **25–26** est ... corporum] est in genere corruptibilium P; in genere corporum est T   **26** Primum ... movens] primus autem motor T ‖ omnino *om.* T   **27** Dicendum] Dico T   **27–28** secundum ... genere] esse in eodem genere secundum substantiam suam T

to those authorities that he speaks in the singular, when he says that there are two powers in our soul or in our intellect, to the extent that the agent intellect is in some way a form with respect to the material intellect, although it is not an informing form. And the Commentator uses such a manner of speaking in *On the Heavens* 1,[76] where he wants it to be the case that heaven is an animate body, and that the moving intelligence is the soul and form of heaven, even though that intelligence is united with heaven only as the appointed mover of heaven. But in the proposed case the agent intellect is not only united with the material intellect as an agent, but also in some way as a form, as will be obvious below.[77]

⟨DOUBT 2: ON THE COMMUNITY OF THE AGENT AND MATERIAL INTELLECTS⟩

50. There is another doubt concerning the agent intellect, concerning the argument of the Philosopher by means of which he proves that it is necessary to posit an agent intellect.[78] For he seems to want it to be the case that in every genus in which there is the receptive potency of some act, in the same genus one should posit an active power reducing that potency to act. But if he understands this of physical genus, this is false. For the sun acts on these things below by reducing matter from potency to act, although the sun is incorruptible, and these things below are generable and corruptible. But the corruptible and the incorruptible differ in their physical genus (from *Metaphysics* 10).[79]

51. Nor is it valid if it is said that the matter of these things below is incorruptible just as the sun is, and therefore the first active and passive are of the same physical genus, since according to this fire would not be able to act on water, since the principle of action of the fire and that of passivity of the water differ just as the corruptible and the incorruptible do, and consequently in physical genus.

52. Moreover, it is not required that the agent and the patient be of the same logical genus, since the first mover, i.e. God, moves the first mobile. But the first mobile is of the genus of bodies. However, the first mover is of no genus at all.

53. It must be said that it is not required that the agent, according to its own substance, be of the same genus as the patient, neither a physical nor a logical genus, as this argument proves, but it suffices that it is of the same analogous

---

[76] Aver. *In De caelo*, 1, perhaps in t. c. 5, 12. 24–14. 64; see also ibid. 2, t. c. 4, 275. 8–276. 24.
[77] See below, para. 82.
[78] Arist. *DA* 3. 5, 430^{a}10–15.
[79] Arist. *Metaph.* 10. 10, 1058^{b}26–9.

quod sit in eodem genere analogo. Unde licet Deus et homo non sint in aliquo uno genere, nec logico nec physico, sunt tamen in uno genere analogo, puta entis.

54. Est etiam sciendum quod accipitur hic 'genus' pro ratione considerandi una unitate analogiae. Unde ad eundem pertinet determinare de corpore mobili in quantum mobile et de primo movente, qui Deus est. | Et eodem modo ad eundem pertinet determinare de intellectu possibili in quantum receptivus est huiusmodi actus naturalis qui est intelligere, et de intellectu agente in quantum est agens et movens talem potentiam ad actum, ita quod sicut in corporalibus ad eundem pertinet determinare de motu et etiam de Deo in quantum primum movens, ita ad eundem pertinet determinare de intellectu materiali, qui est quoddam mobile intellectualiter, et de intellectu agente, non quidem secundum suam quidditatem, sed secundum quod est quoddam principium reductivum talis potentiae ad actum.

⟨DE INTELLECTU SPECULATIVO⟩

55. Per intellectum speculativum intelligit Commentator compositum ex intellectu materiali et intentionibus abstractis universalibus, ut patet ex 5 et 20 et multis aliis commentis 3 *De anima*.[80] Dicit tamen in 5 commento quod licet iste intellectus sit compositus, tamen non resultat tertium ex his ex quibus componitur, sicut accidit in composito ex materia et forma.[81] Quod dicit forsan propter hoc quia non resultat aliquod tertium absolutum ex his secundum eius opinionem. Posuit enim habitus intellectivos esse essentialiter relationes, ut patet ex 7 *Physicorum*, ubi probat quod ad scientiam non est motus,[82] et 5 *Metaphysicae* in fine capituli de 'ad aliquid',[83] et eadem ratione hoc habet dicere de actibus.

56. Aliter istud dictum exponit Albertus, 3 *De anima*, quod hoc dicit quia intellectus non recipit cum transmutatione istas formas intelligibiles, sicut facit materia.[84] Sed istud non salvat quin propter hoc resultet tertium ex his. Et ideo videtur prima expositio convenientior.

---

1 sit] sint T **1–2** Unde ... analogo *om. hom.* T **1** sint] sunt P || uno *om.* O **2** puta] ut puta T **3** etiam] igitur T || sciendum] constituendum (*lectio incerta*) T || accipitur] accipit P **3–4** considerandi una] *inv.* O *et et add.* **3** considerandi] *lectio incerta* T; conterminandi (*lectio incerta*) P **5** mobile] mobili O || eundem] eum T **6** determinare *om.* O || possibili] passibili P || receptivus est] *inv.* T **8** sicut] sic P **9–12** de¹ ... actum] de corpore mobili in quantum mobile et de primo movente, qui Deus est, et eodem modo ad eundem pertinet determinare de intellectu possibili in quantum receptivus est huiusmodi actus naturalis, qui est intelligere, et de intellectu agente, in quantum agens est et movens talem potentiam ad actum O **9** motu] *fortasse scribendum* mobili || etiam *om.* T || quantum] erit *add.* T **10** materiali *om.* P **11** intellectualiter] intellectum T || quidem *om.* P **15** abstractis universalibus] *inv.* O || 20] 10 O **17** tamen non] *inv.* O **18** composito] compositis O || forsan *om.* T **19** ex his *om.* O **20–22** 7 ... aliquid] 5 Metaphysicae in fine capituli de ad aliquid et 7 Physicorum ubi probat quod ad scientiam non est motus T **23** Aliter] tamen *add.* T || quod] quia T || hoc *om.* T || quia] quod PT **25** propter hoc *om.* T || resultet] resultat OP

genus. Because of this, although God and man are not of some one genus, neither a logical nor a physical genus, they are nevertheless of one analogous genus, namely, that of being.

54. It must also be realized that the term 'genus' is taken here to mean a manner of considering things which are one by unity of analogy. Because of this, it pertains to the same scholar to establish definite conclusions about the mobile body, in so far as mobile, and about the first mover, which is God. And in the same way it pertains to the same scholar to establish definite conclusions about the possible intellect in so far as it is receptive of this sort of natural act, namely understanding, and about the agent intellect in so far as it is the agent and mover of such potency towards act, so that just as among bodily things it pertains to the same scholar to establish definite conclusions about motion and also about God in so far as he is the first mover, so it pertains to the same scholar to establish definite conclusions about the material intellect, which is something mobile intellectually, and about the agent intellect, not indeed according to its own quiddity, but in so far as it is a principle capable of reducing such a potency to act.

⟨ON THE SPECULATIVE INTELLECT⟩

55. By speculative intellect the Commentator understands the composite of the material intellect and abstract universal intentions, as is obvious from comments 5 and 20 and many others on *On the Soul* 3.[80] However, he says in comment 5 that although this intellect is composite, nevertheless there does not result a third thing out of these things of which it is composed, as happens in the composite of matter and form.[81] He says this perhaps for this reason, that no third absolute thing results from these according to his opinion. For he claimed that intellectual habits are essentially relations, as is obvious from *Physics* 7, where he proves that there is no motion towards knowledge,[82] and *Metaphysics* 5 at the end of the chapter concerning 'towards something';[83] and for the same reason he has to say this concerning acts.

56. Albert interprets this claim otherwise, on *On the Soul* 3, namely, that Averroes says this because the intellect does not receive these intelligible forms with transmutation, as matter does.[84] But this does not prevent the fact that because of this a third thing results from these. And therefore the first interpretation seems more fitting.

---

[80] Aver. *In DA* 3, t. c. 5, 390. 87–91; t. c. 20, 453. 285–8. See also t. c. 36, 496. 505–497. 507.
[81] Ibid., t. c. 5, 404. 506–8.
[82] Aver. *In Phys*. 7, t. c. 20, fol. 323^{rb}F–^{va}G.
[83] Aver. *In Metaph*. 5, t. c. 20, fol. 129^{rb}F–^{va}H.
[84] Albert the Great, *In DA* 3, tract. 2, cap. 17, 202. 31–90.

57. Istum autem intellectum ponit esse generabilem et corruptibilem et multiplicatum ad multiplicationem hominum, sicut intentiones imaginatae, ex quibus dependet. Tamen non est generabilis nec corruptibilis nec multiplicabilis ratione materialis in eo, scilicet ratione intellectus materialis, sed ratione formalis solum, scilicet ratione intentionum speculativarum, quae sunt generabiles. Aliter frustra poneretur intellectus agens multiplicari in diversis secundum multiplicationem intentionum imaginatarum. Dicit tamen in 5 commento et in 20 quod intellectus speculativus ratione intentionum intellectarum non est simpliciter et absolute corruptibilis, sed solum respectu individui signati, non respectu speciei.[85] Ita quod vult dicere quod intellectus materialis semper habet intentionem equi abstractam et bovis et sic de aliis, non tamen semper habuit eam abstractam a phantasmate meo vel tuo, sed secundum hoc quod copulatur intellectus mihi vel tibi. Sic huiusmodi intentiones sunt generabiles et corruptibiles. Unde ponit philosophiam esse ingenerabilem et incorruptibilem simpliciter. Dicit enim in 5 commento quod si aliqua pars terrae caruerit huiusmodi artificiis, verbi gratia quarta pars septentrionalis, non carebunt eis aliae quartae.[86]

58. Ulterius sequitur ex dicto suo quod haec propositio | 'omne recipiens oportet esse denudatum a natura recepti vel secundum genus vel secundum speciem', quam ponit in 4 commento tertii,[87] falsa sit—saltem in respectivis, quicquid sit de absolutis, ut patet de speciebus diversarum albedinum in eadem parte medii et etiam de diversis formis intelligibilibus eiusdem speciei in eodem intellectu materiali. Sufficit enim in respectivis quod denudetur ab eo quod recipit secundum numerum. Etiam in absolutis non oportet quod recipiens denudetur ab eo quod recipit secundum speciem. Nam superficies existens sub uno gradu albedinis est in potentia receptiva ad alium gradum manente primo gradu quantum ad illud quod perfectionis est in illo; non tamen est in potentia ad aliud individuum albedinis manente gradu priori—gradus enim alius non variat individuum—sicut medium habens speciem unius albi est in potentia ad speciem alterius albedinis differentem numero.

---

2 imaginatae] sunt *add.* O   3 dependet] dependent PT || generabilis nec *om.* OP || corruptibilis . . . multiplicabilis] multiplicabilis nec corruptibilis O   5 intentionum] *corr. ex* intentionis O   6 agens] et quamvis *add.* P || multiplicari] multiplicatur P   8 et absolute *om.* T   9 respectu[1]] ratione T || non respectu] sed solum ratione T   10 abstractam] absolutam T   12 quod] *om.* T || copulatur] corrumpitur T || Sic] sed T   15 artificiis] edificiis T   16 carebunt] carebant O; caruerint P   18 esse denudatum] denudari OP   19 4] 5 T || tertii] libri *add.* T || falsa] figura P || sit[1]] est O   20 speciebus diversarum] diversis speciebus T   21 etiam *om.* T || formis . . . speciei] speciebus intentionalibus eiusdem rei T   23 Etiam] Item T || recipiens] non *add.* P || ab eo] a natura eius T   25 ad[1] *om.* T || primo gradu] *inv.* O; illo gradu T   26 perfectionis] perfectius T || in illo] albedinis PT   27 gradu priori] *inv.* T || alius . . . variat] eius non est ipsum P || sicut] sed P

57. But he claims that this intellect is generable and corruptible and multiplied according to the multiplying of men, just as the imagined intentions are on which it depends. However, it is not generable nor corruptible nor multipliable by reason of what is material in it, that is by reason of the material intellect, but only by reason of what is formal, that is by reason of the speculative intentions, which are generable. Otherwise it would be posited in vain that the agent intellect is multiplied in different men according to the multiplying of the imagined intentions. Nevertheless, he says in comments 5 and in 20 that the speculative intellect, by reason of the understood intentions, is not simply and absolutely corruptible, but only with respect to the given individual, not with respect to a species.[85] So what he wants to say is that the material intellect always has the abstract intention of a horse and an ox and in the same way of other things, but nevertheless it did not always have it abstracted from my phantasm or yours, but according to the fact that the intellect is conjoined with me or you. So such intentions are generable and corruptible. Because of this he claims that philosophy is simply ingenerable and incorruptible. For he says in comment 5 that if any part of the earth, for instance the northern quarter, lacks constructions of a certain kind, the other quarters will not lack them.[86]

58. Furthermore, it follows from his claim that this proposition, 'every recipient should be stripped bare of the nature of the thing received, either according to genus or according to species', which he posits in comment 4 of the third book,[87] would be false—at least in relational things, whatever might be the case concerning absolutes, as is obvious in the case of the species of different whitenesses in the same part of a medium and also of different intelligible forms of the same species in the same material intellect. For it suffices in relational things that it should be stripped bare of that which it receives according to number. Also in absolutes it is not required that the recipient should be stripped bare of that which it receives according to species. For a surface existing under one degree of whiteness is in receptive potency to another degree while the first degree remains as to the perfection that is in it; nevertheless it is not in potency to another individual of whiteness while the prior degree remains—for another degree does not change the individual—just as a medium having the species of one white thing is in potency to the species of another whiteness, differing from it in number.

---

[85] Aver. *In DA* 3, t. c. 5, 407. 589–96; t. c. 20, 448. 136–449. 159.
[86] Ibid., t. c. 5, 408. 615–19.
[87] Ibid., t. c. 4, 385. 67–8.

⟨DE INTELLECTU IN HABITO⟩

59. Per intellectum in habitu intelligit Commentator intellectum informatum per habitus scientificos et morales, ita quod intellectus speculativus est in plus quam intellectus in habitu, se habens ad intellectum in habitu sicut consequens ad antecedens.[88] Dicitur enim 'intellectus speculativus' quicumque intellectus informatus intentione intellecta sive secundum actum sive secundum habitum sive habitu complexo sive incomplexo, ita quod communis est omni intellectui aliquid intelligenti, sive laico sive clerico. Sed 'intellectus in habitu' dicitur | intellectus habituatus per aliquos vel saltem aliquem habitum scientificum, qui intellectus, si sit omnino perfectus, erit habituatus per omnes habitus speculativos—et per consequens morales. Nam secundum commentatorem Averroem, in prologo 8 *Physicorum*,[89] et idem habetur a Commentatore 10 *Ethicorum*,[90] virtutes intellectuales praesupponunt morales.

60. De isto tamen intellectu in habitu est sciendum secundum Commentatorem, 36 commento 3 *De anima*,[91] ⟨quod⟩ intellecta a nobis duobus modis fiunt in nobis. Quaedam enim fiunt naturaliter, ita quod ea non accipimus a doctore aliquo vel per inquisitionem invenimus ipsa, cuiusmodi sunt dignitates | et principia prima, quorum cognitio non dependet nisi a lumine intellectus agentis et cognitione sensitiva. Alia fiunt in nobis voluntarie, quae vel per doctrinam vel inveniendo per inquisitionem, quorum notitia deducitur ex notitia principiorum, ita quod notitia talium dependet tamquam ex causa totali ex primis propositionibus seu verius ex intellectu materiali habituato illis primis propositionibus et intellectu agente. Subiectum autem tam illarum propositionum quam intellectus agentis est intellectus materialis, [et] sicut tam lux quam species coloris habent diaphanum pro subiecto. Lux etiam habet quendam modum formae respectu speciei coloris— et color quodam modo respectu materiae—pro quanto | habet rationem perfecti et color respectu eius rationem imperfecti. 'Omnia enim duo'—ut dicit Commentator—'quorum est unum subiectum, et unum est perfectius altero, necesse est ut respectus perfectioris ad imperfectius sit sicut respectus formae ad materiam'[92] seu instrumentum, licet imperfectius non sit vere materia nec vere instrumentum.

---

5 Dicitur *om.* P || enim] tamen P   6 actum ... habitum] habitum sive secundum actum T   7 communis] commune T   9 habituatus] informatus T || saltem] aliquem aliquos habitus *add. et del.* O || si] *suppl. s.l.* O   10 erit] *scripsimus*; est OPT   11 Averroem] Averrois P   14 intellectu] *suppl. i.m.* P   15 36] *corr. s.l. ex* 13 O || anima] intelligente (*lectio incerta*) *add. et del.* P || quod] *supplevimus*; *om.* OPT || a *om.* PT   16 in nobis *om.* T || enim *om.* O   17–18 principia prima] *inv.* T; principia O   18 a] ex T || et] a *add.* O   19 vel¹] solum T   20 inveniendo] inventionem O || inquisitionem] acquisitionem T || notitia²] primorum *add.* T   21 notitia talium] *inv.* T || ex¹] est T   22 illis] vel P || et] ex *add.* T   23 Subiectum] solum P || illarum] primarum *add.* T || quam] qua P   24 et] *delevimus*; *scrips.* OPT   25 subiecto] aliquo *add. i.m.* P || formae *om.* T   26 et¹] *fortasse scribendum* ut   26–27 et² ... imperfecti *om. hom.* O   27 rationem *om.* P || enim] autem OP   27–28 Commentator *om.* OP   28 altero] alio T   30 nec] vel T || vere² *om.* T

⟨ON THE INTELLECT IN HABIT⟩

59. By 'intellect in habit' the Commentator understands the intellect informed by scientific and moral habits, so that the speculative intellect encompasses more than the intellect in habit, being related to the intellect in habit as the consequent is to the antecedent.[88] For any intellect informed by an understood intention, either according to act or according to habit (either by a complex or a non-complex habit), is called 'speculative intellect', so that it is common to every intellect, whether lay or clerical, that understands something. But the intellect habituated by means of some number of scientific habits (or at least of some one) is called the 'intellect in habit', which intellect, if it were entirely perfect, would be habituated by means of all speculative habits—and consequently by moral ones. For according to the commentator Averroes, in the prologue to the eight books of the *Physics*[89] (and the same can be obtained from the Commentator in *Ethics* 10),[90] intellectual virtues presuppose moral ones.

60. However, concerning this intellect in habit it must be realized that according to the Commentator (comment 36, *On the Soul* 3)[91] things understood by us come to be in us in two ways. For some come to be naturally, so that we do not receive them from any teacher or find them out by investigation; of this sort are dignities and first principles, cognition of which does not depend on anything except on the light of the agent intellect and on sensitive cognition. Others come to be in us voluntarily; these arise either by learning or through finding out by investigation, and cognition of them is deduced from the cognition of principles, so that the cognition of such things depends, so to speak, on the first propositions just as if on its total cause, or, more accurately, on the material intellect, as habituated by those first propositions, and on the agent intellect. But the subject both of those propositions and of the agent intellect is the material intellect, just as both light and the species of colour have the transparent medium for their subject. Light is also in some way form in relation to the species of colour—and colour is in some way form in relation to matter—inasmuch as it has the nature of the perfect and inversely colour in relation to light has the nature of the imperfect. 'For in the case of every two things'—as the Commentator says—'of which one is the subject and one is more perfect than the other, it is necessary that the relation of the more perfect to the less perfect should be just like the relation of form to matter'[92] or instrument, although in reality the less perfect is neither matter nor instrument.

---

[88] It is not clear where in *De anima* 3 Averroes suggests this.
[89] Aver. *In Phys. Prol.*, fol. 1^{va}I.
[90] Aver. *In Eth. Nic.* 10, cap. 8, fol. 155^{va}G–H.
[91] Aver. *In DA* 3, t. c. 36, 496. 490–3.
[92] Ibid. 499. 571–4.

Igitur sequitur quod lux respectu coloris aliquo modo habeat rationem formae. Tertio licet lux et color habeant unum subiectum, lux tamen est quodam modo efficiens respectu coloris, hoc est, facit colorem actu visibilem secundum eum. Sic proportionaliter est in proposito, quod intellectus agens et intentiones omnes intellectae habent intellectum materialem pro subiecto. Et ideo cum intellectus agens sit perfectior intentionibus intellectis, habet quodam modo rationem formae respectu intentionum intellectarum, et cum hoc causat istas intentiones intellectas in intellectu materiali. Et est satis simile hinc inde hoc excepto quod intellectus agens non est forma inhaerens et informans intellectum materialem sicut lux diaphanum. Et quia intellectus agens unitur nobis sicut forma, de qua unione clarius in articulo sequenti dicetur,[93] ideo possumus in nobis generare intellecta quando volumus.

⟨DE INTELLECTU ADEPTO⟩

61. Per intellectum adeptum intelligit Commentator dispositionem intellectus materialis perfectissimam, videlicet quando copulatur sibi intellectus agens non solum ut agens, sed etiam ut eius forma propria in actu, secundum quam dispositionem cognoscit substantias separatas, quae est eius perfectissima operatio in quantum homo.[94] Et quia intellectus materialis hominis non est a principio in ista dispositione qua intellectus agens sibi unitur perfecte ut forma in actu, postea tamen adipiscitur intellectum agentem ut formam eius in actu, ideo proprie dicitur 'intellectus adeptus'.

⟨OPINIO AVERROIS DE COGNITIONE SUBSTANTIARUM SEPARATARUM IN 3 *DE ANIMA*⟩

62. Ad cuius evidentiam est sciendum quod omnes Peripatetici posuerunt quod intellectus noster materialis cognoscit substantias separatas, tamen diversi propter diversas rationes. Commentator autem respondet rationibus Alexandri et Avempace probantibus quod intellectus noster coniunctus potest intelligere substantias separatas, 36 commento.[95] Tenet tamen conclusionem quam ipsi tenuerunt, et videtur inniti rationi Themistii per locum a maiori, quae est ista: virtus immaterialis

---

1 lux] lumen OP || rationem] *lectio incerta* P; respectum O   2 Tertio *om.* P || unum] idem O || est . . . modo] quodam modo est O   3 est] etiam P   4 agens *om.* T   6 rationem] respectum OP   7 intentionum intellectarum] earum O || istas] ipsas T   8 est *om.* P || hoc *om.* T   9 et] vel T || sicut] *corr. i.m. in* sed P   10 quia] sicut T   10–11 clarius . . . dicetur] statim clarius dicetur et T; clarius inferius patebit O   11 possumus] possimus T   12 volumus] volimus T   16 etiam *om.* OP || eius] est O   20 adipiscitur] adipiscit P || eius *om.* T   25 noster *om.* O   25–26 diversi . . . rationes] diversimode ex diversitate rationum T   26 autem] etiam P || et] Avicennae *add. et del.* P   27 probantibus] probantes PT   28 commento] et *add.* T || tamen *om.* T   29 rationi] *corr. ex* ratione P

Therefore it follows that light in relation to colour has in some way the nature of form. Thirdly, although light and colour have one subject, light, however, is in some way an efficient cause in relation to colour—that is, it makes colour actually visible, according to him. So it is proportionally the same in the proposed case that the agent intellect and all understood intentions have the material intellect for their subject. And therefore since the agent intellect is more perfect than understood intentions, it has in a way the nature of a form in relation to understood intentions, and in addition to this it causes those understood intentions in the material intellect. And these two cases are similar enough to one another, with this exception, that the agent intellect is not a form inhering in and informing the material intellect as light does the transparent medium. And because the agent intellect is united with us as a form is, which union will be discussed more clearly in the following article,[93] therefore we can generate understood things in ourselves when we want to.

⟨ON THE ACCOMPLISHED INTELLECT⟩

61. By accomplished intellect the Commentator understands the most perfect disposition of the material intellect, namely when the agent intellect is conjoined with it not only as agent, but also as its proper form in act, according to which disposition it cognizes separate substances, which is its most perfect operation inasmuch as it is man.[94] And because the material intellect of man is not from the beginning in this disposition by which the agent intellect is united with it perfectly as a form in act, but later acquires the agent intellect as its form in act, therefore it is correctly called 'accomplished intellect'.

⟨OPINION OF AVERROES CONCERNING THE COGNITION OF SEPARATE SUBSTANCES IN *ON THE SOUL* 3⟩

62. As evidence for this it must be realized that all the Peripatetics posited that our material intellect cognizes separate substances, although different philosophers did so for different reasons. But the Commentator responds in comment 36[95] to the arguments of Alexander and Avempace which establish that our intellect when conjunct can understand separate substances. However, he maintains the conclusion which they maintained themselves, and he seems to rely on the argument of Themistius by the 'from the greater' rule, which is this: an immaterial

---

[93] See below, paras. 61–8.
[94] Cf. Aver. *In DA* 3, t. c. 5, 411. 703–6; t. c. 36, 484. 151–485. 158.
[95] Ibid., t. c. 36, 482. 81–487. 234; 488. 263–495. 459.

quae comprehendere potest minus perfectum potest comprehendere magis perfectum, licet non econverso.[96] Et ideo cum intellectus materialis sit virtus abstracta et potest comprehendere materialia, dignius est quod immaterialia.

63. Sed opponit contra se sic: si intellectus noster materialis naturaliter intelligat res abstractas, sequitur, cum intellectus materialis a principio fuerit nobiscum copulatus, quod a principio haberemus cognitionem substantiarum separatarum.[97] Et dicit Commentator quod haec dubitatio difficilis est, et quod causa ambiguitatis et laboris expositorum Aristotelis circa istam materiam est quod nullum sermonem de hoc invenerunt ab Aristotele, licet se promisit hoc declarare.[98] |

64. Responsio autem Commentatoris[99] ad rationem prius positam[100]—cuius virtus stat in hoc: ex quo intellectus materialis naturaliter potest cognoscere substantias separatas, quare non a principio potest cognoscere substantias separatas, sed in fine—consistit in hoc quod sicut intellecta speculativa copulantur nobiscum per formas imaginabiles—quod dicit, ut credo, pro tanto quia cognitio intellectus materialis, quae fit per intellecta speculativa, augetur per augmentationem cognitionis virtutis phantasticae, quae fit per intentiones imaginatas—sic intellectus agens ad generationem et augmentationem intellectorum speculativorum copulatur cum intellectu nostro materiali non solum ut agens, sed ut forma illuminans et irradians intellectum, ita quod istud lumen perfectius et perfectius de die in diem copulatur in ratione formae illustrantis ipsi intellectui materiali. Unde dicit[101] quod quando intellecta omnia speculativa sunt in nobis in potentia solum, tunc intellectus agens solum copulatur nobis ut forma in potentia; quando autem quaedam | intellecta speculativa sunt in nobis in potentia et quaedam in actu, tunc intellectus agens copulatur nobis imperfecte, et movemur ad copulationem perfectam; cum autem omnia speculativa fuerint in intellectu nostro materiali actu existentia— accipiendo actum pro habitu perfecto acquisito, ita quod completur motus intellectus in habitu—tunc copulatur nobis intellectus agens perfecte ut forma in actu.

1 comprehendere potest] *inv.* O || potest²] et *add.* O; etiam *add.* T   1–2 comprehendere² ... perfectum] magis perfectum comprehendere O   1 magis] maius P   2 cum ... materialis] intellectus materialis cum O   3 et *om.* P || est quod] quod et O; est quam P   4 se] Commentator *add.* T   4–5 intelligat] intelligit T *et* substantias vel *add.*   5 sequitur] sequeretur P || intellectus] noster *add.* T || a ... nobiscum] fuerit nobis a principio T   6 haberemus ... separatarum] intelligeremus substantias separatas T   7 Et *om.* T || difficilis est] *inv.* T; difficilis P   7–8 ambiguitatis ... laboris] difficultatis et ambiguitatis T   8 materiam] copulationem P   9 de hoc *om.* P || promisit] promiserit OT || declarare] declaraturum O   10 autem *om.* O   10–11 cuius virtus *om.* O   11 ex quo *om.* T || intellectus] naturalis materialiter *add. et del.* P   12 a] in OP   12–13 substantias ... fine *om.* T; illas O   13 consistit ... quod] responsio, inquam, stat in hoc quod T; solutio quia O || copulantur] copulatur P   14 imaginabiles] imaginatas O || ut ... tanto] pro tanto ut credo T   15 augmentationem] augmentum T   15–16 cognitionis *om.* T   16 virtutis] virtus T || phantasticae] coniungitur cognitionis *add. et* coniungitur *del.* T   17–18 copulatur] coniungitur T   20 copulatur] illuminatur T   22 solum ... nobis] copulatur nobis solum T; copulatur nobis O   23 speculativa *om.* O; speculabilia T   25 speculativa] speculabilia T || nostro *om.* P || materiali] in *add.* O || existentia *om.* O   26 actum] actu T

power which can comprehend something less perfect can comprehend something more perfect, although the reverse is not true.[96] And therefore since the material intellect is an abstract power and can comprehend material things, it is more fitting that it should understand immaterial things.

63. But he counters against himself in this way: if our material intellect naturally understands abstract things, it follows, since the material intellect has been conjoined with us from the beginning, that we would have cognition of separate substances from the beginning.[97] And the Commentator says that this is a troublesome doubt, and that the cause of ambiguity and labour for interpreters of Aristotle concerning this matter is that they have found no discussion of this in Aristotle, although he promised to explain it.[98]

64. However, the response of the Commentator[99] to the argument set out before[100]—and its power rests on this: since the material intellect can naturally cognize separate substances, for which reason it cannot cognize separate substances from the beginning, but at the end—consists in this, that just as speculative understood things are conjoined with us by means of imaginable forms—which he says, as I believe, to the extent that the cognition of the material intellect which occurs by means of speculative understood things is increased by means of the increase of the cognition of the imaginative power, which occurs by means of imagined intentions—so the agent intellect is conjoined with our material intellect in order to generate and increase the speculative understood things; and it is conjoined not only as agent, but as form illuminating and irradiating the intellect, so that this light, more and more perfectly from day to day, is conjoined with the material intellect itself in the guise of an enlightening form. Accordingly he says[101] that when all speculative understood things are in us in potency only, then the agent intellect is conjoined with us only as a form in potency; but when some speculative understood things are in us in potency and some in act, then the agent intellect is conjoined with us imperfectly, and we are moved towards perfect conjoining; but when all speculative things are actually existing in our material intellect—understanding by an act a perfect acquired habit, so that the motion of the intellect in habit is completed—then the agent intellect is conjoined with us perfectly as a form in act. But this new conjoining is the cause of a new

---

[96] Ibid. 487. 235–9; 488. 251–7.
[97] Ibid. 488. 257–62.
[98] Ibid. 487. 218–20.
[99] Ibid. 499. 578–500. 598.
[100] See above, para. 63.
[101] Aver. *In DA* 3, t. c. 36, 500. 599–606.

Ista autem copulatio nova est causa novae intellectionis, scilicet substantiarum separatarum secundum eum, et non econverso, secundum quod ponit Avempace.[102] Causa autem copulationis intellectus agentis in ratione formae effectiva non est danda nisi per accidens. Intellectus enim agens est per se causa, licet non totalis, intellectorum speculativorum, et in generando active ista intellecta in intellectu materiali et augendo actuat intellectum materialem denudando eum a potentia. Ex hoc autem quod magis actuatur, natus est perfectius istud lumen recipere ut formam illustrantem ipsum—formam dico non inhaerentem, sed assistentem, sicut si lumen in medio irradiaret medium per assistentiam absque hoc quod inhaereret. Quando autem totaliter est denudatus intellectus materialis a potentia, quod accidit in termino perfectionis intellectus in habitu, tunc primo intellectus materialis est dispositus ut lumen intellectus agentis, quod est ipsemet intellectus agens, ut formam in actu et perfecte recipiat. Et tunc per intellectum agentem tamquam per propriam formam omnia intelligimus | quae intelligimus.

65. Per hoc solvit ad formam rationis, dicens[103] quod haec est causa quare non intelligimus a principio substantias separatas, quia non coniungitur nobis intellectus agens in principio ut forma in actu. Et ideo per ipsum non possumus pro tunc intelligere substantias separatas. Sed cum intellectus agens nobis coniungitur sicut forma in actu perfecte omnibus modis quibus potest copulari, tunc per ipsum tamquam per formam intelligimus substantias separatas. Et hoc accidit solum in termino motus intellectus in habitu, scilicet quando intellectus materialis est perfectus per omnes habitus speculativos, ut dictum est.[104]

66. Dicit etiam Commentator quod sic 'intellectus agens sit forma in nobis, et nullus modus est secundum quem generetur forma in nobis nisi iste'.[105] Dicit etiam parum ante finem illius commenti 36 3 *De anima* quod 'fiducia in continuationis possibilitate intellectus agentis nobiscum est in declarando quod respectus eius ad hominem est respectus formae et agentis, non agentis tantum'.[106]

67. Est etiam intelligendum quod non est sua intentio quod intellectus noster materialis coniunctus, quando est in dispositione adeptionis, [quod] intelligat substantias separatas solum ut relucent in phantasmatibus et in intellectis speculativis, ut quidam dicunt, sed in se quasi ingrediendo aliam regionem, quod patet per ipsum, 20 commento 3 *De anima* parum post principium. Dicit enim quod 'scientia | existens in nobis in dispositione adeptionis dicitur aequivoce cum scientia exi-

1 scilicet *om.* O 5 intellectorum] intellectivorum P 7 est] magis et *add.* T ‖ istud] idem *add.* T 9 irradiaret] irradicaret P 11 intellectus¹ *om.* T 12 ipsemet] ipse P 14 propriam formam] *inv.* O 15 ad *om.* P ‖ haec *om.* T 17 agens] a p *add. et del.* P ‖ per] secundum T 17–18 non ... tunc] pro tunc non possum T 18–19 cum ... sicut] quando intellectus agens coniungitur nobis ut T 19 potest] nobis *add.* T 20 intelligimus] intelligemus T ‖ substantias separatas] huiusmodi substantias O ‖ accidit solum] *inv.* O 23 sic] sicut P ‖ sit *om.* O 24 generetur forma] *inv.* T; generatur forma OP 25 illius commenti] ibi commento T ‖ 3] libri *add.* T 26 possibilitate] positae T 27 non agentis *om.* T 28 etiam] igitur T ‖ sua intentio] *inv.* O 29 quod] *delevimus*; *scrips.* OPT 31 ut ... dicunt *om.* T 32 enim *om.* PT

understanding, that is, of separate substances, according to Averroes, and not the reverse, according to what Avempace claims.[102] But the efficient cause of the conjoining of the agent intellect as a form cannot be provided except by accident. For the agent intellect is by itself the cause, although not the total cause, of speculative understood things, and in the active generation of these understood things in the material intellect and in the increasing of them makes actual the material intellect by stripping it bare of potency. But because of its being made more actual, it is apt by nature to receive this light more perfectly as a form that illuminates it—a form, I say, not inhering, but assisting, just as if light in a medium were to irradiate the medium by means of assistance, without its inhering. But when the material intellect is totally stripped bare of potency, which happens at the end of the perfection of the intellect in habit, then first the material intellect is disposed so that it may receive the light of the agent intellect, which is the agent intellect itself, as a form in act and perfectly. And then it is by means of the agent intellect, just as if by means of a proper form, that we understand everything which we understand.

65. By this he gives a solution to the form of the argument, saying[103] that this is the reason why we do not understand separate substances from the beginning, because the agent intellect is not conjoined with us from the beginning as a form in act. And therefore by means of it we cannot, at that time, understand separate substances. But when the agent intellect is conjoined with us as a form in act perfectly in all ways in which it can be conjoined, then by means of it just as if by means of a form we understand separate substances. And this happens only at the end-point of the motion of the intellect in habit, that is when the material intellect is perfected by means of all speculative habits, as has been said.[104]

66. The Commentator also says that in this way 'the agent intellect is a form in us, and there is no way according to which it could be generated as a form in us except for this one'.[105] He also says just before the end of this comment 36 on *On the Soul* 3 that his 'belief in the possibility of the continued connection of the agent intellect with us rests on the claim that its relation to man is the relation of form and agent, not agent alone'.[106]

67. It must also be understood that it is not his conception that our conjunct material intellect, when it is in a state of accomplishment, understands separate substances only as they manifest themselves in phantasms and in speculative understood things, as some say, but understands them in themselves as if entering another region, which he makes obvious in *On the Soul* 3, comment 20, just after the beginning. For he says that 'knowledge existing in us in a state of accomplishment is not the same kind of knowledge as that which exists by

---

[102] Ibid. 501. 623–9.
[103] Ibid. 3, t. c. 36, 501. 630–9.
[104] See above, para. 64.
[105] Aver. *In DA* 3, t. c. 36, 499. 586–500. 592.
[106] Ibid. 502. 661–4.

stente per naturam et disciplinam'.[107] Similiter 36 commento eiusdem statim post principium movet quaestionem sub hac forma dicens: 'debemus cogitare utrum sit possibile quod intellectus qui est in nobis intelligat res abstractas a materia, secundum quod sunt abstractae a magnitudine, non secundum comparationem ad alterum'.[108] Et loquitur de intellectu materiali, ut patet in exequendo quaestionem. Postea determinat partem affirmativam.[109] Et per consequens intelligit quod intellectus noster materialis coniunctus in dispositione adeptionis non intelligit solum substantias separatas ut relucent in phantasmate, sed in se et absolute.

68. Dicit etiam in fine illius commenti, loquens de intellectu materiali in dispositione adeptionis, quod 'sua intellectio non est aliquid scientiarum speculativarum'[110] etc. Si tamen illa cognitio esset substantiarum separatarum solum ut relucent in effectibus, iam illa cognitio esset speculativa et pertineret ad metaphysicum.

⟨OPINIO AVERROIS DE COGNITIONE SUBSTANTIARUM
SEPARATARUM IN 12 *METAPHYSICAE*⟩

69. Licet ista sit sententia Commentatoris circa possibilitatem cognitionis substantiarum separatarum per intellectum nostrum materialem et etiam ultimata eius sententia quantum ad ea quae dixit in 3 *De anima*, | tamen alibi, puta in 12 *Metaphysicae*,[111] suam intentionem circa hoc perfectius declarat, et ideo forsan percipiens quod non satis se declaravit in 3 *De anima*, dixit in ultimo verbo 36 commenti 3 *De anima*, ubi de ista materia ultimo in illo libro tangit, sic: 'Hoc igitur apparuit nobis in hoc quaesito modo, et si post apparuerit nobis plus, scribemus.'[112]

70. Sciendum quod intentio ultima Commentatoris circa modum et possibilitatem cognitionis substantiarum separatarum ab intellectu materiali nostro est quod intellectus noster materialis, quando denudatus est omnino a potentia, scilicet in termino motus intellectus in habitu, tunc intelligit se ipsum tamquam primum intelligibile, et in intelligendo se intelligit intellectum agentem et omnes substantias superiores abstractas. Secundum enim sententiam Commentatoris quaelibet intelligentia intelligens substantiam abstractam inferiorem intelligit superiorem, licet non econtra. Quod haec sit eius intentio probo per ipsum, 12 *Metaphysicae*, commento 17 in fine, ubi dicit sic: 'Si iste intellectus', id est materialis, 'denudetur

---

1 36 commento] commento 98 O   **3** nobis] utrum *add.* T   **6** intelligit] intendit T   **7** noster *om.* O || intelligit solum] *inv.* T   **9** in[1] ... illius] ibi in fine T   **10** intellectio non] intentio non P; intellectione O   **11** solum *om.* T   **17** materialem *om.* O   **18** in[2] *om.* T   **20** se *om.* T || declaravit] declaraverat T || verbo] *suppl. i.m.* P   **20–21** 36 commenti] *inv.* T   **21** materia *om.* O || ultimo ... libro] *scripsimus*; ultimo in primo libro P; quantum ad librum illum ultimo O; ultimo T   **23** quod] modus ultimus et *add.* T || Commentatoris] *om.* T   **23–24** modum ... cognitionis] cognitionem T   **24** ab ... nostro *om.* T   **25–26** noster ... intellectus *om. hom.* O   **27** in *om.* OT   **27–28** substantias] *om.* T   **29** abstractam] absolutam T || intelligit] etiam *add.* T   **30** Quod] Et *ante* Quod *add.* T || probo] probatio T || per ipsum *om.* T   **31** 17] *scripsimus*; 18 OPT

nature and science'.[107] Similarly in comment 36 of the same book immediately after the beginning he raises a question in this form, saying: 'we must consider whether it is possible that the intellect which is in us understands things abstracted from matter, in so far as they are abstracted from magnitude, not according to a comparison with something else'.[108] And he speaks about the material intellect, as is obvious in the unfolding of the question. Later he determines the affirmative part.[109] And consequently he understands that our conjunct material intellect, in a state of accomplishment, does not understand separate substances only as they manifest themselves in phantasm, but in themselves and absolutely.

68. He also says at the end of this comment, speaking about the material intellect in a state of accomplishment, that 'its understanding is not something that belongs to the speculative sciences'[110] etc. However, if this cognition were of separate substances only as they manifest themselves in effects, this cognition would already be speculative and would pertain to the metaphysician.

⟨OPINION OF AVERROES CONCERNING THE COGNITION OF SEPARATE SUBSTANCES IN *METAPHYSICS* 12⟩

69. Although this is the stated opinion of the Commentator concerning the possibility of the cognition of separate substances by means of our material intellect, and also his last stated opinion as far as what he says on *On the Soul* 3 goes, nevertheless elsewhere, namely in *Metaphysics* 12,[111] he explains his conception concerning this more perfectly, and therefore, perhaps perceiving that he did not explain himself clearly enough in *On the Soul* 3, he said the following in the last word of comment 36 on *On the Soul* 3, where he touches on this matter for the last time in that book: 'Concerning this question this, therefore, has become clear to us now, and if more becomes clear to us later, we shall write about it.'[112]

70. It must be realized that the last conception of the Commentator concerning the manner and the possibility of cognition of separate substances by our material intellect is that our material intellect, when it is entirely stripped bare of potency, that is at the end of the motion of the intellect in habit, then understands itself as a first intelligible thing, so to speak, and in understanding itself understands the agent intellect and all higher abstract substances. For according to the stated opinion of the Commentator any intelligence understanding a lower abstract substance understands the higher, although the reverse is not the case. That this is his conception I prove by what he says himself at the end of comment 17 on *Metaphysics* 12, where he says the following: 'If this intellect', that is the material,

---

[107] Ibid., t. c. 20, 445. 57–9.
[108] Ibid., t. c. 36, 480. 16–20.
[109] Ibid. 481. 48–57.
[110] Ibid. 501. 640–1.
[111] Aver. *In Metaph.* 12, t. c. 17, fols. 302^{vb}K–303^{rb}D.
[112] Aver. *In DA* 3, t. c. 36, 502. 664–6.

apud perfectionem humanam a potentia, necesse est ut destruatur ab eo haec actio quae est alia ab eo, et tunc aut non intelligemus per hunc intellectum omnino, aut intelligemus secundum quod actio eius est substantia eius. Sed impossibile est ut in aliqua hora non intelligamus per ipsum. Relinquatur igitur, cum iste intellectus fuerit denudatus a potentia, ut in|telligamus per ipsum secundum quod actio est substantia eius et est ultima prosperitas.'[113] Patet igitur per intentionem Commentatoris quod ultima prosperitas intellectus nostri materialis coniuncti, quae consistit solum in cognitione substantiarum separatarum, consistit in actione intellectus materialis quae est eius substantia. Sed nulla intellectio est substantia alicuius nisi ubi intellectus et intellectum sunt idem. Igitur ipse vult dicere quod intellectus noster materialis, quando copulatur cum intellectu agente et substantiis separatis, intelligit primo se.

71. Sciendum tamen hic quod intellectio qua intellectus materialis intelligit se, cum fuerit denudatus a potentia, non est substantia ipsius intellectus materialis, cum illa intellectio sit nova in isto supposito, intellectu materiali praecedente in eodem. Pro tanto tamen vocat cognitionem istam substantialem pro quanto sola intellectio illa est eadem cum substantia intellectus ubi intellectus et intellectum sunt idem, quod universaliter est verum secundum eum in omni substantia separata praeterquam in intellectu materiali propter eius potentialitatem.

72. Quod haec sit intentio sua habetur expressius eodem duodecimo, 39 commento, ubi dicit primo quod 'intellectus in nobis non intelligit se donec admiscetur cum intellecto et imaginetur, et intelligat ipsum in actu, non quando est in potentia antequam intelligat'.[114] Istam admixtionem vocat intellectorum speculativorum et intellectus | agentis cum eo in ratione formae illustrantis ipsum, per quem denudatur omnino a potentia. Vult igitur quod intellectus materialis in postremo intelligat se ipsum.

73. Et quod in illa intellectione consistat felicitas nostra secundum eum probo per hoc quod dicit post in eodem commento. Dicit enim sic: 'Si voluptas Dei per comprehensionem sui ipsius est aequalis voluptati quam nos habemus cum intellectus in nobis comprehendit se, et est quando denudatur a potentia, hoc autem

---

1 destruatur] abstrahatur T   2 intelligemus] intelligimus P   3 intelligemus] intelligimus P || eius[1] *om.* O   3–6 Sed ... eius *om. hom.* O   4–5 Relinquatur ... ipsum *om. hom.* T   6 per] secundum O   8 separatarum] abstractarum P   9 alicuius] intelligens actu P   10 et] est T   11 quando] coniungitur et *add.* T   16 Pro ... tamen] sed (*suppl. i.m.*) pro tanto O || substantialem] substantiam eius *fortasse scribendum*   17 est eadem] *inv.* O || cum *om.* T || ubi] unde T   18 eum] et *add.* T   19 potentialitatem] possibilitatem T   20 Quod ... expressius] Et haec est intentio sua, quod probo. Nam expresse habetur T   20–21 39 commento] *inv.* O; commento 36 T   21 primo *om.* T || admiscetur] adipiscetur O *et* admixtionem *add. i.m.*   22 intellecto] intelligendo O   23 admixtionem] intellectionem T   24 eo] ipso O || quem] quae P; *fortasse scribendum* quam   25 intelligat] intelligit T   27 intellectione] intentione (*lectio incerta*) P || consistat] consistit T || probo] *iter.* T   29 nos *om.* T   30 in nobis] *om.* T || quando] intellectus *add.* T

'is stripped bare of potency in its human perfection, it is necessary that this action which is different from it is removed from it, and then either we do not understand entirely by means of this intellect, or we understand in so far as its action is its substance. But it is impossible that at some time we do not understand by this intellect. Therefore it remains, when this intellect has become stripped bare of potency, that we understand by it in so far as its action is its substance and is its final achievement.'[113] It is obvious, therefore, according to the conception of the Commentator, that the final achievement of our conjunct material intellect, which consists only in the cognition of separate substances, consists in the action of the material intellect, which is its substance. But no understanding is the substance of anything except where the intellect and the understood thing are the same. Therefore he wants to say that our material intellect, when it is conjoined with the agent intellect and separate substances, understands itself first.

71. However, here it must be realized that this understanding by which the material intellect understands itself, when it has become stripped bare of potency, is not the substance of the material intellect itself, since that understanding is a new one in this supposit, with the material intellect preceding it in the same supposit. However, he calls this cognition substantial to the extent that only this understanding is the same as the substance of the intellect, where the intellect and the understood thing are the same, which is universally true according to him in every separate substance except in the material intellect because of its potentiality.

72. That this is his conception is put more explicitly later in the twelfth book, comment 39, where he says first that 'the intellect in us does not understand itself until it is mixed up with the understood thing and imagines it, and it understands itself in act, not when it is in potency before it understands'.[114] He specifies this mixing-up as being that of speculative understood things and the agent intellect with it in so far as it is a form enlightening it, by means of which it is entirely stripped bare of potency. Therefore he wants it to be the case that the material intellect understands itself in the end.

73. And that according to him it is in this understanding that our happiness consists, I prove by means of this point, which he puts later in the same comment. For he says the following: 'If the pleasure that God has by means of comprehension of himself is equal to the pleasure which we have when the intellect in us comprehends itself, and this is when it is stripped bare of potency, but this

---

[113] Aver. *In Metaph.* 12, t. c. 17, fol. 303 ra C–rb D.
[114] Ibid., t. c. 39, fol. 322 ra C–rb D.

in nobis parvo tempore existit, ⟨in⟩ Deo autem semper, valde est mirabile.'[115] Ex ista auctoritate plane apparet quod secundum eum felicitas nostra consistit in actu quo intellectus materialis, postquam est denudatus ab omni potentialitate, intelligit se, ita quod sicut ponit quod ultima perfectio cuiuslibet substantiae separatae consistit in cognoscendo se—ita quod idem est cognoscens et cognitum primum—in cognoscendo tamen se cognoscit omnes substantias superiores, ita ponit in intellectu materiali, qui est ultima secundum eum omnium intelligentiarum, quod sua ultima perfectio consistit in intelligendo se et in cognoscendo se cognoscit omnes substantias superiores.

74. Haec tamen est differentia inter intellectum materialem et alias substantias separatas, quod ultima perfectio aliarum substantiarum separatarum est substantia earum et eis coaeterna. Et hoc est quia sunt actus per essentiam. In intellectu autem materiali propter eius potentialitatem, propter quam primo cognoscit res extra se, eius ultima perfectio non est eius substantia nec sibi coaeterna, sibi tamen est possibilis huiusmodi intellectio qua intelligit se, et hoc solum quando denudatus est ab omni potentia.

fin. O **75.** Similiter, 5|1 commento duodecimi, dicit Commentator quod 'multitudo intellectorum in eodem intellectu, sicut est in intellectu in nobis, consequitur alietatem quae invenitur in eo, scilicet intellectus et intellecti in nobis'.[116] Quod patet 'quoniam cum intellectus et intellectum fuerint adunata, perfecta adunatione contingit ut intellecta multa illius intellectus adunentur et fiant unum et simplex omnibus modis'.[117] Ex ista auctoritate apparet quod intentio Commentatoris est quod idem sit intellectus et intellectum in nobis, et quod omnia intellecta in nobis sint adunata in illo uno, quod non accidit in aliquo actu intelligendi nostro nisi in dispositione adeptionis. Igitur etc.

76. Dico igitur quod sententia Commentatoris in hac materia consistit in hoc quod, cum intellectus noster materialis sit omnino denudatus a potentia, tunc intellectus materialis in lumine intellectus agentis intelligit se; in intelligendo autem se omnes substantias separatas intelligit. Ipse enim sic actuatus non solum est talis substantia, sed est imago repraesentativa intellectus agentis, et per consequens in cognoscendo se ipsum cognoscit intellectum agentem. Haec enim cognitio illi
T 28ᵛᵃ naturaliter est annexa. In cognoscendo autem intellectum | agentem per eandem rationem substantiam aliam superiorem cognoscit et sic usque ad primum. In co-

---

1 in²] *supplevimus cum Averroe*; *om.* OPT ‖ mirabile] et *add.* O **2** ista] hac O **4** separatae] creatae O **7** qui] quae PT **8** intelligendo] cognoscendo T ‖ se¹] *om.* T **11** separatas] superiores T ‖ ultima] *corr. ex* ultimata P **12** earum] eorum T **14** eius²] sua T ‖ sibi¹] ei O ‖ sibi² *om.* O; si P **15–16** denudatus est] *inv.* O **18** eodem] eorum T **19** eo] nobis T **22** est *om.* T **24** sint] sunt T ‖ aliquo] alio *add.* T ‖ nostro *om.* T **27** omnino ... potentia] denudatus a potentia omnino T **28** in² *om.* T **29** omnes ... intelligit] intelligit substantias omnes separatas T ‖ Ipse] ipsa T ‖ enim] est *add.* P ‖ actuatus] actuata T **33** substantiam ... cognoscit] cognoscit substantiam aliam superiorem T ‖ et sic] sicque T

exists in us for a short time, but in God always, this is much to be wondered at.'[115] From this authority it plainly appears that according to him our happiness consists in the act whereby the material intellect, after it is stripped bare of all potentiality, understands itself, so that just as he posits that the ultimate perfection of any separate substance consists in cognizing itself—so that the knower and the first known thing are the same—but in cognizing itself it cognizes all higher substances, so he posits that in the material intellect, which is, according to him, the last of all intelligences, its ultimate perfection consists in understanding itself, and in cognizing itself it cognizes all higher substances.

74. But there is this difference between the material intellect and other separate substances, that the ultimate perfection of other separate substances is their substance and coeternal with them. And this is because they are acts essentially. But in the material intellect, on account of its potentiality, because of which it first cognizes things outside itself, its ultimate perfection is not its substance or coeternal with it, but an understanding of the sort by which it understands itself is possible for it, and this is only when it is stripped bare of all potency.

75. Similarly, in comment 51 on the twelfth book, the Commentator says that 'a multitude of understood things in the same intellect, just as is the case in the intellect in us, follows the difference which is found in it, that is between the intellect and the understood thing in us'.[116] This is obvious, 'since when the intellect and the understood thing are unified, once the union is completed, it happens that many things understood by that intellect are unified and become one and simple in all ways'.[117] From this authority it is clear that the conception of the Commentator is that the intellect and the understood thing in us are the same, and that all understood things in us are unified in that one thing, which does not happen in any act of understanding that belongs to us except in a state of accomplishment. Therefore etc.

76. I say, therefore, that the stated opinion of the Commentator on this matter consists in the claim that, when our material intellect is stripped bare of potency, then the material intellect understands itself in the light of the agent intellect; but in understanding itself it understands all separate substances. For it is itself, when in act in this way, not only such a substance, but the representative image of the agent intellect, and consequently in cognizing itself it cognizes the agent intellect. For this cognition is naturally annexed to it. But in cognizing the agent intellect by the same token it cognizes another higher substance, and so all the way to the first. In cognizing itself, it also cognizes all these lower things. For in

---

[115] Ibid., fol. 322^{rb}F–^{va}G.
[116] Ibid., t. c. 51, fol. 336^{vb}L–M.
[117] Ibid.

gnoscendo etiam se cognoscit omnia ista inferiora. Nam in ipso sunt pro statu adeptionis intentiones intelligibiles omnium. Et ideo sicut Deus in cognoscendo se per ideas in eo cognoscit naturaliter omnia alia extra se tamquam obiecta secundaria secundum theologos, licet Philosophus et Commentator hoc negarent, quod aliquid intelligit extra se, sic intendit Commentator quod intellectus pro statu adeptionis in cognoscendo se tamquam primum obiectum omnia alia hic materialia per species prius acquisitas, quae ipsum informant, intelligit. Hanc credo esse ultimam sententiam Commentatoris circa hanc materiam.

⟨CONTRADICTIO AVERROIS⟩

77. Tamen sententia sua circa hanc materiam in 12 *Metaphysicae*, quae est eius ultima, videtur non concordare sententiae suae 3 *De anima*, nec etiam cum intentione Philosophi ibidem. Quod non concordet cum dicto suo ibidem probo. Nam in 36 commento 3 *De anima* dicit parum ante finem quod, 'cum intellectus agens efficitur nobis forma in actu, tunc per illum intelligimus omnia quae intelligimus'.[118] Dicit etiam ibidem prius quod 'nos agimus per intellectum agentem nostram propriam actionem'.[119] Ex quo concludit quod intellectus agens est forma in nobis per quem intellectus materialis intelligit substantias separatas.[120] Ex quibus videtur quod de intentione eius sit quod intellectus noster materialis pro statu adeptionis per intellectum agentem tamquam per formam repraesentantem substantias separatas ipsas intelligit. Sed secundum intentionem suam in duodecimo ipsemet intellectus materialis iam denudatus a potentia est intelligens et intellectus et etiam forma repraesentans substantias separatas.[121] Istae autem duae sententiae non concordant, ut videtur.

78. Praeterea, videtur quod sententia sua in 12 *Metaphysicae* non solum repugnat sibi ipsi in 3 *De anima*, sed etiam Aristoteli. Nam Aristoteles in 3 *De anima* dicit quod intellectus materialis intelligit se sicut intelligit alia;[122] sed non intelligit alia a se, scilicet materialia, nisi per intentiones abstractas a rebus, quae intentiones sunt aliae a rebus quas intelligit; igitur nec intelligit se nisi per intentionem abstractam ab aliis. Sed certum est quod nostra felicitas non consistit in |

---

1 etiam] autem T || ista *om.* T   2 intelligibiles] intellectuales T   3 ideas] *corr. in* ideata T || in eo] Deo T   5 intelligit] intelligat T || Commentator] *suppl. i.m.* P   6 primum *om.* P   6–7 materialia] intelligit *add.* T   7 prius *om.* T || intelligit] *om.* T || credo esse] *inv.* T   8 hanc] istam T   10 hanc] illam P || materiam *om.* P   11 ultima] ultimata P   13 in *om.* T || dicit . . . finem] parum ante finem dicit T   14 intelligimus] intelligemus P   14–15 intelligimus] intelligemus P   17 quem] *fortasse scribendum* quam   18 quod[1] *om.* T || de . . . sit] de eius intentione esse T || quod[2] *om.* T || intellectus . . . materialis] intellectum nostrum materialem T   20 intelligit] intelligere T   21 intellectus[2]] intellecta T   22 repraesentans] alias *add.* P   24 *Metaphysicae om.* T   26 materialis] noster T   26–27 sed . . . se *om.* T   28 intentiones *om.* T || nec] non T

itself are, in a state of accomplishment, intelligible intentions of all things. And therefore just as according to the theologians God, in cognizing himself, by means of the ideas in him cognizes naturally all other things outside himself as secondary objects, so to speak, although the Philosopher and the Commentator would deny that he understands anything outside himself, so the Commentator thinks that the intellect, in a state of accomplishment, in cognizing itself as the first object, so to speak, understands thereby all other material things down here by means of their previously acquired species, which inform it. I believe this to be the final stated opinion of the Commentator concerning this matter.

⟨CONTRADICTION OF AVERROES⟩

77. However, his stated opinion concerning this matter in *Metaphysics* 12, which is his final one, seems not to agree with his stated opinion in *On the Soul* 3, nor even with the view of the Philosopher in the same place. I prove that it does not agree with what he had said in the same place. For in comment 36 on *On the Soul* 3 he says just before the end that 'when the agent intellect becomes with respect to us a form in act, then by means of it we understand everything which we understand'.[118] He also says earlier in the same place that 'we perform our own proper action by means of the agent intellect'.[119] From this he concludes that the agent intellect is a form in us by means of which the material intellect understands separate substances.[120] Accordingly it seems that it is his conception that our material intellect in a state of accomplishment understands the separate substances by means of the agent intellect as if by means of a form that represents them. But according to his conception in the twelfth book, the material intellect itself, already stripped bare of potency, is the thing that understands and the understood thing, and also the form representing separate substances.[121] But these two stated opinions, as it seems, do not agree.

78. Moreover, it seems that his stated opinion in *Metaphysics* 12 is incompatible not only with what he says himself in *On the Soul* 3, but also with Aristotle. For Aristotle in *On the Soul* 3 says that the material intellect understands itself just as it understands other things;[122] but it does not understand things other than itself, that is material things, except by means of intentions abstracted from things, which intentions are different from the things which it understands; therefore it does not understand itself either except by means of an intention abstracted from other things. But it is certain that our happiness does not consist in that act by

---

[118] Aver. *In DA* 3, t. c. 36, 501. 636–9.
[119] Ibid. 499. 588–500. 589.
[120] Ibid. 500. 589–90.
[121] See above, para. 70.
[122] Arist. *DA* 3. 4, 430ᵃ2–3.

actu illo quo intellectus materialis intelligit se per intentiones abstractas a rebus materialibus. Igitur non est de intentione Philosophi quod ultima felicitas nostra consistat in actu quo intellectus materialis intelligit se.

⟨AD RATIONES PROBANTES CONTRADICTIONEM AVERROIS⟩

79. Ad ista. Ad primum[123] dico quod Commentator ibi non intelligit quod per intellectum agentem tamquam per propriam formam intelligat omnia sicut per formam repraesentativam omnium. Nam si sic, cum intellectus agens per Commentatorem intelligat se—nam scientia in actu et scitum in ipso sunt idem per Commentatorem, 3 *De anima*, 19 commento in fine[124]—sequeretur quod intellectus agens intelligeret ista materialia. Cuius contrarium dicit in principio eiusdem commenti, dicens quod intellectus agens nihil intelligit ex eis quae hic sunt.[125] | Nec intelligit Commentator quod intellectus materialis intelligat per intellectum agentem tamquam per formam quae sit principium cognoscendi substantias separatas et alia cognoscibilia ab eo. Nam nullus ponit in homine nisi unam potentiam cognitivam abstractam. Licet enim intellectus agens secundum intentionem Commentatoris sit virtus cognitiva, non tamen est in homine principium cognoscendi, sed solum intellectus materialis. Et de illo est quaestio Commentatoris quo modo intelligit substantias separatas.

80. Dico igitur quod Commentator intelligit quod intellectus agens est forma per quam intellectus materialis intelligit, quia est dispositio in qua vel sub qua appropriata sibi intelligit quicquid intelligit. Sicut lumen est dispositio sub qua diaphanum recipit speciem coloris, sic intellectus materialis, quicquid videt, videt in lumine vel sub lumine intellectus agentis, quod lumen non est aliud quam ipse intellectus agens.

81. Ad aliud[126] dicendum quod intellectus materialis non intelligit se sicut alia pro quanto intelligit se per intentiones abstractas a rebus materialibus, quoniam, ut dicit Commentator, intellectus ipse abstractus est et separatus, et per consequens actu intelligibile, propter quod non intelligitur per abstractionem intentionis alicuius rei materialis, quae est intelligibilis in potentia, sicut patet 15 et 16 commento 3 *De anima*.[127] Pro tanto igitur potest dici quod intellectus intelligit se sicut alia pro quanto intellectio rerum materialium est dispositio necessaria respectu intellectionis sui ipsius.

---

1 illo] in *add*. T **1–3** per . . . se *om. hom*. T **6** sicut] sed P **8** nam scientia] scientia enim T || et] ut T || scitum] situm P **8–9** per Commentatorem] secundum ipsum T **9** 19 commento] *inv*. T **12** intelligat] intelligit P **14** nisi *om*. T **17** solum] solus P || est *om*. P **21** sub *om*. T **23** vel . . . lumine² *om*. T **25** sicut] sed P **30** Pro] per P **31** intellectio] intentio P || respectu] puta P

which the material intellect understands itself by means of intentions abstracted from material things. Therefore it is not the conception of the Philosopher that our ultimate happiness consists in the act whereby the material intellect understands itself.

⟨IN ANSWER TO THE ARGUMENTS PROVING THE CONTRADICTION OF AVERROES⟩

79. In answer to these. In answer to the first[123] I say that the Commentator there does not think that by means of the agent intellect just as if by means of its own proper form the material intellect understands all things just as it would by means of a form representative of all things. For if this were the case, since the agent intellect understands itself according to the Commentator—for knowledge in act and the known thing are the same in the intellect according to the Commentator in *On the Soul* 3 at the end of comment 19[124]—it would follow that the agent intellect would understand these material things. He says the opposite of this at the beginning of the same comment, saying that the agent intellect understands none of the things that are here.[125] Neither does the Commentator think that the material intellect understands by means of the agent intellect just as if by means of a form which is the principle of cognizing separate substances and other things cognizable by it. For no one posits that there is in man more than one abstract cognitive power. For although the agent intellect according to the conception of the Commentator is a cognitive power, it is not, however, the principle of cognizing in man, but only the material intellect is such. And the question of the Commentator is about this—that is, how the material intellect understands separate substances.

80. Therefore I say that the Commentator thinks that the agent intellect is a form by which the material intellect understands, because it is a disposition that is appointed to it, in which or under which it understands whatever it understands. Just as light is the disposition under which the transparent medium receives the species of colour, so the material intellect sees whatever it sees in the light or under the light of the agent intellect, which light is nothing other than the agent intellect itself.

81. In answer to the other argument[126] it must be said that the material intellect does not understand itself just as it does other things, inasmuch as it understands itself by means of intentions abstracted from material things, since, as the Commentator says, the intellect is itself abstract and separate, and consequently intelligible in act, for which reason it is not understood by means of the abstraction of the intention of a material thing, which is intelligible in potency, just as is obvious in comments 15 and 16 on *On the Soul* 3.[127] Therefore it can be said that the intellect understands itself just as it does other things only to the extent that the understanding of material things is a necessary disposition with respect to the understanding of itself.

---

[123] See above, para. 77.
[124] Aver. *In DA* 3, t. c. 19, 443. 87–8.
[125] Ibid. 441. 15–16.
[126] See above, para. 78.
[127] Aver. *In DA* 3, t. c. 15, 434. 6–14; t. c. 16, 435. 20–8.

⟨QUADRUPLEX STATUS INTELLECTUS HOMINIS⟩

82. Ex praedictis potest colligi quod quadruplex est status nostri intellectus. Unus et primus dum est in potentia ad intelligendum ante intelligere. Secundus quando est in actu cognitionis cuiuscumque. Tertius quando est habituatus per habitus scientificos, non tamen omnes, sed est adhuc in motu ad aliquem habitum cognitivum. Ultimus et quartus quando motus iam terminatus est ipsius intellectus in habitu, et perfectus est intellectus per omnes habitus. In primo gradu intellectus materialis non attingit intellectum agentem aliquo modo sicut formam. In secundo gradu et tertio, dum proficit in cognoscendo, aliquo modo attingit eum ut formam, sed imperfecte, et quanto magis perficitur tanto perfectius attingit eum ut formam. In quarto autem gradu, habitis omnibus intelligibilibus in actu, tunc in toto intellectus agens est sibi coniunctus ut forma. Secundum primum statum dicitur intellectus noster 'materialis' tantum. Quantum ad secundum statum dicitur 'intellectus speculativus'. Secundum tertium statum dicitur 'intellectus in habitu'. Secundum quartum dicitur 'intellectus adeptus', quia adeptus est intellectus agens ipsi intellectui materiali ut forma in actu, ex qua adeptione intellectus materialis cognoscit se et omnes substantias superiores. Iste autem status cognitionis est de quo habet intelligi quod omnes | homines natura scire desiderant, et est felicitas ultima hominis secundum intentionem Averrois.

⟨DE INTELLECTU PASSIVO⟩

83. Per intellectum autem passivum intelligit Commentator virtutem imaginativam, ut habetur 20 commento 3 *De anima*. Dicit autem in fine illius commenti quod 'per istum intellectum homo differt ab aliis animalibus'.[128] Quod tamen non habet intelligi quod primo et ultimate distinguatur homo ab aliis per illum intellectum, sed per intellectum materialem, ut habetur in 1 commento illius tertii[129] et etiam in 5, ubi supponit quod intellectus materialis sit prima perfectio hominis, ut patet in quaestione secunda quam ibi movet.[130] Verumtamen per intellectum passivum distinguitur homo ab aliis animalibus, ut probat in fine 20 commenti per hoc quoniam aliter intellectus materialis copularetur aliis animalibus sicut uni

---

2 nostri intellectus] *inv.* T   **3** Unus et *om.* T ‖ primus] est *add.* T ‖ ad ... intelligere] ante intelligere ad intelligendum T   **4** Tertius] est *add.* T   **5** aliquem] alium P   **6** Ultimus ... quartus] quartus et ultimus T ‖ motus iam] *inv.* T ‖ ipsius *om.* P   **7** perfectus ... intellectus] intellectus est iam perfectus T   **9** gradu] modo T   **10** perficitur] proficit T ‖ tanto] ac T ‖ eum] ipsum T   **11** autem *om.* T ‖ habitis] scilicet *add.* T   **12** sibi] tamen T   **13** statum *om.* T   **14** statum dicitur *om.* T   **15** dicitur *om.* T ‖ est] ipse *add.* T   **17** se et *om.* T ‖ substantias] intelligentias P ‖ cognitionis] adeptionis T   **18** natura] ultima T ‖ et est] etc. P   **18–19** felicitas ultima] *inv.* T   **22** illius] 19 T   **23** ab] animalibus *add. et del.* P   **24–25** quod ... intellectum¹] primo et ultimate hominem per illum intellectum distingui ab aliis animalibus T   **25** tertii] De anima *add.* T   **26** etiam *om.* T   **27** patet *om.* T   **29** aliter ... copularetur] intellectus materialis non copulatur T ‖ uni *om.* T

⟨THE FOURFOLD STATE OF THE INTELLECT OF MAN⟩

82. From what was said earlier it can be gathered that the state of our intellect is fourfold. One, and the first, while it is in potency to understanding before it understands. Second, when it is in the act of cognition of anything at all. Third, when it is habituated by scientific habits, not all, however, but when it is still in motion towards some cognitive habit. Fourth and last, when the motion of the intellect itself in habit is now ended, and the intellect has been perfected by means of all habits. In the first degree the material intellect does not touch the agent intellect as a form in any way. In the second degree and the third, while it advances in cognizing, it does touch it as a form in some way, but imperfectly, and the more it is perfected, the more perfectly it touches it as a form. But in the fourth degree, when it possesses all intelligible things in act, then the agent intellect is totally conjunct with it as a form. When it is in the first state our intellect is called 'material' only. When it is in the second state it is called 'speculative intellect'. When it is in the third state it is called 'intellect in habit'. When it is in the fourth it is called 'accomplished intellect', because the agent intellect is accomplished with respect to the material intellect itself as a form in act, and because of that accomplishment the material intellect cognizes itself and all higher substances. But this state of cognition is of that of which it must be understood that all men by nature desire to know, and is the ultimate happiness of man according to the conception of Averroes.

⟨ON THE PASSIVE INTELLECT⟩

83. By passive intellect, however, the Commentator understands the imaginative power, as one learns from comment 20 on *On the Soul* 3. But he says at the end of that comment that 'by this intellect man differs from the other animals'.[128] However, this should not be understood in the sense that first and principally man is distinguished from the others by that intellect, but by the material intellect, as one learns from comment 1 of that third book[129] and also from comment 5, where he takes it for granted that the material intellect is the first perfection of man, as is obvious in the second question which he raises there.[130] Nevertheless it is by the passive intellect that man is distinguished from the other animals, as he proves at the end of comment 20 by this argument: since otherwise the material intellect would be conjoined with the other animals as it is conjoined with a

---

[128] Ibid., t. c. 20, 449. 173–5; 454. 315–16.
[129] Ibid., t. c. 1, 379. 21–2.
[130] Ibid., t. c. 5, 392. 159.

homini.[131] De ista acceptione intellectus, quia realiter virtus sensitiva est, idcirco circa declarationem eius naturae non insisto.

⟨PUNCTUS 2 ARTICULI 2: SENTENTIA AVERROIS⟩

84. Istis suppositis, scilicet diversis acceptionibus 'intellectus', supposita etiam expositione 'intellectivae' prius posita, videlicet quod per 'intellectivam' intelligatur forma quae est principium cognoscendi quidditates rerum, ex istis manifestum est quod per 'intellectivam' intelligit Commentator intellectum materialem. Solus enim intellectus materialis secundum eum est in nobis principium cognoscendi quidditates. Dico igitur quod intentio Commentatoris in ista materia est ista, quantum ad conclusionem principalem, quod intellectiva seu intellectus materialis, quae idem sunt apud eum, est forma corporis humani informans ipsum modo quo supra exponitur.

⟨CONCORDIA ET DISCORDIA AVERROIS CUM FIDE CATHOLICA⟩

85. Circa quod sciendum quod opinio sua in ista materia non discordat ab opinione vera et catholica nisi in duobus. Convenit enim cum opinione catholica in hoc quod sicut catholici ponunt quod intellectiva est perfectio formalis et prima hominis intrinseca homini per quam distinguitur primo specifice a quocumque alio, ita posuit Commentator. Unde in 5 commento 3 *De anima*, in secunda quaestione quam movet, supponit quod intellectus materialis sit prima perfectio hominis.[132] Et in 1 commento eiusdem dicit quod per hanc virtutem differt homo ab aliis animalibus.[133] Et 1 tractatu *De substantia orbis*, parum ante finem, dicit quod homo est intelligens per partem in ipso, non sic caelum.[134] In alio etiam convenit cum vera opinione, pro quanto dicit intellectum esse incorruptibilem, sicut catholici dicunt.

P 220ʳᵃ 86. In duobus tamen discordat, videlicet in hoc quod ponit | intellectum in nobis non solum incorruptibilem, sed etiam ingenerabilem et aeternum. Nam sequens sententiam sui magistri in 1 *De caelo et mundo* nihil posuit aeternum ex parte post quin posuit aeternum ex parte ante.[135] In alio etiam discordat a vera opinione quod ipse non posuit intellectum nostrum materialem numerari ad numerationem corporum particularium, sed posuit unum intellectum numero materialem in omnibus
T 29ʳᵇ hominibus. |

1 virtus ... est] est virtus sensitiva T || idcirco *om.* P 2 eius naturae] *inv.* T 4 scilicet diversis] *inv.* T 9 igitur] secundum hoc *add.* P 11 quae] qui P || idem sunt] est idem T 14 Circa quod] ubi *et* est *add.* T 17 primo specifice] *inv.* T 19 sit] est T 22 intelligens] intellectivus T 23 convenit] dicit T 25 In ... videlicet] sed in duobus discordat, scilicet T || discordat] discordet P 26 incorruptibilem] *corr. s.l. ex* corruptibilem P || etiam *om.* P || Nam] non P 27 sui magistri] *inv.* T 28 quin] illud *add.* T || posuit] posuerit T 29 nostrum materialem *om.* T || numerari] *suppl. i.m.* P 30 numero materialem] immaterialem numero P 30–31 in ... hominibus] in omni homine P

man.[131] Concerning this meaning of intellect, I shall not proceed with an explanation of its nature, since it is really a sensitive power.

⟨POINT 2 OF ARTICLE 2: THE STATED OPINION OF AVERROES⟩

84. With these things in place, that is, the different meanings of 'intellect', as well as the exposition of 'intellectual soul' set out earlier, namely that by 'intellectual soul' a form is understood which is the principle of cognizing the quiddities of things—from these it is manifest that by 'intellectual soul' the Commentator understands the material intellect. For only the material intellect, according to him, is in us the principle of cognizing quiddities. Therefore I say that the conception of the Commentator on this matter is this, regarding the principal conclusion, that the intellectual soul or the material intellect, which are in his view the same, is the form of the human body, informing it in the way which is expounded above.

⟨AGREEMENT AND DISAGREEMENT OF AVERROES WITH THE CATHOLIC FAITH⟩

85. Concerning this, it must be realized that his opinion on this matter is not in disagreement with true and Catholic opinion except on two points. For he agrees with Catholic opinion in this, that just as Catholics posit that the intellectual soul is a formal perfection and the first perfection of man, intrinsic to man, by which he is first specifically distinguished from anything else, so posited the Commentator. Accordingly in comment 5 on *On the Soul* 3, in the second question which he raises, he assumes that the material intellect is the first perfection of man.[132] And in comment 1 of the same book he says that by this power man differs from other animals.[133] And in the first treatise of *On the Substance of the Celestial Sphere*, just before the end, he says that man is intelligent by a part in himself, but this is not the case with the heavens.[134] In another point, also, he agrees with true opinion, to the extent that he says that the intellect is incorruptible, as Catholics say.

86. On two points however he is in disagreement, namely in that he posits that the intellect in us is not only incorruptible, but also ungenerable and eternal. For following the stated opinion of his master in *On the Heavens* 1 he posited that nothing is eternal into the future except what he posited to be eternal into the past.[135] On another point he is also in disagreement with true opinion, that he did not posit that our material intellect is numbered according to the numbering of particular bodies, but he posited a material intellect that is one in number in all men.

---

[131] Ibid., t. c. 20, 454. 315–18.
[132] Ibid., t. c. 5, 392. 159.
[133] Ibid., t. c. 1, 379. 21–2.
[134] Aver. *De sub. orb.* 1, fol. 5^{va}H–I.
[135] Arist. *De caelo*, 1. 10, 279^{b}17–33; Aver. *In De caelo*, 1, t. c. 102, 195. 42–196. 66.

⟨RATIONES AVERROIS PRO UNITATE INTELLECTUS MATERIALIS⟩

87. Ad hoc ponendum movetur propter has rationes. Prima est ista: si intellectus esset numeratus in omnibus hominibus, esset intellectum in potentia tantum sicut singulare, et per consequens motivum intellectus; ex quo infert quod idem esset motivum et motum.[136]

88. Ad evidentiam huius consequentiae Commentatoris et aliarum quae sequuntur est sciendum quod ipse non posuit individuari nisi formam materialem eductam de potentia materiae, nec pluralitatem individuorum sub specie nisi in corruptibilibus. Istud secundum patet ex 1 *Caeli et mundi*.[137] Primum etiam patet ex illo capitulo 3 *De anima* 'Quoniam aliud est magnitudo et magnitudinis esse',[138] ubi plane vult quod in separatis a materia non est alia intentio individui et speciei, sicut accidit in corporalibus.[139] Unde licet non posuerit substantiam individuari per quantitatem, quia contrarium dicit 7 *Metaphysicae*, 2 commento—dicit enim manifestum esse per se quod individuum substantiae est prius individuo accidentis[140]—tamen non posuit aliam formam individuatam nisi corporalem et extensam, cuiusmodi formam non posuit intellectum materialem. Si tamen esset numeratus ad numerationem hominum, secundum sententiam suam esset forma materialis et extensa.

89. Hoc intellecto, probatur faciliter consequentia, quoniam intellectus materialis est in potentia ut intelligat et moveatur tamquam ab obiecto a quacumque forma materiali, praesupposito lumine intellectus agentis. Si igitur intellectus materialis esset quaedam forma corporalis, sequeretur quod idem esset movens et motum.

90. Secundo arguit sic, reducendo ad hoc inconveniens quod idem reciperet se, dato quod intellectus materialis numeraretur.[141] Consequentia patet ex praedictis,[142] quoniam ex quo intellectus materialis est receptivus cognitionis cuiuslibet formae materialis, et intellectus materialis est forma materialis, supposito quod sit numerabilis, per ipsum, sequetur quod est receptivus cognitionis sui ipsius. Sed ubi cognoscens et cognitum sunt idem, cognitio media est idem cum extremis. Igitur eo ipso quod recipit cognitionem sui ipsius, recipit se ipsum, quod est impossibile.

91. Tertio reducit ad inconveniens quod reciperet et cognosceret in quantum

---

2 hoc] autem *add*. T   3 in[1] ... hominibus] etc. P || in[2] ... tantum] tantum in potentia T   5 esset *om*. T || et] mobile *add*. T   6 consequentiae *om*. P || Commentatoris *om*. T || aliarum] *scripsimus*; aliorum PT   8 eductam] deductam P   10 illo] primo P || Quoniam] autem *add*. T   10–11 et . . . esse *om*. T   13 individuari] *corr. s.l. ex* individuam P   14 esse] est T || est prius] *inv*. T   15 formam individuatam] individuatam substantiam T   18 materialis] *corr. i.m. ex* substantialis P   19–20 materialis *om*. T   20 moveatur] moveat P   21 praesupposito] *scripsimus*; supposito T; praesupposita P   21–22 materialis] agens T   22 sequeretur] sequitur T   24 reciperet] recipet T   25 materialis] reciperet *add. et del*. P   26 quoniam] quantum T   30 quod[1]] quo P   32 reciperet] recipet T

⟨AVERROES' ARGUMENTS FOR THE UNITY OF THE MATERIAL INTELLECT⟩

87. He is moved to uphold this by the following arguments. The first is this: if the intellect were numbered in all men, it would be something understood in potency only as a singular is, and consequently something capable of moving the intellect; from which he infers that the same thing would be capable of moving and being moved.[136]

88. As regards the evidence for this consequence of the Commentator's, and for others which follow, it must be realized that he did not posit that anything is individuated except the material form which is elicited from the potency of matter, nor did he posit a plurality of individuals in a species except in the case of corruptible things. This second point is obvious from *On the Heavens* 1.[137] The first is also obvious from that chapter of *On the Soul* 3 'Since magnitude and being of magnitude are different',[138] where he plainly wants it to be the case that in things separate from matter there is not a different intention of the individual and the species, as happens in corporeal things.[139] Accordingly although he did not posit that substance is individuated by quantity, since he says the opposite in *Metaphysics* 7, comment 2—for he says that it is immediately manifest that the individual of a substance is prior to the individual of an accident[140]—nevertheless he did not posit another individuated form except a corporeal and extended one, and he did not posit the material intellect to be this sort of form. If, however, it were numbered according to the numbering of men, according to his stated opinion it would be a material and extended form.

89. This being understood, the consequence is easily proved, since the material intellect is in potency to understanding and to being moved by any material form just as if by its object, presupposing the light of the agent intellect. If, therefore, the material intellect were a corporeal form, it would follow that the same thing would be a mover and moved.

90. Secondly he argues in this way, leading to this absurdity, that the same thing would receive itself if it were the case that the material intellect were numbered.[141] The consequence is obvious from what was said earlier,[142] because from the fact that the material intellect is receptive of the cognition of every material form, and the material intellect is a material form, supposing that it is numerable, according to him, then it follows that it is receptive of the cognition of itself. But where the knower and the known thing are the same, the intermediate cognition is the same thing as the extremes. Therefore, just because it receives cognition of itself, it receives itself, which is impossible.

91. Thirdly he reduces the argument to this absurdity, that the material intellect

---

[136] Aver. *In DA* 3, t. c. 5, 402. 432–8.
[137] Aver. *In De caelo*, 1, t. c. 94, 176. 46–177. 74.
[138] Arist. *DA* 3. 4, 429^{b}10.
[139] Aver. *In DA* 3, t. c. 9, 421. 25–422. 32.
[140] Aver. *In Metaph.* 7, t. c. 2, fol. 153^{va}I–^{vb}K.
[141] Aver. *In DA* 3, t. c. 5, 402. 438–40.
[142] See above, paras. 9, 88.

hoc, et sic non distingueretur a sensu.[143] Consequentia patet, quia omnis cognitio quae respicit hic et nunc ad sensum pertinet. Prima consequentia probatur, quia receptum recipitur per modum recipientis. Sed intellectus materialis per te est singularis. Ergo species quam recipit erit singularis et in essendo et in repraesentando ex eadem causa qua in sensu.

92. Quarto arguit reducendo ad hoc inconveniens quod in intentionibus seu speciebus intelligibilibus in abstrahendo speciem a specie esset processus in infinitum.[144] Consequens est falsum et implicans contradictionem, quia ordini repugnat infinitas. Consequentia probatur, quia tunc species in intellectu tuo et meo distinguerentur numero et convenirent specie. Igitur contingeret abstrahere unam speciem ab illis duabus speciebus. Illa species abstracta per intellectum meum et tuum per eandem rationem est alia et alia, quia in alio et alio intellectu. Igitur per eandem rationem ab illis | duabus speciebus abstractis contingit abstrahere aliam speciem, quae per eandem rationem esset alia et alia, abstracta per intellectum tuum et meum. Et sic processus esset in infinitum etc.

93. Quinto sic: sequeretur quod scientia esset qualitas activa, quod est falsum, vel quod discipulus non addisceret a magistro.[145] Consequentia patet, quoniam si intellectus sit alius in te et in me, oporteret quod, si causetur doctrina ab intellectu uno in alium, hoc oportet esse per unum principium activum. Et propter istud posuit Plato quod scire nihil aliud est quam reminisci.

94. Sexto et ultimo arguit quod per intellectum iudicamus res infinitas numero, ut patet in propositione universali quam format intellectus. Sed per virtutem singularem non cognoscimus infinita.[146] Tenuit ergo Averroes quod intellectus unus numero correspondet omni homini.

⟨MODUS PONENDI AVERROIS⟩

95. Modus autem ponendi suus fuit iste. Posuit enim intellectum materialem sicut quamcumque aliam intelligentiam non habere aliquam intentionem superadditam speciei, sed per eandem intentionem esse intelligentiam et hanc, ita quod sua haeccitas est sua quidditas, non superaddita quidditati, sicut posuit in corporalibus quod per aliam intentionem caro est caro et haec caro, ut patet in 3 *De anima*

2 nunc] non P || ad ... pertinet] pertinet ad sensum T || Prima *om.* P 4 erit] est T || in[1] *om.* P || in[2] *om.* P 5 ex ... sensu *om.* T 6–7 intentionibus ... speciebus] speciebus seu intentionibus T 6 seu] in *add. et del.* P 7 intelligibilibus] intellectualibus T || processus] procedere P 8 implicans] implicat T 8–9 repugnat] infinite *add. et del.* P 9 probatur] patet (*lectio incerta*) T 10 distinguerentur] distinguitur P 11–12 meum ... tuum] tuum et meum T 13 aliam] et aliam *add.* T 14–15 quae ... meum *om.* T 15 esset *om.* T || etc. *om.* T 16 sequeretur] vel *add.* P 17 a *om.* T || quoniam] quia T 18 causetur] causaretur T 18–19 intellectu uno] *inv.* T 19 hoc ... esse] quod hoc esset T || istud] hoc T 20 est] esset T 21 arguit] arguitur T 26 suus *om.* T 27 sicut] sed P || habere] haberet P 29 superaddita] superadditum P || sicut] sed P 30 et] est *add.* T || in *om.* T

would receive and cognize in so far as it is singular, and thus it would not be distinguished from sense.[143] The consequence is obvious, in that every cognition which concerns the here and now pertains to sense. The first consequence is proved, in that the thing received is received according to the way of the receiver. But the material intellect, according to you, is singular. Therefore the species which it receives will be singular, both in being and in representation, for the same reason as in sense.

92. Fourthly he reduces the argument to this absurdity, that in intentions or intelligible species, in abstracting a species from a species there would arise an infinite progress.[144] The consequent is false and implies a contradiction, since infinity is incompatible with order. The consequence is proved, since then the species in your intellect and mine would be distinguished in number and would agree in species. Therefore it would happen that you could abstract one species from those two species. That species abstracted by my intellect and yours is by the same token two different things, because it is in two different intellects. Therefore by the same token it is possible to abstract another species from those two abstracted species, and this species would, by the same token, be two different things, abstracted by your intellect and mine. And so there would be an infinite progress, etc.

93. Fifthly as follows: it would follow that knowledge would be an active quality, which is false, or that the pupil would not learn from the master.[145] The consequence is obvious, since if the intellect were different in you and in me, it would be required that, if learning were caused by one intellect in another, this would be required to be by means of one active principle. And because of this Plato posited that to know is nothing other than to remember.

94. Sixthly and lastly he argues that by means of the intellect we judge infinite things in number, as is obvious in a universal proposition which the intellect forms. But by means of a singular power we do not cognize infinite things.[146] Averroes therefore held that an intellect that is one in number corresponds to every man.

⟨AVERROES' WAY OF UPHOLDING⟩

95. His way of upholding was this. For he posited that the material intellect, like any other intelligence, does not have any intention superadded to the species, but by means of the same intention is an intelligence and this one, so that its hecceity is its quiddity, not something superadded to quiddity, as he posited in the case of corporeal things, where by a different intention flesh is flesh and this flesh, as is obvious in *On the Soul* 3 'Since magnitude and being of magnitude are

---

[143] Aver. *In DA* 3, t. c. 5, 402. 441–6.
[144] Ibid. 411. 713–17.
[145] Ibid. 717–21.
[146] Ibid., t. c. 19, 441. 37–42.

'Quoniam aliud est magnitudo et magnitudinis esse'.[147] Hunc autem intellectum posuit habere naturalem inclinationem et dependentiam ad corpus organicum perfectum potentiis sensitivis hominis, quas posuit alterius speciei omnino a potentiis sensitivis cuiuslibet alterius animalis, ut patet ex fine 20 commenti.[148] Ita quod haec fuit imaginatio eius quod sicut secundum opinionem nostram catholicam haec intellectiva nostra, quia est singularis, distinguendo singulare contra speciem, est actus huius corporis totius primo tamquam primi perfectibilis, est etiam ipsa tota forma seu perfectio cuiuslibet partis ex consequenti—non tamen dependet in suo esse ab hac parte materiali vel illa, licet sit actus et forma secundum se totam cuiuslibet partis materialis—ita posuit intellectum materialem, quem non posuit esse individuatum per aliam intentionem a specie sua, esse per naturam actum et perfectionem naturae humanae in suppositis tamquam sui primi perfectibilis, sed huius hominis vel illius solum ex consequenti. Et in hoc stat sua intentio, sicut credo.

⟨PUNCTUS 3 ARTICULI 2: RATIONES CONTRA AVERROEM⟩

⟨RATIONES AVERROIS⟩

96. Contra opinionem suam arguo primo per rationes suas proprias. Prima dubitatio quam | movet contra se in 5 commento est ista: intellectus agens est aeternus per ipsum et materialis similiter. Igitur intellectus speculativus erit aeternus, et similiter intellecta speculativa.[149] Consequens est falsum per eum. Consequentia patet etiam per eum, quia ab aeterno non procedit actio nova, ut frequenter habetur ab eo, 8 *Physicorum*.[150]

97. Secunda dubitatio quam facit contra se ipsum est magis difficilis, et est ista: cum intellectus materialis | sit prima perfectio hominis ex definitione animae, 2 *De anima*,[151] quae est communis omni animae, intelligere autem sit secunda perfectio hominis, cum secunda perfectio sit alia et alia in alio et alio, per ipsum, sequeretur quod prima perfectio erit alia.[152]

98. Item, reducit ad multa inconvenientia, si intellectus sit unus numero in omnibus. Primum est: cum Socrates sit homo et Plato sit homo per illum intellectum materialem, et intellectus ille est unus numero in utroque, sequetur quod Socrates et Plato erunt unus homo numero.[153]

99. Aliud inconveniens est: cum quando forma rei est, tunc res est; intellectus autem materialis, cum sit aeternus, praecessit Socratem et est forma Socratis; ergo Socrates fuit antequam esset.[154]

---

1 et . . . esse *om.* T   **4** cuiuslibet . . . animalis] *suppl. i.m.* P || cuiuslibet *om.* T || 20] 8 *add. et del.* P   **7** primi] primo T   **19** erit] est T   **21** quia] quod P   **21–22** habetur . . . eo] dicit T   **23** ipsum *om.* T   **24** sit] est P   **25** animae] intellectivae *add.* T   **27** sequeretur] sequitur T   **29** est] quod *add.* T   **30** intellectus *om.* T || unus *om.* T || sequetur] sequitur T   **31** erunt] erit T   **32** est: cum] tunc T

different'.[147] But he posited that this intellect has a natural inclination towards and dependence on an organic body that is perfected by man's sensitive powers, which he posited to be of another species entirely from the sensitive powers of any other animal, as is obvious from the end of comment 20.[148] So that this was the way he pictured it, that just as according to our Catholic opinion this our intellectual soul, because it is singular, by distinguishing the singular from the species, is the act of this whole body firstly, as if of the first perfectible thing, and it is also itself the total form or perfection of every part derivatively—but it does not depend in its being on this or that material part, although it is an act and a form, according to its whole self, of every material part—in the same manner he posited the material intellect, which he did not posit to be individuated by another intention from its species, to be by nature an act and perfection of human nature in supposits as if of its first perfectible thing, but of this or that man only derivatively. And his conception, as I believe, consists in this.

⟨POINT 3 OF ARTICLE 2: ARGUMENTS AGAINST AVERROES⟩

⟨AVERROES' ARGUMENTS⟩

96. Against his opinion I argue first by means of his own arguments. The first doubt which he raises against himself in comment 5 is this: the agent intellect is eternal according to him, and similarly the material intellect. Therefore the speculative intellect will be eternal, and similarly the speculative understood things.[149] The consequent is false according to him. The consequence is also obvious according to him, because a new action does not proceed from an eternal thing, as he says frequently in *Physics* 8.[150]

97. The second doubt which he raises against himself is more troublesome, and it is this: since the material intellect is the first perfection of man, from the definition of the soul, *On the Soul* 2,[151] which is common to every soul, but to understand is the second perfection of man, since the second perfection is different in different things, according to him, it would follow that the first perfection would be different.[152]

98. Again, it leads to many absurdities, if the intellect is one in number in all men. The first is: since Socrates is a man and Plato is a man by means of that material intellect, and that intellect is numerically one in both of them, it would follow that Socrates and Plato would be one man in number.[153]

99. Another absurdity is this: when the form of a thing exists, the thing exists; but the material intellect, since it is eternal, preceded Socrates and is the form of Socrates; therefore Socrates existed before he exists.[154]

---

[147] See above, para. 88.
[148] Aver. *In DA* 3, t. c. 20, 454. 315–18.
[149] Ibid., t. c. 5, 391. 117–392. 157.
[150] e. g. Aver. *In Phys.* 8, t. c. 4, fol. 341 ᵛᵃ1.
[151] Arist. *DA* 2. 1, 412ᵇ4–6.
[152] Aver. *In DA* 3, t. c. 5, 392. 158–393. 175.
[153] Ibid. 392. 165–6.
[154] Ibid. 166–7.

100. Tertio sequeretur quod Socrates in quantum homo esset incorruptibilis, licet non in quantum animal.[155] Consequens falsum. Consequentia patet, quoniam est homo per intellectum materialem, qui est incorruptibilis.

101. Quarto sequeretur quod necessario ego acquirerem scientiam quando tu acquireres, et obliviscerer te obliviscente.[156]

102. Ex quo ulterius deducunt alii quod contrariae opiniones essent in eodem receptivo primo. Consequentiae istae patent. Prima quia impossibile est eidem simul acquiri et non acquiri. Similiter impossibile est idem secundum idem oblivisci et non oblivisci. Secunda consequentia patet, quoniam certum est quod diversi homines habent contrarias opiniones. Certum etiam est quod intellectus materialis est primum receptivum istarum opinionum et per te est unus numero in diversis opinantibus.

103. Sexto et ultimo arguit sic: cuicumque perfectibili correspondet perfectio quae est forma immaterialis et separata, tali non correspondet nisi unum perfectibile, ut ponit exemplum de motoribus corporum caelestium, in quibus non correspondet uni motori nisi unum mobile, nec uni nautae simul nisi una navis. Igitur cum intellectus materialis sit substantia immaterialis, per eum, sibi uni existenti non correspondebit nisi unum perfectibile.[157]

⟨RATIONES ALBERTI⟩

104. Praeterea, contra istam opinionem arguit Albertus, 3 *De anima*, per quattuor rationes. Prima est ista: omne compositum efficitur hoc aliquid per suam formam substantialem, quae est sua prima perfectio. Sed hic homo est hoc aliquid et singularis, numero distinctus ab alio. Igitur forma istius est singularis et distincta a forma alterius. Forma autem sua est intellectus materialis. Igitur etc.[158]

105. Secunda ratio sua est haec: principia particularium sunt particularia per Philosophum 7 *Metaphysicae* contra Platonem.[159] Igitur cum intellectus materialis sit forma huius individui et illius, oportet quod sit singularis, particularis et distinctus in hoc et in illo.[160]

106. Tertia ratio sua est ultima ratio supra posita quam allegat Commentator contra se,[161] et ideo transeo. |

107. Quarta ratio sua est ista: cum animalitas in homine individuetur et numeretur in diversis suppositis hominis, humanitas autem non individuatur nec

---

2 Consequens] est *add.* T   6 contrariae ... essent] essent contrariae opiniones T   7 Consequentiae istae] *inv.* T   ‖   Prima] Primo T   ‖   quia *om.* P   7–8 eidem simul] simul idem T   8 est *om.* T   9 quoniam] quia T   10 etiam est] *inv.* T   11 est² *om.* P   ‖   unus] unum P   12 opinantibus] opinionibus P   14 est *om.* P   ‖   tali] *sc.* perfectioni   15 in quibus] quod P   21 Prima] ratio *add.* T   23 singularis¹] singulariter P   ‖   alio] homine *add.* T   24 sua] istius T   25 sua ... haec *om.* T   ‖   particularia] 7 Metaphysicae *add.* T   26 7 *Metaphysicae om.* T; 7 P   ‖   Igitur cum] *inv.* T   27 singularis] et *add.* T   29 sua *om.* T   29–30 ratio ... transeo] Commentatoris supra posita T   31 sua *om.* T

100. Thirdly it would follow that Socrates as man would be incorruptible, although not as animal.[155] The consequent is false. The consequence is obvious, since he is a man by means of the material intellect, which is incorruptible.

101. Fourthly it would necessarily follow that I would acquire knowledge when you acquired it, and I would forget it as you forgot it.[156]

102. From this others further deduce that there would be contrary opinions in the same first recipient. These consequences are obvious. The first because it is impossible for something to be acquired by and not acquired by the same thing at the same time. Likewise it is impossible for the same thing, with respect to the same thing, to forget and not to forget. The second consequence is obvious, since it is certain that different people have contrary opinions. It is also certain that the material intellect is the first recipient of these opinions and according to you is one in number in different people with opinions.

103. Sixthly and lastly he argues as follows: to any perfectible thing to which there corresponds a perfection which is an immaterial and separate form, to this sort of perfection only one perfectible thing corresponds, as he posits the example of the movers of celestial bodies, among which only one mobile corresponds to one mover, and only one ship to one sailor at any one time. Therefore since the material intellect is an immaterial substance, according to him, to it, being one thing, there will correspond only one perfectible thing.[157]

⟨ALBERT'S ARGUMENTS⟩

104. Moreover, Albert argues against this opinion in *On the Soul* 3, by means of four arguments. The first is this: every composite is made this certain thing by means of its substantial form, which is its first perfection. But this man is this certain and singular thing, distinct in number from another. Therefore his form is singular and distinct from the form of another. But his form is the material intellect. Therefore etc.[158]

105. His second argument is this: the principles of particular things are particular according to the Philosopher in *Metaphysics* 7, against Plato.[159] Therefore since the material intellect is the form of this and that individual, it is required that it is singular, particular, and distinct in this and that individual.[160]

106. His third argument is the last argument set out above which the Commentator alleges against himself,[161] and so I pass over it.

107. His fourth argument is this: since animality in a man is individuated and numbered in different supposits of man, but humanity is not individuated or

---

[155] Ibid. 167–9.
[156] Ibid. 393. 177–81.
[157] Aver. *In DA* 3, t. c. 5, 403. 473–84.
[158] Albert the Great, *In DA* 3, tract. 2, cap. 7, 187. 47–56.
[159] Arist. *Metaph.* 7. 13, 1038^{b}9–10.
[160] Albert the Great, *In DA* 3, tract. 2, cap. 7, 187. 58–64.
[161] Ibid. 65–78; above, para. 103.

numeratur—nam intellectus materialis, per quem homo est homo, unus numero est in omnibus—sequeretur quod natura generis individuaretur, et differentia maneret universalis non-individuata, sequeretur etiam quod species componeretur ex individuato secundum esse et ex non-individuato, similiter componeretur ex corruptibili et incorruptibili, quae omnia videntur absurda.[162]

⟨RATIONES ALIORUM⟩

108. Iterum arguunt alii dicentes hoc esse ficticium quod aliquid per se subsistens et separatum sit forma et perfectio alicuius quod est per se unum, quia per se unum fit ex duobus quia hoc actu, hoc potentia, ex 7 et 8 *Metaphysicae*.[163]

109. Praeterea, ficticium videtur esse quod aliquid unum per se subsistens copuletur tot corporibus loco et tempore distantibus et distinctis.

110. Praeterea, impossibile est aliquid unum numero inveniri in diversis suppositis nisi in sola natura divina propter eius illimitationem. Igitur cum intellectus materialis sit forma limitata, non potest esse unus numero in diversis.

111. Iterum, quae est causa effectiva istius unionis vel copulationis intellectus materialis cum corpore Socratis vel Platonis? Non intellectus agens, quia intellectus materialis prius nobis copulatur quam agens, ex 20 commento.[164] Nec aliqua alia substantia aeterna est causa huiusmodi copulationis, quoniam haec copulatio est nova, et ab aeterno et immutabili non procedit actus novus secundum eum. Substantiae autem aeternae sunt immutabiles et per se et per accidens secundum ipsum. Nec generans est causa effectiva huiusmodi copulationis. Nam cum generans sit corporeum, eius actus terminatur solum ad formam corpoream. Nec intellectus materialis copulat se ipsum cum corpore, quoniam nulla forma copulata cum materia est causa effectiva copulationis propriae cum alio. Igitur ista copulatio non est nisi ficticium, quia dictum sine omni ratione.

---

1 homo¹ *om.* P   **2** sequeretur] *scripsimus*; sequetur P; sequitur T   **2–3** quod . . . sequeretur *om. hom.* T   **3** etiam *om.* P   ‖   componeretur] componitur T   **4** individuato²] et *add.* T   **7** dicentes *om.* T   **8–9** quia . . . hoc²] quarum unum actu et aliud T   **9** 8] enim (*lectio incerta*) *add. et del.* P   ‖   Metaphysicae] Praeterea, unumquodque movens determinat sibi certam proportionem mobilis. Unde si essent plures stellae, non moverent nisi cum fatigatione. Intellectus vero determinat sibi certum numerum corporum *add.* T   **10** aliquid] aliquod P   **12** inveniri] invenire P   **12–13** suppositis] numero *add.* T   **14** forma] il *add. et del.* P   ‖   esse . . . diversis] in diversis esse unus numero T   **16** intellectus¹] *lectio incerta* T   **17** prius] *scripsimus*; primo PT   **17–18** aliqua . . . substantia] alia substantia alia P   **18** huiusmodi] istius T   **19** immutabili] *scripsimus*; incommutabili T; immutabilis P *et* a tali autem substantia immutabili *add. i.m.* P   ‖   actus novus] aliquid novum T   **20** aeternae] separatae P; secundum eum *add.* T   ‖   immutabiles] et aeternae immutabiles *add.* T   **20–21** secundum ipsum *om.* T   **21** huiusmodi] istius T   **22** eius] causa T   **24** copulationis propriae] *inv.* T   ‖   alio] materia T   **25** non . . . ratione] impossibilis T

numbered—for the material intellect, by means of which man is man, is one in number in everyone—it would follow that the nature of the genus would be individuated, and the difference would remain universal and non-individuated, and it would also follow that the species would be composed of something individuated according to being and of something non-individuated, and would similarly be composed of a corruptible thing and an incorruptible thing, all of which seems to be absurd.[162]

⟨ARGUMENTS OF OTHERS⟩

108. Others again argue by saying that this is fictitious, that anything subsisting by itself and separate is the form and perfection of something that is one thing by itself, because something that is one thing by itself comes to be from two things, since one is act and the other potency, from *Metaphysics* 7 and 8.[163]

109. Moreover, it seems to be fictitious that some one thing subsisting by itself would be conjoined with so many bodies distant and distinct in place and time.

110. Moreover, it is impossible for something that is one in number to be found in different supposits, except in the divine nature alone on account of its illimitation. Therefore since the material intellect is a limited form, it cannot be one in number in different things.

111. Again, what is the efficient cause of this union or conjoining of the material intellect with the body of Socrates or Plato? Not the agent intellect, because the material intellect is conjoined with us before the agent, from comment 20.[164] Nor is some other eternal substance the cause of such a conjoining, since this conjoining is new, and from an eternal and immutable thing there does not proceed a new act according to him. Eternal substances, however, are immutable both by themselves and by accident according to him. Nor is a generator the efficient cause of such a conjoining. For since the generator is corporeal, its act results only in a corporeal form. Nor does the material intellect conjoin itself with a body, since no form conjoined with matter is the efficient cause of its own conjoining with something else. Therefore this conjoining is nothing but a fictitious thing, since it is proposed without any reason.

---

[162] Albert the Great, *In DA* 3, tract. 2, cap. 7, 187. 79–91.
[163] Arist. *Metaph.* perhaps at 7. 13, 1039^{a}3–5; 8. 5, 1045^{a}23–33.
[164] Aver. *In DA* 3, t. c. 20, 447. 109–11.

⟨PUNCTUS 4 ARTICULI 2: AD RATIONES CONTRA AVERROEM⟩

⟨AD RATIONES AVERROIS⟩

112. Ad primum[165] respondet Commentator quod intellectus speculativus constituitur per duo subiecta, a quorum uno habet esse verum, et per illud subiectum intelligit rem extra, quae est obiectum motivum eius sub lumine intellectus agentis—res enim extra est causa agens una cum intellectu agente intellecta speculativa. Et quia eo quod res est vel non est, est oratio vera vel falsa|—veritas enim est adaequatio rei et intellectus—ideo dicit quod intentiones intellectae habent suam veritatem ab isto subiecto, puta a re, extendendo 'subiectum' ad obiectum. Aliud subiectum habent intellecta speculativa a quo habent quod sunt unum entium in mundo, videlicet quod sunt universalia in actu distincta contra particularia, et ut sic non sunt in rebus secundum ipsum, sed in intellectu solummodo. Licet subiectum secundo modo dictum sit incorruptibile, subiectum tamen primo modo dictum est corruptibile.[166] |

113. Ad formam argumenti dicendum quod, si intellecta speculativa solum dependerent ex intellectu agente et materiali, bene sequeretur quod essent aeterna. Sed quia cum intellectu agente et materiali concurrunt phantasmata necessario sicut causa partialis ad generationem intellectorum speculativorum, ideo cum ista phantasmata sint nova et transmutabilia, sequitur quod intellecta speculativa sunt nova et non aeterna. Exemplum, licet sol sit aeternus et sit causa effectiva in generatione hominis vel asini, quia tamen non est causa totalis, sed cum ipso concurrunt alia agentia corruptibilia, nihil prohibet effectum productum esse corruptibilem. Sic hic.

114. Ad secundum[167] dicendum, cum accipitur quod perfectio secunda numeratur in diversis hominibus, igitur et prima, quod non sequitur, sed est fallacia consequentis. Secunda enim perfectio praesupponit primam et in ea fundatur, et ideo ex numeratione primae perfectionis sequitur numeratio secundae, sed non econtra. In eodem enim intellectu possunt esse plures actus intelligendi, saltem successive, et etiam simul secundum aliquos. Unde stante unitate primae perfectionis, ex distinctione phantasmatum sequitur distinctio actuum intelligendi, qui sunt perfectiones secundae. Et ideo dico quod, licet eadem sit perfectio prima in

---

3 primum] in oppositum *add.* T   4–5 subiectum] solum P   6 agens] *suppl. i.m.* P   7 quia] ab *add.* T || est³] dicitur T || enim] *scripsimus*; etiam PT   8 adaequatio] ad esse T || intellectus] et *add.* T || intentiones] intellectiones T   9 'subiectum'] solum P   10 habent² *om.* P || sunt] sint T   11 videlicet] secundum *add.* T   14 corruptibile] *corr. ex* incorruptibile P   15 formam] igitur *add.* T   16 dependerent] dependent T || aeterna] aeternae T   17 Sed] quodlibet T || concurrunt] requiritur P   18 ista] huiusmodi T   19 sint] sunt P   19–20 sequitur . . . aeterna *om.* P   19 sunt] essent T   21 vel asini *om.* T   22 agentia] particularia *add.* T   25 diversis] subiectis vel *add.* T   26 enim] causa P   27 numeratione] numeratio primae P   29 etiam *om.* P || simul . . . aliquos] secundum aliquos simul T || primae] personae (*lectio incerta*) P   30 qui] quae P   31 secundae] hominis *add.* T || eadem sit] *inv.* T

⟨POINT 4 OF ARTICLE 2: IN ANSWER TO THE ARGUMENTS AGAINST AVERROES⟩

⟨IN ANSWER TO AVERROES' ARGUMENTS⟩

112. To the first[165] the Commentator responds that the speculative intellect is constituted by two subjects, from one of which it has true being, and by means of that subject it understands an external thing, which is an object capable of moving it under the light of the agent intellect—for the external thing is an agent cause together with the agent intellect of the speculative understood things. And since a spoken proposition is true or false in so far as a thing is or is not—for truth is the correspondence of a thing and the intellect—therefore he says that understood intentions have their truth from this subject, that is from the thing, by extending 'subject' to the object. Speculative understood things have another subject, from which they have that they are among beings in the world, that is that they are universals in act distinct from particulars, and as such they are not among extramental things according to him, but only in the intellect. Although subject said in the second way is incorruptible, nevertheless subject said in the first way is corruptible.[166]

113. In answer to the form of the argument it must be said that, if speculative understood things depended only on the agent intellect and the material intellect, it would rightly follow that they would be eternal. But because phantasms necessarily concur as a partial cause, together with the agent intellect and the material intellect, of the generation of speculative understood things, therefore since these phantasms are new and transmutable, it follows that speculative understood things are new and not eternal. For example, although the sun is eternal and is an efficient cause in the generation of a man or a donkey, since however it is not the total cause, but together with it other corruptible agents concur, nothing prohibits the effect produced from being corruptible. So in this case.

114. In answer to the second argument[167] it must be said that, when it is adduced that the second perfection is numbered in different men, therefore the first is too, it does not follow, but there is a fallacy of the consequent. For the second perfection presupposes the first and is founded in it, and therefore from the numbering of the first perfection follows the numbering of the second, but not the reverse. For in the same intellect there can be several acts of understanding, at least successively, and even at the same time according to some. Accordingly, given the unity of the first perfection, from the distinction among phantasms follows the distinction among acts of understanding, which are second perfections. And therefore I say that, although the first perfection is the same in two supposits

---

[165] See above, para. 96.
[166] Aver. *In DA* 3, t. c. 5, 400. 376–90.
[167] See above, para. 97.

duobus suppositis hominis, tamen quia diversorum hominum sunt diversa phantasmata, ideo actus intelligendi, qui sunt perfectiones secundae hominis, necessario in diversis suppositis numerantur.

115. Ad tertium[168] dicendum quod licet Socrates per idem sit homo et Plato, non tamen per idem Socrates est hic homo et Plato ille. Haeccitas autem in hoc et illo sub specie hominis solum est ratione corporis, non ratione intellectus, et ideo non sequitur quod Socrates et Plato sint unus homo numero. Exemplum, per eandem formam numero manus mea est manus et pes meus est pes, supposito quod in me non sit alia forma ab intellectiva; non propter hoc sequitur | quod manus mea et pes sint unum numero.

116. Ad quartum[169] dico quod nihil valet, quoniam idem argumentum potest fieri contra opinionem catholicam, in alia tamen forma, arguendo sic: quando forma rei est, res est; sed intellectiva Socratis est incorruptibilis secundum fidem, Socrates corruptibilis; igitur Socrates erit quando non erit. Dico igitur ad formam argumenti 'quando forma rei est, res est', hoc est verum de forma educta de potentia materiae.

117. Ad quintum[170] dico quod idem sequitur contra nos, si ratio valeret, quoniam forma per quam Socrates est homo est incorruptibilis per nos; sensitiva autem vel corporeitas in homine est corruptibilis. Respondeo quod, licet forma per quam Socrates est homo sit incorruptibilis, 'homo' tamen, quia nominat compositum ex illa forma incorruptibili et corpore corruptibili, hoc compositum est per se corruptibile.

118. Ad sextum[171] dicendum quod non sequitur quod ego acquirerem scientiam per hoc quod alius acquireret etc., quia nullus acquirit scientiam nisi ex phantasmatibus causatis ab imaginativa sua. Et haec est causa quare intellectus separatus a Socrate non reminiscitur eorum quorum Socrates habuit notitiam, quia virtus phantastica et per consequens phantasmata Socratis, corrupto Socrate, corrupta sunt, sine quibus intellectus nullam intellectionem habere potest quae illis phantasmatibus corresponderet. Dico igitur quod quia diversa sunt phantasmata in diversis hominibus, ideo diversae sunt intellectiones, licet intellectus materialis, qui est receptivus earum, sit omnino idem.

---

2 qui] quae P || hominis *om.* T **4** dicendum *om.* P || per] id *add.* P **5** per ... Socrates] Socrates per idem T **6** et[1]] in *add.* T || intellectus] hominis T **8** meus *om.* T **9** me] homine T || non[2] ... hoc] nec tamen T || sequitur *om.* T **11** Ad] *suppl. s.l.* P **11–12** potest fieri *om.* P **12** opinionem] fidem T || catholicam] *aliquid illegibile add. et del.* P || in ... forma] in tantum P || arguendo] arguo P **13** rei] *corr. s.l. ex* vel P || est[2]] *suppl. s.l.* P **14** Socrates[1]] autem est *add.* T || quando ... erit] *suppl. i.m.* P || quando] postquam T || igitur[2] *om.* T **15** argumenti] quod *add.* T || est verum] habet intelligi T **17** dico] dicitur P || ratio] non P **18** incorruptibilis] corruptibilis P || sensitiva] sensitivum T **19** corruptibilis] *scripsimus*; corruptibile PT || Respondeo] Dico *et igitur add.* T **24** etc. *om.* T **27–28** corrupta sunt] *inv.* T **28** intellectionem] intentionem P **29** corresponderet] correspondent T || in] hominibus *add. et del.* P **30** sunt *om.* P **31** receptivus] receptivum P || omnino idem] *inv.* T

of man, nevertheless in that different men have different phantasms, therefore the acts of understanding, which are second perfections of man, are necessarily numbered in different supposits.

115. In answer to the third argument[168] it must be said that although Socrates is man in virtue of the same thing by which Plato is man, nevertheless it is not in virtue of the same thing that Socrates is this man and Plato that. But hecceity in this and that individual in the species of man occurs only because of the body, not because of the intellect, and therefore it does not follow that Socrates and Plato are numerically one man. For example, by what is numerically the same form my hand is a hand and my foot is a foot, supposing that in me there is not another form than the intellectual soul; it does not follow on account of this that my hand and foot are numerically one.

116. In answer to the fourth argument[169] I say that it is invalid, since the same argument can be made against Catholic opinion, but in another form, arguing as follows: when the form of a thing exists, the thing exists; but the intellectual soul of Socrates is incorruptible according to faith, Socrates corruptible; therefore Socrates will exist when he will not exist. Therefore I say in answer to the form of argument 'when the form of a thing exists, the thing exists', this is true of a form elicited from the potency of matter.

117. In answer to the fifth argument[170] I say that the same conclusion follows against us, if the argument were valid, since the form by means of which Socrates is man is incorruptible according to us; but the sensitive soul or corporeity in man is corruptible. I respond that, although the form by means of which Socrates is man is incorruptible, man, however, in that 'man' names the composite of that incorruptible form and a corruptible body, is by itself, being this composite, corruptible.

118. In answer to the sixth argument[171] it must be said that it does not follow that I would acquire knowledge because another acquired it etc., since no one acquires knowledge except from phantasms caused by his imaginative power. And this is the reason why the intellect after it has been separated from Socrates does not remember the things of which Socrates had cognition, since Socrates' imaginative power and consequently his phantasms are corrupted, once Socrates is corrupted, and without them the intellect can have no understanding which would correspond to those phantasms. Therefore I say that since there are different phantasms in different men, therefore there are different understandings, although the material intellect, which is their recipient, is entirely the same.

---

[168] See above, para. 98.
[169] See above, para. 99.
[170] See above, para. 100.
[171] See above, para. 101.

119. Et ad confirmationem huius, cum dicit quod contrariae opiniones non possunt esse in eodem susceptivo primo,[172] dico quod dummodo illud susceptivum sit communicabile diversis suppositis, nihil prohibet. Exemplum, generare et non-generare contradicunt, tamen haec est vera 'Deus generat' et haec similiter 'Deus non generat', nec video quin posset concedi, quicquid dicat Magister Sententiarum. Vel 'Deus est nascibilis ⟨et⟩ 'Deus est innascibilis': ratione diversarum proprietatum in diversis personis divinis possunt haec praedicata opposita verificari. Sic in eodem intellectu numero communicabili diversis suppositis, ratione distinctionis istorum suppositorum et phantasmatum in illis suppositis, possunt esse opiniones contrariae, non quod contrarientur respectu eius, sed quod essent contrariae in eodem intellectu secundum unum et idem suppositum, in eodem tamen intellectu secundum diversa supposita non contrariantur.

120. Ad ultimam Commentatoris[173] dico ad maiorem quod ipsa est vera, ubi comparatur perfectio vel forma abstracta ad suum primum perfectibile, sicut patet in exemplis adductis. Sed primum perfectibile ab intellectu materiali non est Socrates vel Plato nec universale abstractum per intellectum, sed ipsa natura | humana, quae una est secundum se et quidditatem in omnibus suppositis, licet numeraliter distinguatur in diversis. Et ipsa ut sic una est primum perfectibile ab intellectu materiali, et ipsa ut sic non numeratur nec est singularis singularitate determinata sub specie. Potest tamen bene dici 'singularis' singularitate vaga.

⟨AD RATIONES ALBERTI⟩

121. Ad primam rationem Alberti[174] dicendum quod maior est falsa, haec scilicet, quod hoc compositum 'homo' sit hoc aliquid—intelligendo per 'hoc aliquid' aliquod singulare—contentum sub specie hominis per formam suam, scilicet per intellectum materialem, sed est homo per intellectum materialem, hic homo per differentiam individualem ex parte materiae hominis.

122. Ad secundum[175] dico quod Aristoteles loquitur ibi contra Platonem et utitur universali secundum opinionem Platonis, qui posuit universale esse quoddam subsistens extra animam cuiuscumque speciei et illud esse communicabile diversis suppositis et necessarium propter scientiam et generationem. Contra quam opinionem de universali dicit Philosophus: principia particularium sunt particularia. Et

---

1 Et *om.* T   2 in *om.* P || quod *om.* P   3 diversis] multis T || generare] generative P   3–4 non-generare] non generative P; non *add. et del.* P   4 contradicunt] et *add.* T || Deus[1]] Pater T   5 nec] non P || posset] possit T   6 et] *supplevimus; om.* PT   7 in] et T || praedicata opposita] supposita praedicata T || verificari] de Deo *add.* T   8 communicabili] a *add.* P   13 ultimam] ultimum T || quod . . . vera *om.* T   14 comparatur perfectio] *iter. et corr.* P || sicut] sed P   16 Socrates] forma P || nec] vel T   18 est] sit P || primum] *corr. ex* principium primum P   20 determinata] determinate T   23 hoc[1] *om.* T   24 contentum] contractum T   25 materialem[2]] et *add.* T   26 differentiam] aliam *add.* P   29 animam *om.* T   30 generationem] *lectio incerta* P   31 sunt] semper P

119. And in confirmation of this, when he says that contrary opinions cannot be in the same first susceptive thing,[172] I reply that as long as that susceptive thing is communicable to different supposits, nothing prohibits this. For example, to generate and not-to generate are contradictory, yet this is true: 'God generates' and this similarly: 'God does not generate', and I do not see why it should not be conceded, whatever the Master of Sentences says. Or 'God is able to be born' and 'God is not able to be born': because of different properties in different divine persons these opposite predicates can be verified. So in numerically the same intellect, which is communicable to different supposits, because of the distinction of these supposits and the phantasms in these supposits, there can exist contrary opinions, not in that they are contrary with respect to it, but in that they would be contrary in the same intellect according to one and the same supposit, yet in the same intellect according to different supposits they are not contrary.

120. In answer to the Commentator's last argument[173] I say in answer to the major premiss that it is true, where a perfection or abstract form is compared with its first perfectible, as is obvious from the examples cited. But the first perfectible by the material intellect is not Socrates or Plato nor the universal abstracted by the intellect, but human nature itself, which is one according to itself and its quiddity in all supposits, although numerically it is distinguished in different supposits. And human nature as it is in this way one is the first perfectible by the material intellect, and as such it is not numbered nor singular by a singularity determined in a species. However, it can rightly be called 'singular' by a vague singularity.

⟨IN ANSWER TO ALBERT'S ARGUMENTS⟩

121. In answer to Albert's first argument[174] it must be said that the major premiss is false, namely this, that this composite 'man' is this certain thing—understanding by 'this certain thing' something singular—contained in the species of man because of his form, namely because of the material intellect, but he is man because of the material intellect, this man because of the individual difference belonging to the matter of man.

122. In answer to the second argument[175] I say that Aristotle speaks there against Plato and uses a universal according to the opinion of Plato, who posited that a universal is something of any species subsisting outside the soul and that it is communicable to different supposits and necessary on account of knowledge and generation. Against that opinion regarding the universal the Philosopher says: the principles of particulars are particulars. And this is true if one distinguishes a

---
[172] See above, para. 102.
[173] See above, para. 103.
[174] See above, para. 104.
[175] See above, para. 105.

verum est distinguendo particulare contra universale Platonicum. Distinguendo tamen particulare contra universale quod non habet in se principium individuans superadditum speciei seu quidditati, non est verum, saltem in homine, qui est in confinio materialium et immaterialium, compositum ex natura corporali corruptibili et natura spirituali incorruptibili. Et ideo necesse est quod eius principia non 5 habeant omnino omnem conformitatem ad invicem quam habent principia aliorum compositorum ex forma educta de potentia materiae et materia.

123. Ad aliam rationem Alberti[176] patet per idem. Non enim est inconveniens quod natura generis sit individuata secundum esse, et natura differentiae non-individuata; similiter quod species componatur ex universali non-individuato nec 10 individuabili et natura individuata. Sed diceret Averroes quod hoc accidit necessario in homine et in nullo alio, et hoc propter ordinem universi, qui requirit quod in aliquo uno materialia et immaterialia un|iantur, ut in homine. Propter quod oportet quod principium formale in homine, quod est de numero immaterialium, retineat conditionem immaterialium, quae est non-numerari in eadem specie. Principium 15 autem materiale numerabile est.

⟨AD RATIONES ALIORUM⟩

124. Ad rationes aliorum. Ad primum,[177] cum dicitur quod hoc est ficticium quod aliquid subsistens et separatum sit forma alicuius quod est per se unum, concedo. Et minorem nego quantum ad hoc quod assumitur quod intellectus mate- 20 rialis est subsistens separatum. Non enim est separatum nec separabile a suo primo perfectibili, sed necessario et aeternaliter sibi copulatum et coniunctum secundum viam Commentatoris. Et quando ulterius dicitur quod principia compositi unius sunt actus et potentia,[178] concedo. Sed non oportet quod actus ille | sit inhaerens potentiae. Nam hoc non possunt catholici dicere de intellectiva, cum per se sub- 25 sistere per naturam et inhaerere per naturam sint opposita circa idem. Dicant ergo catholici quo modo ex intellectiva—non obstante quod sit subsistens—et corpore humano fit unum, et similem modum et etiam veriorem modum unitatis poterit Commentator assignare. Et dico 'veriorem', quoniam cum ad unitatem compositi requirantur inclinatio, dependentia et ordo naturalis inter formam et materiam, 30

1 contra] contingit (vel concludit vel convenit) P   2 individuans] individuationis T   4 confinio] confinium P || natura] materiali et incor add. et del. P   5 spirituali] et add. P   7 et] ex ipsa add. T   8 Alberti] ultimam add. P   10 componatur] computatur P   11 individuabili] indivisibili T   12 universi] universum P   13 uno] suo P || uniantur] uniuntur P || ut] puta T   16 numerabile] numerale T   20 Et] sed T || minorem nego] inv. T   22 aeternaliter] naturaliter P || copulatum . . . coniunctum] coniunctum et copulatum T   23 compositi unius] inv. T   25 potentiae] potentiam P || dicere] divinae (lectio incerta) P   26 et] alterius add. T   28 fit] sint P || etiam om. T || veriorem] apparentiorem T || modum unitatis om. T   29 'veriorem'] apparentiorem T   30 requirantur] requiratur T || inclinatio] et add. et del. P || materiam] naturam P

particular over against a Platonic universal. Yet if one distinguishes a particular over against a universal which does not have in itself an individuating principle superadded to its species or quiddity, it is not true, at least in man, who is on the boundary of material and immaterial things, a composite of a corruptible corporeal nature and an incorruptible spiritual nature. And therefore it is necessary that his principles do not have entirely all the conformity with each other which the principles of other things have, if they are composites of a form elicited from the potency of matter and of matter.

123. The answer to another of Albert's arguments[176] is obvious for the same reason. For it is not an absurdity that the nature of a genus is individuated according to being, and the nature of a difference non-individuated; similarly that a species is composed of a universal which is non-individuated nor able to be individuated and an individuated nature. But Averroes would say that this happens necessarily in man and in nothing else, and this because of the order of the universe, which requires that in some one thing material and immaterial things should be united, as in man. Because of this it is required that the formal principle in man, which is among the number of immaterial things, retains the condition of immaterial things, which is not-to be numbered in the same species. But the material principle is numerable.

⟨IN ANSWER TO THE ARGUMENTS OF OTHERS⟩

124. In answer to the arguments of others. In answer to the first,[177] when it is said that it is fictitious that something subsisting and separate is the form of something that is one by itself, I concede it. And I deny the minor premiss in so far as it is assumed that the material intellect is a separate subsisting thing. For it is not separate nor separable from its first perfectible thing, but necessarily and eternally it is conjoined and conjunct to it according to the views of the Commentator. And when it is later said that the principles of one composite are act and potency,[178] I concede it. But it is not required that this act should be inhering in the potency. For Catholics cannot say this of the intellectual soul, since to subsist by itself by nature and to inhere by nature are opposites with respect to the same thing. Therefore let Catholics try to say in what manner one thing comes to be from the intellectual soul—notwithstanding that it is subsisting—and the human body, and the Commentator will be able to offer a similar manner and even a truer manner of unity. And I say 'truer', since as for the unity of a composite thing inclination, dependence, and natural order between form and matter are required, the material

---

[176] See above, para. 107.
[177] See above, para. 108.
[178] See above, ibid.

intellectus materialis plus dependet a suo primo perfectibili quam anima mea secundum catholicos dependeat a suo perfectibili, quia anima mea potest subsistere sine aliquo perfectibili, et aeternaliter subsisteret, postquam esset separata, nisi accideret novum miraculum et valde magnum ad hoc quod uniatur. Non sic diceret Averroes de intellectu materiali respectu sui primi perfectibilis quod posset esse, si natura humana non esset, quoniam secundum eum cum ultimus eius finis sit cognitio substantiarum separatarum, hanc cognitionem habere non potest per eum, nisi quando terminatus est motus intellectus in habitu et perfectus, quae cognitio haberi non potest sine conversione ad phantasmata secundum eum. Et phantasmata non sunt nisi in corpore. Et ideo ponit quod intellectus non reminiscitur post mortem. Unde diceret Averroes quod, licet intellectus materialis sit subsistens, tamen non est hoc aliquid perfectum in specie, sed principium speciei. Verumtamen difficile est intelligere quo modo ex forma non-inhaerente, sed subsistente, et materia fiat unum. Sed magis est difficile hoc intelligere de intellectiva et corpore secundum opinionem catholicam, ut declaratum est,[179] quam secundum opinionem Commentatoris. De ista autem unione dicit Augustinus, 21 *De civitate Dei*, capitulo 2, quod modus quo corporibus adhaeret spiritus est ineffabilis nec ab homine comprehendi potest.[180]

125. Dico ergo quod propter naturalem inclinationem et dependentiam intellectus materialis a corpore, qua et in esse et in operatione sua finali a corpore organico huiusmodi virtutes sensitivas habente dependet, quae sunt praeparationes necessariae respectu cuiuscumque actionis eius, ita quod intelligere non est eius, sed dependet essentialiter ex corpore tamquam ab eo quod operatur, ideo ex his fit unum. Et ad hanc intentionem dicit Aristoteles, 1 *De anima*, quod si intelligere sit imaginari vel non sit sine imaginatione, impossibile est quod sit extra corpus.[181] Per quod vult dicere: intelligere non est proprium intellectui, sed est totius coniuncti primo sicut eius quod primo intelligit. Unde dico quod huiusmodi naturalis dependentia | et ordo principiorum hominis ad invicem, quae non invenitur in cumulo lapidum, qui sunt simul sine omni commixtione naturali vel dependentia ad invicem, sufficit ad hoc quod homo sit vere unum ens definibile et subiectum demonstrationis. Non tamen est homo ita vere unum sicut aliae species animalis, sed inter omnia alia animalia maiorem distinctionem naturarum et potentiarum in se complectitur. Et si dicatur: quanto dicetur aliquid simplicius tanto perfectius, ergo, cum homo inter animalia sit animal perfectius, ergo et simplicius, dicendum

1–2 secundum . . . mea] *om. hom.* P *et* quae *add.*   3 esset] est T   5 primi *om.* T || perfectibilis] scilicet *add.* T   6 non] *suppl. s.l.* P   7 cognitio] coniunctio P   8 motus intellectus] eius motus T   13 difficile] *lectio incerta* T   14 fiat] fit P || difficile hoc] hoc definibile T   15 opinionem] fidem T   16 Commentatoris] Averrois T || unione] *corr. ex* opinione P   17 2] 22 T   20 qua] quae P || et[1] *om.* T   21 habente] habentem P   22 eius[2]] nisi quo primo *add.* T   24 intentionem] sententiam T   25 sit . . . imaginatione] sine imaginatione sit T   26 dicere] quod *add.* T   31 aliae] alia T   32 alia *om.* T   33 Et . . . dicatur *om.* P || dicetur *om.* T   34–78.1 ergo[1] . . . perfectius *om. hom.* T   34 et] est P

intellect depends more on its first perfectible thing than my soul, according to Catholics, depends on its perfectible thing, because my soul can subsist without any perfectible thing, and would subsist eternally after it were separated, unless a new and very great miracle were to happen in order for it to be joined. Averroes would not say this of the material intellect, in relation to its first perfectible thing, that it could exist, if human nature did not exist, since according to him as its final end is the cognition of separate substances, it cannot have this cognition, according to him, except when the motion of the intellect in habit has reached its end and is perfect, and this cognition cannot be possessed without turning towards phantasms, according to him. And phantasms do not exist except in the body. And therefore he posits that the intellect does not remember after death. Therefore Averroes would say that, although the material intellect is a subsisting thing, yet it is not this certain thing complete in a species, but the principle of a species. Nevertheless it is difficult to understand in what manner one thing comes to be from a form that is non-inhering, but subsisting, and from matter. But it is more difficult to understand this of the intellectual soul and the body according to Catholic opinion, as has been explained,[179] than according to the opinion of the Commentator. However, of this union Augustine says (*On the City of God* 21, chapter 2) that the manner in which the spirit adheres to bodies is inexpressible and cannot be comprehended by man.[180]

125. I say therefore that on account of the natural inclination and dependence of the material intellect on the body, by which both in its being and in its final operation it depends on an organic body having sensitive powers of this kind, which are necessary preparations with respect to any of its actions, so that to understand does not belong to it, but depends essentially on the body as if on that which performs it, therefore from the material intellect and the body one thing comes to be. And with respect to this conception Aristotle says (*On the Soul* 1) that if to understand is to imagine or does not come to pass without imagination, it is impossible that it exists outside the body.[181] By means of this he wants to say: to understand is not proper to the intellect, but belongs to the whole conjunct first just as to that which first understands. Consequently I say that natural dependence of this sort and the mutual order of the principles of man, which is not found in a pile of stones, which are together without any natural commixing or mutual dependence, suffices for the fact that man is truly one being, definable and the subject of demonstration. Yet man is not truly one in the same way as the other species of animal, but among all other animals he embraces in himself a greater distinction of natures and powers. And if it is said: the simpler something is said to be the more perfect it is, therefore, since among animals man is the more perfect animal, therefore also the simpler, it

[179] See above, para. 124.
[180] Aug. *De civ. Dei*, 21. 2, ii. 488.
[181] Arist. *DA* 1. 1, 403^{a}8–10.

quod haec regula 'quanto simplicius, tanto perfectius' habet intelligi in substantiis separatis, non in compositis istis corruptibilibus. Causa huius differentiae est ista quia in substantiis separatis primum quod est simplicissimum et principium aliorum omnium est perfectissimum, quoniam actualissimum. Et ideo per recessum ab eo per compositionem maiorem vel minorem dicitur unaquaeque substantia separata magis et minus perfecta, ita quod simplicior quia propinquior perfectissimo 'perfectior', compositior quia remotior ab eo 'imperfectior'. Sed in compositis materialibus 'simplicius' et 'compositius' accipiuntur per comparationem ad materiam, quae est principium simplex omnium materialium, ita quod forma quae minus elevatur supra materiam constituit compositum magis simplex, sicut patet in elementis. Quanto autem forma magis elevatur supra conditiones materiae tanto maiorem distinctionem et compositionem facit cum materia. Quia igitur materia, quae est primum in illo ordine, est simplicissimum in illo ordine, ideo quanto simplicius est aliquid de corporalibus tanto imperfectius, et quanto compositius tanto perfectius.

126. Sed dicetur: per eandem rationem qua ponitur intellectus materialis—non obstante quod sit substantia per se subsistens—esse formam et principium formale hominis, per eandem rationem oporteret hoc ponere de intellectu agente, et sic duae substantiae subsistentes essent de intrinseca compositione hominis, et per consequens homo non esset vere unum.

127. Praeterea, cum intelligentia movens caelum de necessitate naturae moveat, per hanc rationem sequeretur quod corpus caeleste, ut in se comprehendit intelligentiam moventem, sit per se unum ens, et sic nulla substantia separata esset per se in genere substantiae sicut species, sed solum per reductionem sicut principium generis, quod communiter habetur pro falso.

128. Ad primum[182] dico quod non sequitur nec est simile, quia intellectus agens in sua operatione prima, quae est eius finalis perfectio, non dependet a corpore nec a copulatione sua cum intellectu materiali. Perfectio enim finalis eius est speculatio Dei et substantiarum separatarum superiorum ipso. Nihil enim inferius ipso intelligit. In ista autem operatione non dependet a copulatione eius cum intellectu materiali nec cum corpore, immo sua copulatio ad corpus et abstractio phantasmatum perpetua et continua est quaedam sequela ad eius operationem | principalem, sicut motus caeli perpetuus consequitur primam operationem intelligentiarum, qua intelligunt Deum, ut statim dicetur.[183]

---

2 compositis istis] *inv.* T ‖ Causa] autem *add.* T   4 omnium *om.* T   5–6 separata] *suppl. i.m.* P   7 'perfectior' *om.* T ‖ 'imperfectior'] in perfectione T   11 in] de P   12 distinctionem ... compositionem] compositionem et distinctionem T   13 quanto] quando P   17 esse formam] est forma P   21 intelligentia] *lectio incerta* P   22 per] secundum T   23 substantia *om.* P   24 esset] esse P   25 falso] *corr. i.m. ex illegibili* P   27 operatione] actione T   28 finalis eius] *inv.* T   29 separatarum] vel *add.* T   30 operatione] eius *add.* T   32 perpetua ... continua] continua in perpetua P

must be said that this rule 'as much the simpler, so much the more perfect' must be understood in relation to separate substances, not in these corruptible composites. The cause of this difference is this, that in separate substances the first, which is the simplest and the principle of all the others, is the most perfect, since it is the most actual. And therefore every separate substance is said to be more or less perfect on account of the fact that it retreats from the first substance because of its greater or lesser composition, so that the simpler is said to be 'more perfect' in that it is nearer to the most perfect, the more composite 'more imperfect' in that it is more remote from it. But in material composites 'simpler' and 'more composite' are understood by comparison with matter, which is the simple principle of all material things, so that a form which is less elevated above matter constitutes a more simple composite, as is obvious in the case of the elements. But the more a form is elevated above the conditions of matter, the greater is its distinction from matter and the greater is the composition that it makes with matter. For this reason since matter, which is first in that order, is the simplest in that order, therefore to the extent that something from among corporeal things is simpler, to that extent it is more imperfect, and to the extent that it is more composite, to that extent it is more perfect.

126. But it will be said: by the very same argument by which the material intellect is posited to be the form and the formal principle of man—notwithstanding that it is a substance subsisting by itself—by the same argument it would be required to posit this of the agent intellect, and so there would be two subsisting substances that belong to the intrinsic composition of man, and consequently man would not be truly one thing.

127. Moreover, since the intelligence that moves heaven moves it by the necessity of nature, by the same argument it would follow that a heavenly body, in so far as it encompasses in itself the moving intelligence, would be a being that is one by itself, and so no separate substance would be by itself in the category of substance as a species, but only by reduction as a principle of the category, which is commonly held to be false.

128. In answer to the first[182] I say that it does not follow, nor is it similar, since the agent intellect in its first operation, which is its final perfection, does not depend on the body nor on its conjoining with the material intellect. For its final perfection is the contemplation of God and of the separate substances higher than itself. For it understands nothing lower than itself. In this operation, however, it does not depend on its conjoining with the material intellect nor with the body, but rather its conjoining with the body and the perpetual and continuous abstraction of phantasms is a sort of sequel to its principal operation, just as the perpetual motion of heaven follows from the first operation of the intelligences, by which they understand God, as will be said immediately.[183]

---

[182] See above, para. 126.
[183] See below, para. 131.

129. Sed dicetur: si intellectus agens non sit principium intrinsecum homini, cum intelligere hominis essentialiter dependeat | ab intellectu agente sicut ab uno principio per se requisito ad intellectionem, sequitur quod intelligere nostrum non est in potestate voluntatis nostrae.

130. Dicendum quod non sequitur, quoniam, licet intellectus agens non sit principium intrinsecum homini, tamen actio intellectus agentis est in potestate nostra. Nam intellectus agens necessitate naturali phantasmata actu existentia in virtute phantastica abstrahit et ponit in intellectum materialem. Sed post cognitionem rerum conversio ad haec phantasmata est in potestate nostra, et ideo intelligere haec intelligibilia et illa est in potestate nostra. Exemplum, licet sol sit extrinsecum mihi, supposito tamen quod semper sol necessario luceret necessitate naturali, in potestate mea esset semper videre colores. Sic hic.

131. Ad aliud[184] dicendum quod non est simile quoniam intelligentia motrix caeli nec in esse nec in sua operatione prima, quae est speculari Deum, dependet ex suo movere caelum. Sed suum movere caelum consequitur suam operationem primam, ita quod suum intelligere Deum est causa motus sui perpetui. Et ideo intelligentia movens caelum unitur caelo ut motor tantum, et eodem modo unitur intellectus agens corpori humano et intellectui materiali. Non sic autem intellectus materialis unitur corpori humano, quoniam tam in operatione sua perfectissima quam in esse ex corpore dependet, ita quod sua copulatio corpori praecedit sicut causa omnem eius operationem.

132. Ad aliud,[185] cum dicitur quod haec opinio est ficticia pro quanto ponit unam substantiam copulari tot corporibus distantibus etc., diceret Averroes quod multo est hoc rationabilius quam sit modus quem ponunt catholici. Nam ex quo entia nolunt male disponi, ex fine 12 *Metaphysicae*,[186] ordo et connexio partium universi hoc exigit, cum superiora entia sint immaterialia, aeterna et non-numerabilia in eadem specie, inferiora autem sint materialia, corruptibilia et plura in eadem specie, quod est dare aliquam speciem compositam comprehendentem in se intrinsece utramque naturam, in qua copulantur et connectuntur superiora inferioribus, sicut medium componitur ex extremis. Et illa species media erit numerabilis secundum differentias corporales, innumerabilis autem et non-multiplicabilis secundum formam. De hoc autem quod additur quod unitur distinctis et distantibus loco et tempore,[187] hoc non est inconveniens. | Nam ex quo eius unitas est solum specifica, non individualis, prout 'individuum' aliquam intentionem addit supra speciem, ut dictum est,[188] ponere aliquid tale correspondere diversis corporibus

---

1 dicetur] dices T || homini *om.* T   **4** voluntatis nostrae] nostra T   **8** intellectum materialem] *fortasse scribendum* intellectu materiali   **12** mea] nostra T || esset semper] *inv.* T   **22** ficticia] ficticium P   **23** substantiam] intelligentiam T || distantibus etc. *om.* T   **24** multo] multum P   **25** nolunt] volunt P   **26** sint] sunt P || aeterna *om.* P   **27** sint *om.* T   **28** comprehendentem] *scripsimus*; comprehendens PT   **29** connectuntur] committuntur P   **30–31** numerabilis] innumerabilis P   **33** est solum] *inv.* T

129. But it will be said: if the agent intellect is not a principle intrinsic to man, whereas man's understanding essentially depends on the agent intellect as on one principle necessarily required for understanding, it follows that our understanding is not in the power of our will.

130. It must be replied that it does not follow, since, although the agent intellect is not a principle intrinsic to man, nevertheless the action of the agent intellect is in our power. For the agent intellect by natural necessity abstracts phantasms that actually exist in the imaginative power and puts them in the material intellect. But after the cognition of things the turning towards these phantasms is in our power, and therefore to understand these intelligible things and those is in our power. For example, although the sun is extrinsic to me, nevertheless supposing that necessarily the sun would always shine by natural necessity, it would always be in my power to see colours. So in this case.

131. In answer to another argument[184] it must be said that there is no similarity since an intelligence that is a mover of heaven does not depend on its moving of heaven either in being or in its first operation, which is to contemplate God. But its moving of heaven follows its first operation, so that its understanding of God is the cause of its perpetual motion. And therefore an intelligence moving heaven is united with heaven as a mover only, and in the same way the agent intellect is united with the human body and the material intellect. But the material intellect is not united with the human body in this way, since both in its most perfect operation and in being it depends on the body, so that its conjoining with the body precedes as a cause all its operation.

132. In answer to another argument,[185] when it is said that this opinion is fictitious inasmuch as it posits that one substance is conjoined with so many bodies that are distant from each other etc., Averroes would reply that this is much more rational than is the way that Catholics posit. For since beings do not want to be badly disposed, from the end of *Metaphysics* 12,[186] the order and connection of the parts of the universe requires this—since higher beings are immaterial, eternal, and non-numerable in the same species, but lower things are material, corruptible, and many in the same species—that there must be some composite species which intrinsically in itself encompasses both natures, and in which superior things are conjoined and connected with inferior, just as the intermediate is composed from the extremes. And this intermediate species will be numerable according to corporeal differences, but innumerable and non-multiplicable according to form. But about what is added, that it is united with things that are distinct and distant in place and time,[187] this is not an absurdity. For since its unity is only specific, not individual, in so far as 'individual' adds some intention to the species, as has been said,[188] to posit that something of this sort corresponds to different bodies distant in

---

[184] See above, para. 127.
[185] See above, para. 109.
[186] Arist. *Metaph.* 12. 10, 1076^{a}3–4.
[187] See above, para. 109.
[188] See above, para. 95.

loco et tempore distantibus et distinctis numero, quae sunt eius perfectibilia secundario et ex consequenti, non est aliquod inconveniens, sed multum conveniens. Sed ex alia parte, quod Deus immediate ageret in corpus humanum vel in materiam, quod etiam animam intellectivam ex nihilo de novo crearet, quod etiam Deus eo ipso quod agens particulare, scilicet homo generans, aliquam dispositionem 5 induceret in materiam determinatam, licet per actum deformem et non placentem Deo, crearet de novo animam infundendo in sua materia, ita quod, ut aliqui dicunt, illa dispositio prius inducta per agens particulare est dispositio quae est necessitas respectu infusionis intellectivae a Deo—ista omnia diceret Commentator solum esse ficta et nullo modo consona rationi naturali. 10

133. Ad aliud,[189] cum dicitur quod nulla una natura numero limitata potest inveniri in diversis suppositis, concederet Commentator etiam in natura illimitata. Negat enim trinitatem personarum in divinis 12 *Metaphysicae*, 39 commento.[190] Verumtamen licet non possit una natura numero saltem limitata esse in diversis eius suppositis, quia esse naturae limitatae primo inest supposito et non inest natu- 15 rae nisi quia supposito, tamen nihil prohibet unam formam numero numerositate specifica, non numerositate superaddita speciei, plures materias simul perficere tamquam eius perfectibilia secundaria, ex quibus in suo esse non dependet. Unde diceret Averroes forte quod multo rationabilius videtur [quod] una⟨m⟩ forma⟨m⟩ cuius ratio singularitatis est ratio eius quidditatis et per consequens non determi- 20 natur ad locum nec ad tempus, copulari diversis corporibus numero et loco distinctis et distantibus simul tamquam secundario perfectibilibus ab ipsa, quam unam formam individuam et numeratam ad numerationem materiae totam et totaliter simul perficere diversas partes eiusdem individui, quoniam ex secundo sequitur quod idem, licet per accidens, simul movetur et quiescit, quod Commentator ex 25 positione sua non concederet sequi magis quam concederet de motore, qui solum coniungitur caelo per motum, de quo dicit quod non movetur per se nec per accidens.

134. Ad ultimum,[191] cum quaeritur de causa copulationis intellectus materialis nobis, diceret quod causa finalis est connexio et ordo partium universi, quae 30 exigunt | quod sit aliquod medium inter corporalia corruptibilia et incorporalia et perpetua in sui compositione comprehendens utramque naturam istorum extremo-

---

1 distantibus et *om.* P   3 immediate *om.* T   4 ex] de T   5 quod] est *add.* T   7 sua] illa T   8 prius inducta] praeinducta P || particulare] naturale T   9 intellectivae] in Deo *add. et del.* P || solum *om.* T   10 ficta] fictitia T   11 una natura] *inv.* T || potest] poterit P   12 Commentator] et *add.* P || etiam... natura] in natura etiam P   13 personarum... divinis] personae divinae (*lectio incerta*) P || 39 commento] *inv.* T   14 una natura] *inv.* T   15 eius *om.* T   19 diceret... forte] forte diceret Averroes T || multo] multum P || [quod]... forma⟨m⟩] quod una forma PT; quod *delevimus et* una forma *correximus in* unam formam   20 eius *om.* T   20–21 determinatur] nec *add.* T   21 ad² *om.* P   22 et *om.* T || ipsa] ipso T   24 quoniam] quantum T   26 sua] eius P   27 coniungitur] *corr. i.m. ex* cogitur P || non movetur] nec numero P; nec *add.* T   29 de *om.* T   30 connexio] commixtio P   31 exigunt] exigit T || et¹ *om.* P || incorporalia] incorruptibilia P

space and time and distinct in number, which are its perfectible things secondarily and derivatively, is not something absurd, but very fitting. But on the other part, that God would act immediately on the human body or on matter, that he would also create the intellectual soul anew from nothing, that also God, just because a particular agent, that is a generating man, induces some disposition in determinate matter, although by an act that is deformed and not pleasing to God, creates a soul anew by infusing it in its matter, so that, as some say, that disposition first induced by the particular agent is a disposition which is a necessity with respect to the infusion of the intellectual soul by God—the Commentator would say that all this is only fictitious and in no way in harmony with natural reason.

133. In answer to another argument,[189] when it is said that no nature that is numerically one and that is also limited can be found in different supposits, the Commentator would also concede this in the case of an unlimited nature. For he denies the trinity of persons in the divine nature (*Metaphysics* 12, comment 39).[190] Nevertheless although a nature that is numerically one, at least if it is limited, cannot be in different supposits belonging to it, since the being of a limited nature first inheres in a supposit and does not inhere in a nature unless because it inheres in a supposit, still nothing prohibits a form that is numerically one by a specific numerosity, and not by a numerosity that is superadded to the species, from perfecting several matters at the same time as its secondary perfectibles, on which it does not depend in its being. Hence Averroes would perhaps say that it seems much more rational for one form whose property of singularity is the property of its quiddity, and consequently is not determined in terms of place nor in terms of time, to be conjoined at the same time with numerically different bodies and distinct and distant in place just as if with things secondarily perfectible by it, than for one form which is individual and numbered according to the numbering of matter to perfect as a whole and wholly at the same time different parts of the same individual. For from the second alternative it follows that the same thing, although by accident, at the same time moves and is at rest, which the Commentator from his position would not concede to follow more than he would concede it of a mover, which is conjoined with heaven only by motion, of which he says that it is not moved by itself nor by accident.

134. In answer to the last argument,[191] when a question is raised about the cause of the conjoining of the material intellect with us, he would say that the final cause is the connection and order of the parts of the universe, which require that there is an intermediate between corporeal corruptible things and incorporeal and perpetual things, and encompasses in its composition the natures of both these

---

[189] See above, para. 110.
[190] Aver. *In Metaph.* 12, t. c. 39, fol. 322^(va)I.
[191] See above, para. 111.

rum. De causa effectiva huiusmodi copulationis credo quod diceret quod eius non est causa effectiva nisi per accidens. Sicut enim ignis, quantum est ex parte sua, semper arderet—quod autem non ardet modo hoc combustibile vel aliud et postea ardet, huius non est causa effectiva nisi per accidens, scilicet qui combustibile apponit igni—sic hic naturaliter intellectus materialis perficit corpus humanum, ita quod ex parte | sua nihil deficit quin semper quodcumque corpus humanum perficeret. Quia tamen non potest corpus perficere nisi existat in actu, sicut ex alia parte ignis non potest comburere nisi combustibili sibi approximato, ideo sicut approximans combustibile igni est causa per accidens combustionis de novo nec est alia causa effectiva per se, ita generans corpus Socratis est causa per accidens copulationis intellectus materialis cum Socrate, nec est illius copulationis danda alia causa effectiva per se.

⟨DE COPULATIONE INTELLECTUS CUM INDIVIDUO⟩

135. Sciendum tamen est de ista copulatione quod Commentator varie loquitur de ea. Aliquando enim dicit quod intellectus in potentia, per quem intelligit intellectum materialem, prius nobis copulatur quam intellectus agens, ut patet 20 commento longe ante medium, ubi dicit: 'Secundum nostram opinionem et Themistii intellectus qui est in potentia prius copulatur nobis quam intellectus agens.'[192] Aliquando vero videtur dicere contrarium, scilicet quod intellectus agens prius nobis copulatur quam intellectus materialis. Nam dicit in fine 18 commenti quod 'intellectus qui dicitur abstrahere intellectum et creare eum necesse est ut praecedat in nobis intellectum qui est recipere eum'.[193]

136. Propter quod notandum quod intellectus materialis copulatur nobis secundum eius sententiam tripliciter. Primo per naturam, de qua copulatione dicit 20 commento parum post medium: 'Et forte innuit intellectum in sua prima continuatione quae est per naturam.'[194] Et ista copulatio fit in primo instanti generationis hominis. Nam ex quo prima perfectio hominis est intellectus materialis per ipsum, in 5 commento,[195] et per perfectionem illam distinguitur ab omnibus aliis animalibus, ut dicit 1 commento,[196] sequitur quod per hanc copulationem primo fit aliquid et ponitur in specie hominis. Secunda copulatio intellectus materialis est nobiscum per phantasmata, secundum quam dicitur intellectus speculativus. Ta-

---

1 huiusmodi] istius T || eius] quod *add.* T   3 vel] nihil P || aliud] illud T || et *om.* T   5 igni] igitur T   6 humanum] semper *add.* T   8 comburere] agere P   9 igni] igitur T || combustionis] calefactionis P   10 effectiva . . . se] per se effectiva T   11 Socrate] corpore Socratis T || est . . . copulationis] illius copulationis est T   14 est *om.* T   14–15 de . . . ea] quod de ista copulatione varie loquitur Commentator T   15 ea] *lectio incerta* P   16 copulatur] copulari P || intellectus agens] intellectum agentem P || patet] ex *add.* T   17 nostram opinionem] *inv.* T   18 prius] primum P   20 copulatur] copuletur T   21 creare] causare T   21–22 praecedat . . . nobis] in nobis praecedat T   25 innuit intellectum] *inv.* T   26–27 generationis] generationum (*lectio incerta*) P   29 dicit] in *add.* T || fit] sit T   30 est] fit T   31 nobiscum] nobis T

extremes. Concerning the efficient cause of this sort of conjoining, I believe that he would say that it does not have an efficient cause except by accident. For just as fire, as far as fire itself is concerned, would always burn—but that it does not now burn this or that combustible and later it does, there is no efficient cause of this except by accident, namely the one who brings the combustible near fire—so in this case the material intellect naturally perfects the human body, so that for its part nothing is lacking that would prevent it from always perfecting any human body whatsoever. Since, however, it cannot perfect a body unless it exists in act, as in the other case the fire cannot burn up anything except after the combustible has been brought near it, therefore as the one that brings the combustible near the fire is the accidental cause of a new burning nor is there another essential efficient cause, so he who generates Socrates' body is the accidental cause of the conjoining of the material intellect with Socrates, nor should another essential efficient cause of this conjoining be given.

⟨ON THE CONJOINING OF THE INTELLECT WITH AN INDIVIDUAL⟩

135. Nevertheless it must be realized concerning this conjoining that the Commentator speaks about it in various ways. For sometimes he says that the intellect in potency, by which he understands the material intellect, is conjoined with us before the agent intellect, as is obvious from comment 20 long before the middle, where he says: 'According to our opinion and that of Themistius the intellect which is in potency is conjoined with us before the agent intellect is.'[192] Sometimes, however, he seems to say the contrary, namely that the agent intellect is conjoined with us before the material intellect is. For he says at the end of comment 18 that 'as to the intellect which is said to abstract the understood thing and to create it, it is necessary that it precedes in us the intellect which exists to receive it'.[193]

136. On account of this it must be noted that according to his stated opinion the material intellect is conjoined with us in three ways. First by nature, of which conjoining he says in comment 20 just after the middle: 'And perhaps he indicates the intellect in its first continuation which is by nature.'[194] And this conjoining comes to be in the first instant of the generation of man. For since the first perfection of man is the material intellect according to him, in comment 5,[195] and by that perfection man is distinguished from all other animals, as he says in comment 1,[196] it follows that by this conjoining something first comes to be and is placed in the species of man. The second conjoining of the material intellect with us is by phantasms, according to which conjoining it is called speculative intellect.

---

[192] Aver. *In DA* 3, t. c. 20, 447. 109–11.
[193] Ibid., t. c. 18, 440. 86–8.
[194] Ibid., t. c. 20, 450. 209–11.
[195] Ibid., t. c. 5, 392. 159.
[196] Ibid., t. c. 1, 379. 21–2.

lem enim colligationem naturalem posuit inter intellectum materialem et virtutem phantasticam quod virtus phantastica in actu nata est movere intellectum, licet non nisi lumine intellectus | agentis; intellectus etiam materialis in actu praesupponit virtutem phantasticam in actu. Similiter intentiones intellectae numerantur secundum numerum intentionum imaginatarum. Tertio copulatur intellectus materialis nobiscum in ratione obiecti intelligibilis. Prima eius copulatio est secundum esse, secunda et tertia secundum operationem, sed diversimode. Secunda enim operatio consistit in cognitione rerum materialium per intentiones abstractas a phantasmatibus, sed tertia in cognitione intellectus materialis non per abstractionem nec per intentionem mediam, sed sine medio, ita quod idem erit intellectus et intellectum et ratio intelligendi, in qua intellectione, ut supra dictum est,[197] posuit consistere felicitatem humanam. Item, per primam copulationem intellectus non distinguitur ex parte intellectus Socrates a Platone, licet a quacumque alia specie distinguatur per intellectum. Sed per secundam copulationem et tertiam Socrates distinguitur a Platone ex parte intellectus, quia et intellectus speculativus et adeptus in diversis suppositis hominis numerantur.

137. Similiter est intelligendum secundum sententiam Commentatoris quod intellectus agens copulatur nobis tripliciter. Copulatur enim primo intellectui materiali sicut proprium activum passivo. Causat enim et creat per ipsum in intellectu materiali intellecta speculabilia, per quae intellectus materialis fit in actu. Et in causando ista intellecta fit aliquo modo forma intellectus materialis. Secunda eius copulatio est in termino perfectionis motus intellectus in habitu, et tunc copulatur intellectui materiali ut eius forma perfecte et in actu. Tertia eius copulatio est cum intellectu materiali in ratione obiecti cogniti, quae copulatio est simul tempore cum copulatione eius secunda in ratione formae, tamen natura posterior est.

138. His intellectis dico quod comparando intellectum materialem, secundum quod est forma in nobis in actu, ad intellectum agentem uniformiter, in quantum copulatur intellectui materiali ut forma eius in actu, sic intelligit Commentator, 20 commento,[198] quod intellectus materialis prius copulatur nobis quam intellectus agens. Et hoc est certum, quia intellectus materialis copulatur nobis ut forma in principio generationis nostrae, sed intellectus agens non copulatur nobis ut forma in actu nisi in postremo, scilicet in termino perfectionis intellectus in habitu. Comparando autem intellectum materialem intellectui agenti quantum ad primam operationem utriusque, sic intelligit Commentator in 18 commento quod intellectus agens in nobis praecedit intellectum materialem.[199] Et hoc est certum.

---

2 licet] sed T   3 nisi] in *add.* P || etiam] autem T   4 intellectae] in actu *add.* T   6 nobiscum] in nobis T || eius] enim T   8 cognitione] agnitione P || intentiones abstractas] *inv.* T   9 tertia ... cognitione] in tertia copulatione T   12 intellectus] nobis *add.* P   15 et[1] *om.* T   19 sicut] sed P || passivo] et *add.* T || enim ... creat *om.* T   21 causando] creando P || materialis] *suppl. i.m.* P || eius] enim T   34 operationem] perfectionem T || in *om.* T   35 praecedit] in nobis *add.* P

For he posited such a natural binding together of the material intellect and the imaginative power that the imaginative power in act is apt by nature to move the intellect, although not without the light of the agent intellect. The material intellect in act also presupposes the imaginative power in act. Similarly, understood intentions are numbered according to the number of imagined intentions. Thirdly the material intellect is conjoined with us in so far as it is an intelligible object. Its first conjoining is according to being, its second and third according to operation, but in different ways. For the second operation consists in the cognition of material things by means of intentions abstracted from phantasms, but the third in the cognition of the material intellect not by means of abstraction nor by means of an intermediate intention, but without intermediate, so that the intellect and the understood thing and the means of understanding are the same, in which understanding, as was said above,[197] he claimed that human happiness consists. Again, by means of the first conjoining of the intellect Socrates is not distinguished on the part of the intellect from Plato, although he is distinguished by means of the intellect from any other species. But by means of the second and third conjoinings Socrates is distinguished from Plato on the part of the intellect, since both the speculative and the accomplished intellect are numbered in different supposits of man.

137. Similarly, according to the stated opinion of the Commentator, one must understand that the agent intellect is conjoined with us in three ways. For it is first conjoined with the material intellect just as the proper active principle with the passive. For according to him it causes and creates in the material intellect speculative understood things, by means of which the material intellect comes to be in act. And in causing these understood things the agent intellect comes to be in some way the form of the material intellect. Its second conjoining is at the final perfection of the motion of the intellect in habit, and then it is conjoined with the material intellect as its form perfectly and in act. Its third conjoining is with the material intellect in so far as it is a cognized object, which conjoining is temporally simultaneous with its second conjoining in so far as it is a form, yet by nature is later.

138. These things being understood, I say that by comparing the material intellect as a form in us in act with the agent intellect uniformly, as far as it is conjoined with the material intellect as its form in act, so the Commentator understands, comment 20,[198] that the material intellect is conjoined with us before the agent intellect is. And this is certain, because the material intellect is conjoined with us as a form at the beginning of our generation, but the agent intellect is not conjoined with us as a form in act except at the end, namely at the final perfection of the intellect in habit. However, by comparing the material intellect with the agent intellect in terms of the first operation of each, the Commentator understands thus in comment 18[199] that the agent intellect precedes in us the material intellect. And

---

[197] See above, para. 73.
[198] Aver. *In DA* 3, t. c. 20, 447. 109–11.
[199] Ibid., t. c. 18, 440. 86–8.

Nam cognitio intellectus materialis rerum materialium praesupponit naturaliter, etsi forte sint simul | tempore, abstractionem intentionum intellectarum per intellectum agentem a phantasmate. Si autem comparemus intellectum materialem ad agentem in quantum uterque copulatur nobis in ratione obiecti intelligibilis, dico quod omnia ista tria sunt simul tempore, scilicet copulatio intellectus agentis cum materiali in ratione formae in actu perfecto, cognitio intellectus materialis qua immediate se cognoscit, et cognitio intellectus materialis qua cognoscit intellectum agentem et omnes alias substantias immateriales. Primum tamen naturaliter praecedit secundum et tertium sicut causa effectum. Nam copulatio intellectus agentis cum materiali in ratione formae in actu est causa cognitionis intellectus materialis qua cognoscit substantias separatas, sicut Commentator dicit parum ante finem 36 commenti.[200] Secundum etiam praecedit tertium naturaliter sicut causa aliquo modo tertii. Nam per hoc quod intellectus materialis denudatus a potentia se ipsum cognoscit, substantias alias superiores cognoscit, sicut ceterae substantiae separatae, quae semper sunt | in actu, in cognoscendo se ipsas substantias superiores naturaliter cognoscunt, ut prius dictum est.[201]

⟨AD RATIONES PRINCIPALES⟩

139. Ad rationes principales ad primam partem[202] diceret Commentator concedendo conclusionem omnium rationum.

140. Ad illud in oppositum,[203] cum dicebatur quod Aristoteles non sensit quod intellectus materialis sit forma corporis, secundum quod eum exponit Commentator, diceret quod non est verum.

141. Et si dicatur quod Averroes dicit intellectum abstractum a corpore in 12 commento 1 libri *De anima* et multis aliis commentis,[204] dicit etiam quod non est virtus in corpore in 3 commento 3 libri *De anima* et multis aliis locis,[205] dicendum secundum sententiam suam quod per 'abstractum' non intelligit formam separatam secundum esse a corpore, sed per 'abstractum' intelligit formam non-mixtam cum materia, extensam ad extensionem materiae, sicut sunt formae eductae de potentia materiae. Similiter per virtutem in corpore intelligit virtutem corporalem corporali organo utentem in operando. Et ita sunt glossandae auctoritates Philosophi, cum dicit quod nullius corporis est actus et habitus secundum intentionem

---

1 naturaliter] materialiter T   2 tempore] per *add*. T   3–4 materialem . . . agentem] agentem ad materialem T   5 scilicet] sed (*lectio incerta*) T   6 actu perfecto] *inv*. T || cognitio] perfectio T   9 sicut] sed P   11 sicut] sed P || parum . . . finem] in fine T   12 sicut] sed P   14 substantias . . . cognoscit²] cognoscit etiam substantias alias superiores separatas T || sicut] aliud P || ceterae substantiae] substantiae aliae T   15 semper sunt] *inv*. T || ipsas] et sic *add*. T   16 prius . . . est] dictum est prius T   20 illud] aliud P; autem *add*. T   23 quod *om*. P   24 libri *om*. T || et] in *add*. T || commentis] communiter (*lectio incerta*) P || est *om*. T   25 in¹ *om*. T || libri *om*. T || *De anima om*. P || et] in *add*. T || multis] pluribus T || dicendum] quod *add*. T   31 quod] *om*. T

this is certain. For the cognition of the material intellect of material things naturally presupposes, even if perhaps they are temporally simultaneous, the abstraction of understood intentions by the agent intellect from a phantasm. But if we compare the material intellect with the agent as far as each is conjoined with us as an intelligible object, I say that all three of these are temporally simultaneous, namely the conjoining of the agent intellect with the material as a form in a perfect act, the cognition of the material intellect by which it immediately cognizes itself, and the cognition of the material intellect by which it cognizes the agent intellect and all other immaterial substances. However, the first naturally precedes the second and the third as cause precedes effect. For the conjoining of the agent intellect with the material as a form in act is a cause of the cognition of the material intellect by which it cognizes separate substances, as the Commentator says just before the end of comment 36.[200] The second also precedes the third naturally as the cause, in some way, of the third. For the material intellect cognizes other higher substances because of the fact that once it is stripped bare of potency it cognizes itself, just as the other separate substances, which always exist in act, in cognizing themselves naturally cognize the higher substances, as was said before.[201]

⟨IN ANSWER TO THE PRINCIPAL ARGUMENTS⟩

139. In answer to the principal arguments in favour of the first alternative,[202] the Commentator would concede the conclusion of all the arguments.

140. In answer to the argument to the contrary,[203] when it was said that Aristotle did not think that the material intellect is the form of the body, according to how the Commentator expounds him, he would reply that it is not true.

141. And if it is said that Averroes says that the intellect is abstracted from the body in comment 12 of *On the Soul* book 1 and in many other comments,[204] and also says that it is not a power in the body in comment 3 of *On the Soul* book 3 and in many other comments,[205] it must be replied according to his stated opinion that by 'abstracted' he does not understand a form separated from the body according to being, but by 'abstracted' he understands a form non-mixed with matter, extended with the extension of matter, such as are forms elicited from the potency of matter. Similarly, by a power in the body he understands a corporeal power that uses a corporeal organ in its operation. And so are the authorities of the Philosopher to be glossed, when he says that there is no body of which the intellect is the act and habit, according to the conception of the Commentator.

---

[200] Ibid., t. c. 36, 501. 623–9.
[201] See above, paras. 69–70.
[202] See above, paras. 1–3.
[203] See above, para. 4.
[204] Aver. *In DA* 1, t. c. 12, 18. 63–5. See also ibid., t. c. 13, 19. 30–1; 3, t. c. 7, 418. 41; t. c. 14, 432. 34; t. c. 19, 441. 19–21.
[205] Ibid. 3, t. c. 3, 382. 10–11. See also ibid., t. c. 2, 381. 26–32; t. c. 4, 383. 15, 384. 29; t. c. 5, 388. 39–40, 393. 193; t. c. 6, 413. 11; t. c. 14, 432. 120–1.

Commentatoris. Unde licet haec sit definitio universalis animae 'anima est actus corporis', tamen 'actus' seu 'perfectio', ut dicit Commentator, 5 commento 3 *De anima*,[206] aequivoce dicitur, hoc ⟨est⟩ per alium et alium modum, de intellectiva et aliis animabus. 'Et ideo dixit Aristoteles in definitione animae'—ut ipse dicit ibidem—'[quod] quae est prima perfectio ⟨corporis⟩ naturalis organici ⟨quod⟩ nondum est manifestum utrum per omnes virtutes perficitur corpus eodem modo, aut est ex eis ⟨aliqua⟩ per quam corpus non perficitur, aut si perficitur, erit alio modo'.[207]

⟨ARTICULUS 3: DE CONCORDIA ET DISCORDIA AVERROIS CUM ARISTOTELE⟩

142. De tertio principali, utrum opinio Commentatoris concordet in ista materia cum opinione Philosophi quantum ad aeternitatem intellectus materialis et eius unitatem numeralem in omnibus, dicunt aliqui doctores exponentes librum *De anima* quod opinio Commentatoris est erronea et ficticia quantum ad utrumque articulum nec concordans | opinioni Philosophi. Sed omnia dicta Philosophi de anima exponunt secundum verum intellectum quem catholici tenent de ipsa, scilicet quod ipsa incipit esse cum corpore per creationem, est tamen incorruptibilis, et quod numeratur ad numerationem corporum.

143. Pro ista opinione quantum ad primum articulum videtur facere una auctoritas Philosophi, 12 *Metaphysicae*, ubi videtur velle quod nulla forma praecedit compositum, tamen intellectus est posterior composito.[208] Ex qua auctoritate videtur quod Aristoteles posuit intellectivam incipere cum corpore, sed non per generationem, quia de foris venit, ut ipse dicit 16 *Animalium*.[209] Et cum hoc posuit quod non corrumpitur cum corpore et per consequens manet incorruptibilis, cum infra se non habeat materiam, quae est causa corruptionis.

144. Secundum articulum omnino abhorrent, loquendo etiam iuxta rationem naturalem, nec dicunt hoc sensisse Philosophum, sed contrarium. Posuit enim Philosophus quod anima intellectiva est actus primus corporis organici etc. quo vivimus, sentimus et intelligimus. Sed cuiuslibet perfectibilis est propria perfectio correspondens, et ideo intentio Philosophi fuit, ut dicunt, quod animae humanae

---

3 hoc *om.* T || est] *supplevimus*; *om.* PT || per alium] et (*lectio incerta*) passivum T 5 quod¹] *delevimus*; *scrips.* PT || corporis] *supplevimus cum Averroe*; *om.* PT || organici] organi T || quod²] *supplevimus*; *om.* PT 6 nondum est] non est dum P 7 aliqua] *supplevimus cum Averroe*; *om.* PT 12 opinione] intentione P || Philosophi] Aristotelis T || materialis] possibilis T 13 numeralem] naturalem P || omnibus] et *add.* T 14 ficticia] ficta P 16 verum] unum P 18 quod] ipsa *add.* T 19 una *om.* T 23 16] 6 T || *Animalium*] de animalibus T 24 incorruptibilis] incorruptibile P 25 causa] pars T 26 abhorrent] abhorrerent T || iuxta] secundum T 28 Philosophus *om.* T || primus *om.* T 29 perfectibilis] perficit communis P

Accordingly although this is the universal definition of the soul: 'the soul is the act of the body', nevertheless 'act' or 'perfection', as the Commentator says, *On the Soul* 3, comment 5,[206] is predicated equivocally, that is in different ways, of the intellectual soul and of other souls. 'And therefore Aristotle said in the definition of the soul'—as he says himself in the same place—'which is the first perfection of a natural organic body, that it is not yet manifest whether the body is perfected in the same way by all those powers, or there is some one among them by which the body is not perfected, or if it is perfected, it will be in another way.'[207]

⟨ARTICLE 3: ON THE AGREEMENT AND DISAGREEMENT OF AVERROES WITH ARISTOTLE⟩

142. On the third principal point, whether the opinion of the Commentator agrees in this matter with the opinion of the Philosopher regarding the eternity of the material intellect and its numerical unity in all men, some doctors who expound the book *On the Soul* say that the opinion of the Commentator is erroneous and fictitious regarding both articles, and that it does not agree with the opinion of the Philosopher. But they expound all the sayings of the Philosopher about the soul according to the true understanding which Catholics hold about it, namely that it begins to be with the body by creation, but that it is nevertheless incorruptible, and that it is numbered according to the numbering of bodies.

143. In favour of this opinion regarding the first article seems to be one authority of the Philosopher, *Metaphysics* 12, where he seems to want it to be the case that no form precedes the composite, although the intellect is posterior to the composite.[208] From this authority it seems that Aristotle posited that the intellectual soul begins with the body, but not by means of generation, since it comes from outside, as he says himself in *On the Animals* 16.[209] And with this he posited that it is not corrupted with the body and consequently remains incorruptible, since under itself it does not have matter, which is the cause of corruption.

144. The second article they entirely abhor, speaking also in accordance with natural reason, and they do not say that the Philosopher thought this, but the contrary. For the Philosopher posited that the intellectual soul is the first act of an organic body etc. by which we live, sense, and understand. But any perfectible thing has its own corresponding perfection, and therefore the conception of the Philosopher was, they say, that human souls are numbered according to the num-

---

[206] Ibid., t. c. 5, 405. 528–31.
[207] Ibid. 405. 531–6.
[208] Arist. *Metaph.* 12. 3, 1070ᵃ21–2.
[209] Arist. *GA* 2. 3, 736ᵇ27–8.

numerentur ad numerationem corporum. Contra istum articulum etiam adducunt multas rationes, quarum efficaciores sunt superius positae et solutae.[210]

145. Sed quod haec opinio non sit opinio Aristotelis, probo. Primo suppono secundum istos doctores quod in homine non sit alia forma substantialis quam intellectiva quae immediate perficit materiam. Istud concedent et supponunt ubique. Tunc arguo sicut Aristoteles in fine 7 *Metaphysicae*:[211] dissolutis A et B ab invicem, manet A et manet B, et non manet haec syllaba BA; ergo in hac syllaba BA est aliquid praeter B et praeter A quod nec est elementum huius syllabae BA nec est compositum ex elementis, sed forma ipsius. Sic arguo hic: dissolutis ab invicem intellectiva et materia, quam perficit, manet intellectiva per te, et manet materia, quam perficit, et non manet homo; ergo praeter intellectivam et materiam oportet ponere aliquid in homine quod nec sit elementum eius nec compositum ex elementis, sed forma ipsius hominis. Et idem sequitur si ponantur in homine intellectiva et forma mixti, dummodo concedatur quod corpus illud mixtum manet idem numero anima ab ipso separata. Ergo ex quo Philosophus posuit animam intellectivam esse formam corporis, sequitur ex processu suo, ut deductum est,[212] quod non posuit animam manere post separationem eius a corpore.

146. Ad hanc rationem respondent aliqui volentes sustinere opinionem praedictam quod non est simile in exemplo Philosophi et in proposito, quoniam in mixto, de quo arguit ibi Philosophus, et in hac syllaba BA elementa quae manent separata ab invicem omnia habent unum modum principiandi, scilicet causae materialis. Et ideo ibi praeter elementa ista oportet ponere in composito aliquod aliud principium formale. Sed sic non est in proposito, quoniam anima per essentiam est forma et actus, materia autem potentia, et ideo praeter haec non oportet ponere in composito | aliud quod habeat rationem formae.

147. Praeterea, posset dici quod haec ratio est aequaliter efficax contra Commentatorem, quia ipse ponit intellectum non solum manere ante compositum, sed ⟨etiam⟩ post.

148. Contra istam responsionem[213] primo sic: Priscianus in maiori volumine suo dicit quod vocalis se habet ut forma respectu consonantis,[214] et hoc non ob-

1 Contra] et ad T || istum] articulum *add. et del.* P || etiam *om.* T || adducunt] faciunt P 3 opinio¹] vera *add.* T || non ... opinio² *om. hom.* P || probo] probatio T 4 istos doctores] opinionem doctorum T || istos] auctores *add. et del.* P || sit] est P 4–5 substantialis ... intellectiva] ab intellectiva substantialis T 6 sicut] sed P || ab] ad T 7 haec syllaba *om.* T || hac syllaba *om.* T 8 B] A T || A] B T || BA² *om.* P 10 quam perficit *om.* T || te] se T 11 perfecit] perficiebat T || homo *om.* T || ergo] in homine *add.* P || materiam] corpus P 12 aliquid ... homine] in homine aliquid T || eius *om.* T 13 ponantur] ponatur T || homine] scilicet *add.* P 14 illud] idem P 15 numero] post *add.* P || anima ... separata] forma ab ipso separata, scilicet anima T || posuit] ponit P 16–17 esse ... animam *om.* T 22 ibi *om.* T || ista] ipsa T || aliud] ad P 23 essentiam] suam *add.* T 24 haec] *scripsimus*; hoc PT 25 aliud] aliquod aliud principium formale T 27 ante] post P 28 etiam] *supplevimus*; *om.* PT || post] ante P 29 maiori] magno P 30 suo *om.* T || forma] na *add. et del.* P || respectu] cons *add. et del.* P 30–94.1 obstante] absolute P

bering of bodies. Against this article they also adduce many arguments, of which the more effective are posited and resolved above.[210]

145. But I prove that this opinion is not the opinion of Aristotle. First I assume according to these doctors that in man there is not a substantial form other than the intellectual soul which immediately perfects matter. This they concede and assume everywhere. Then I argue just as Aristotle does at the end of *Metaphysics* 7:[211] when A and B are dissolved from each other, A remains and B remains, and this syllable BA does not remain; therefore in this syllable BA there is something besides B and besides A which is neither an element of this syllable BA nor a composite of elements, but the form of it. So I argue here: when the intellectual soul and matter, which it perfects, are dissolved from each other, the intellectual soul remains, according to you, and the matter, which it perfected, remains, and man does not remain; therefore besides the intellectual soul and matter it is necessary to posit something in man which is neither an element of him nor a composite of elements, but the form of man himself. And the same conclusion follows if the intellectual soul and the form of the mixed body are posited in man, as long as it is conceded that that mixed body remains numerically the same when the soul is separated from it. Therefore since the Philosopher posited that the intellectual soul is the form of the body, it follows from his chain of reasoning, as has been deduced,[212] that he did not posit that the soul remains after its separation from the body.

146. Some people wanting to maintain the opinion previously stated respond to this argument that there is no point of similarity in the example of the Philosopher and in the proposed case, since in the mixed body, about which the Philosopher argued there, and in this syllable BA the elements which remain, after they have been separated from each other, all have one way of being a principle, namely that of the material cause. And therefore besides these elements there it is required to posit some other formal principle in the composite. But it is not so in the proposed case, since the soul is essentially form and act, but matter is potency, and therefore besides these it is not required to posit in the composite anything else which would serve as form.

147. Moreover, it could be said that this argument is equally effective against the Commentator, since he posits that the intellect remains not only before the composite, but also after it.

148. Against this response[213] I argue first as follows: Priscian in his larger volume says that a vowel relates as a form to a consonant,[214] and notwithstanding

---

[210] See above, paras. 108–11, 124–34.
[211] Arist. *Metaph.* 7. 17, 1041^{b}12–33.
[212] See above, para. 145.
[213] See above, para. 146.
[214] Priscian, *Gramm.* 1. 17–18, p. 13.

stante vult Philosophus quod, quia dissolutis ab invicem B et A in hac syllaba BA B et A possunt manere separata, propter hoc oportet ponere aliud et aliud principium formale in hac syllaba. Ergo eodem modo in proposito non obstante quod in homine anima sit actus, et materia potentia.

149. Praeterea, arguo istud per rationem non innitendo auctoritati Philosophi sic: manente toto quod entitatem rei constituit, manet res quae constituitur. Nam quod res aliqua | non manet hoc non potest esse nisi propter defectum alicuius principii constitutivi. Sed intellectiva et materia manentibus non manet homo secundum hanc opinionem. Ergo aliquod principium hominis tertium deficit.

150. Dicitur huic quod non requiritur nisi unio, et ipsa non est alia res a principiis hominis.

151. Contra: materia hominis et intellectiva, quae fuit eius forma, manent homine corrupto. Illa unio, cum sit res vera—aliter ab ipsa homo in suo esse non dependeret—non manet. Ergo haec unio est res alia a principiis hominis. Sic arguit Philosophus, 1 *Physicorum*, ad probandum quod privatio sit aliud a materia.[215]

152. Item, si unio necessario requiratur ad constitutionem hominis, quae est res alia, ut probatum est,[216] ab intellectiva et materia hominis, quaero an igitur sit principium intrinsecum vel sit extrinsecum concomitans. Non potest dari quod sit extrinsecum, quoniam cum necessario requiratur ad esse hominis, si esset extrinsecum, consequeretur aliquid intrinsecum homini tamquam eius causam ad quam consequitur. Omne enim posterius aliquo, necessario tamen consequens vel concomitans illud prius, habet in ipso priori causam ratione cuius necessario consequitur. Super ista enim regula fundatur natura demonstrationis 'propter quid'. Ergo, si illa unio sit extrinsecum homini et per consequens posterius quidditate hominis, necesse erit dare causam priorem in homine quare illa unio necessario consequitur hominem. Sed causa quare consequitur non potest dici materia hominis per se nec intellectiva per se, quia ista manet quando non est illa unio. Nec potest dici quod intellectiva unita materiae sit causa illius unionis. Nam tunc quaeram de illa unione quam consequitur an sit intrinsecum homini vel extrinsecum. Si detur intrinsecum, habeo propositum, quod praeter intellectivam et materiam est dare tertium principium intrinsecum homini, quod ipsi negant. Si extrinse-

---

1–2 dissolutis ... manere] dissoluto BA manet B et A T   2 separata] quod *add.* P || aliud[1] ... aliud[2]] sicut T   4 in homine *om.* T || actus] et potentia et *add. et del.* P || materia] corpus T; et *add.* P   5 non ... Philosophi *om.* T || innitendo] *corr. s.l. ex* intendo P   8 constitutivi] constitutum P; illius *add.* T || Sed *om.* T || homo] *scripsimus*; hoc PT   9 hominis *om.* T   10 huic] ad T   13 ab ... esse] homo in suo esse ab ipsa T   14 dependeret] dependet P   15 materia] et forma *add.* T   17 ut ... hominis] ab intellectiva et materia hominis ut probatum est T || igitur *om.* T   18 sit[1]] *scripsimus; om.* P; sicut T || sit[2] *om.* T   19 requiratur] requiritur P   20 homini] hominis T   21 aliquo] *suppl. i.m.* P   22 concomitans] commutans P   23 ista enim] *inv.* T   24 homini *om.* T   26 consequitur[1]] subsequitur T || quare] quam P   26–27 materia ... se[1]] per se materia hominis T   28 intellectiva] quando est *add.* T   29 intrinsecum] extrinsecum T || homini *om.* T || extrinsecum] intrinsecum T   31–96.1 extrinsecum] homini *add.* T

this the Philosopher wants it that, since after B and A have been dissolved from each other in this syllable BA B and A can remain separated, on account of this it is required to posit something else and some other formal principle in this syllable. Therefore in the same way in the proposed case, notwithstanding that in man the soul is act and matter is potency.

149. Moreover, I argue this by an argument, without relying on the authority of the Philosopher, in this way: when everything that constitutes the entity of a thing remains, the thing which is constituted remains. For as to the fact that some thing does not remain, this cannot be except because of a defect of some constitutive principle. But when the intellectual soul and matter remain, man does not remain, according to this opinion. Therefore some third principle of man is missing.

150. It is said in reply to this argument that nothing is required except union, and this is not a thing other than the principles of man.

151. To the contrary: the matter of man and the intellectual soul, which was his form, remain when man is corrupted. That union, since it is a real thing—otherwise man would not depend on it in his being—does not remain. Therefore this union is a thing other than the principles of man. So the Philosopher argues in *Physics* 1 in order to prove that privation is something other than matter.[215]

152. Again, if union were necessarily required for the constitution of man—and union is, as has been proved,[216] something other than the intellectual soul and the matter of man—I ask whether it is therefore an intrinsic principle or an extrinsic, concomitant one. It cannot be replied that it is extrinsic, since as it is necessarily required for the being of man, if it were extrinsic, it would follow from something intrinsic to man just as if from the cause from which it follows. For everything posterior to something but necessarily consequent or concomitant to that prior thing has in that prior thing the cause by virtue of which it necessarily follows. For on this rule is founded the nature of the demonstration of the reason why. Therefore, if that union were extrinsic to man and consequently posterior to the quiddity of man, it would be necessary to stipulate a prior cause in man in order to explain why that union necessarily follows man. But neither the matter of man by itself nor the intellectual soul by itself can be said to be the cause of this, since each of these remains when that union does not exist. Nor can it be said that the intellectual soul united with matter is the cause of that union. For then I shall ask concerning that union from which it follows whether it is intrinsic to man or extrinsic. If it is replied that it is intrinsic, I have my proposed conclusion, that besides the intellectual soul and matter one must stipulate a third principle intrinsic to man, which they deny. If it is replied that it is extrinsic, I shall ask concerning

---

[215] Arist. *Phys.* 1. 7, 190ª17–21.
[216] See above, para. 151.

cum, quaeram de illa unione, sicut de prima, quid est illud in quidditate hominis quod ipsa consequitur. Vel igitur oportebit dare aliam unionem intrinsecam vel erit processus in infinitum in unionibus | realibus. Si ergo concedatur quod haec unio sit intrinsecum quidditati hominis, sequitur primo contra illos quod in homine sit aliud principium constitutivum eius quidditatis ab intellectiva et materia, quod ipsi negant. Sequitur etiam quod intellectiva in compositione hominis se habet ut elementum seu pars materialis quae est in potentia ad istam unionem, et quod unio sit formalissimum principium in homine. Ex quo sequitur ulterius quod quidditas hominis includit formalissime formam respectivam, non absolutam. Et omnia ista sequuntur quia ponitur quod intellectiva est forma hominis, et cum hoc, quod manet eadem numero et materia eius homine corrupto. In aliis enim formis, quae corrumpuntur cum composito, nihil valeret argumentum, quia ibi diceretur quod forma per essentiam est unita materiae, ita quod sua unio cum materia vel inhaerentia materiae non est alia res ab ipsa forma, quod in proposito dici non potest, ut probatum est.[217]

153. Aliter dicitur quod Philosophus intendit probare ibi quod in composito est dare aliquid praeter elementa quae manent. Illud tertium tamen non erit principium constituens, sed erit ipsum totum resultans ex principiis vel forma totius, puta quod in homine praeter intellectivam et corpus oportet ponere humanitatem, quae nec est intellectiva praecise nec materia, sed tertium constitutum ex his. Et hoc bene concederet Philosophus.

154. Sed istud nihil valet quoniam, ut patet ibi de intentione Philosophi,[218] Commentatoris[219] et aliorum expositorum, illud tertium nec erit elementum nec ex elementis, et per consequens per illud tertium nec intelligit totum compositum nec formam totius, sed formam quae est pars totius et constituens totum.

155. Ad aliud,[220] cum dicitur quod haec ratio est aequaliter contra sententiam Commentatoris, dico quod non. Primo quia Commentator non posuit intellectum materialem esse formam adaequatam et propriam alicuius individui, sed naturae specificae, quatenus est incorruptibilis in successione suppositorum. Unde bene concederet Commentator quod, si destruerentur omnia corpora humana, intellectus materialis esse non posset. Sed opinio catholica ponit quod haec anima est perfectio huius perfectibilis primo et adaequata, et tamen quod potest subsistere isto corpore corrupto.

156. Praeterea, supposita responsione quae prius data est[221] quod non est simile

---

2 ipsa] *scripsimus*; ipsum PT || Vel *om.* T || igitur] quod P || dare] vel *add.* T 3 haec] ista T 4 sit] aliquid *add.* T || quidditati] quidditatis P 5 aliud] eius *add.* T || constitutivum] quidditativum T || ab ... materia] a materia et intellectiva T 10 ista *om.* T 13 est] esset P || sua] *aliquid illegibile add. et del.* P || unio] unitas T 14 forma *om.* T 17 aliquid] aliquod T 20 intellectiva] per se *add.* T || praecise ... materia] nec materia praecise T 22 Philosophi] et *add.* T 23 expositorum] est quod *add.* T || erit] est T 34 responsione] ratione P

that union, just as I did concerning the first, what is that in the quiddity of man from which it follows. Therefore, either it will be necessary to give some other intrinsic union, or there will be an infinite regress in real unions. Therefore if it is conceded that this union is intrinsic to the quiddity of man, it follows first against those teachers that in man there is a principle constitutive of his quiddity other than the intellectual soul and matter, which they deny. It also follows that the intellectual soul in the composition of man has the role of an element or a material part which is in potency to this union, and that the union is the most formal principle in man. From this it further follows that the quiddity of man includes most formally a relational form, not an absolute one. And all these things follow because it is posited that the intellectual soul is the form of man, and with this, that it remains the same in number as does its matter when man is corrupted. For in the case of other forms, which are corrupted with the composite, the argument would not be valid, since there it would be said that the form by its essence is united with matter, so that its union with matter or inherence in matter is not a thing other than the form itself, which in the proposed case cannot be said, as has been proved.[217]

153. Otherwise it is said that the Philosopher intends to prove there that in a composite one must stipulate something besides the elements which remain. This third thing, however, will not be a constituent principle, but will be the whole itself resulting from the principles or the form of the whole, namely that in man besides the intellectual soul and the body it is required to posit humanity, which is neither the intellectual soul precisely nor matter, but a third thing constituted from these. And the Philosopher would certainly concede this.

154. But this is not valid since, as is obvious there in accord with the conception of the Philosopher,[218] of the Commentator,[219] and of other interpreters, this third thing will not be an element nor made up of elements, and consequently by this third thing he understands neither the whole composite nor the form of the whole, but a form which is a part of the whole and which constitutes the whole.

155. In answer to another argument,[220] when it is said that this argument is equally against the stated opinion of the Commentator, I reply that this is not the case. First because the Commentator did not posit that the material intellect is a form corresponding to and proper to some individual, but to a specific nature, to the extent that it is incorruptible in the succession of supposits. Accordingly the Commentator would certainly concede that, if all human bodies were destroyed, the material intellect could not exist. But Catholic opinion posits that this soul is the perfection of this perfectible body first and corresponding to it, and nevertheless that it can subsist when this body is corrupted.

156. Moreover, if one assumes the response which was previously given,[221]

---
[217] See above, ibid.
[218] Arist. *Metaph.* 7. 17, 1041^{b}19–27.
[219] Aver. *In Metaph.* 7, t. c. 60, fols. 208^{va}H–209^{ra}C.
[220] See above, para. 147.
[221] See above, para. 146.

de exemplis Philosophi ubi principia quae manent separata sunt omnia principia materialia, et ideo oportet dare aliud principium formale, non sic in homine est de principiis eius quae manent separata. Sic ergo exclusa auctoritate responderet Commentator ad rationem satis colorate et faciliter concedendo conclusionem, scilicet quod in homine necesse est dare aliquod tertium principium aliud a materia prima et intellectiva, quod est intrinsecum quidditati hominis. Posuit | enim Commentator in homine praeter materiam primam et intellectum materialem animam sensitivam perfectissimam, quam posuit formam aliam substantialem ab intellectu materiali et distinctam specie a sensitiva cuiuslibet bruti, ut patet in fine 20 commenti, ut supra allegatum est.[222] Illa autem sensitiva formale est respectu materiae, et si sit quasi materiale respectu intellectus materialis, qui est sua ultima perfectio. Unde non sequitur hic, sicut in argumento Philosophi,[223] quod illud tertium sit forma et perfectio ultima, sicut in exemplis Philosophi. Et causa dicta est,[224] quia ibi omnia quae ponuntur separatim existere se habent in uno genere principiandi, scilicet materiae. Non sic hic, ut dictum est.

157. Iterum, haec opinio quantum ad hoc quod ponit intellectum materialem incipere esse et tamen esse incorruptibilem ex parte post, | nullo modo stat cum opinione Philosophi. Nam ex intentione probat Philosophus, 1 *Caeli et mundi*, quod omne sempiternum ex parte post est sempiternum ex parte ante et econverso.[225]

158. Praeterea, non posuit intellectivam produci per generationem, ut isti concedunt, sed ab extra venire, non per creationem, quia principium apud eum fuit quod ex nihilo nihil fit, ergo aeternaliter praecessit.

159. Iterum, cum Philosophus posuit resurrectionem hominum in identitate numerali impossibilem, posito cum hoc quod homo fuerit ab aeterno, ut posuit Philosophus, sequeretur quod animae infinitae frustrarentur a suis finibus per tempus infinitum et continue naturaliter appeterent quod impossibile esset eas attingere, scilicet unionem earum ad corpora, ad quam naturaliter inclinantur secundum catholicos, quam viam isti doctores imponunt Philosopho.

160. Aliter arguitur quod haec non est opinio Philosophi, quia Philosophus non posuit Deum immediate causare nisi unum effectum et nihil immediate causare in inferioribus, sed mediantibus causis mediis.

161. Sed est istud dubium, quia in fine libelli *De fortuna* videtur ex verbis Phi-

1 sunt omnia] *inv.* T   2 est *om.* T   3 Sic] *suppl. i.m.* P || responderet] respondet P   5 necesse] necessario T || aliud *om.* P   6 quidditati] quidditatis P   8 formam aliam] *inv.* T   9 distinctam] distincta P   10 formale est] *inv.* T   11 quasi *om.* T || qui] quae P || sua] *lectio incerta* T   12 argumento] articulo P   13 sicut] sed P || dicta est] *inv.* T   14 principiandi] percipiendi P   17 incipere *om.* T || incorruptibilem] in materialem T   18–19 Caeli . . . mundi] de caelo et mundo T   23 nihil fit] *inv.* T   24 posuit] posuerit T || resurrectionem] rationem P   25 hoc] homo T   26 sequeretur] sequitur T || tempus] tempore P   27 naturaliter appeterent] *inv.* T   28 corpora] corpus P   29 imponunt] *corr. s.l. ex* proponunt P   31 causare[2]] insunt P || in] istis *add.* T   33 est istud] *inv.* T

that the case of man is not similar to the examples of the Philosopher where the principles which remain separate are all material principles, and it is therefore necessary to stipulate another formal principle, it is not so in man concerning his principles which remain separate. So, therefore, the Philosopher's authority being left aside, the Commentator would reply to the argument in a sufficiently forceful way and easily conceding the conclusion, namely that in man it is necessary to stipulate some third principle other than prime matter and the intellectual soul, that is intrinsic to the quiddity of man. For the Commentator posited in man besides prime matter and the material intellect a most perfect sensitive soul, which he posited to be a substantial form other than the material intellect and distinct in species from the sensitive soul of any brute, as is obvious at the end of comment 20, as was alleged above.[222] But that sensitive soul is a formal principle with respect to matter, even if it is in a sort of way material with respect to the material intellect, which is its ultimate perfection. Accordingly it does not follow in this case, as in the argument of the Philosopher,[223] that this third thing is a form and an ultimate perfection, as in the examples of the Philosopher. And the reason for this has been mentioned,[224] namely, because there all things which are posited to exist separately are related to each other in a single way of being a principle, namely that of matter. Not so in this case, as has been said.

157. Again, this opinion, to the extent that it posits that the material intellect begins to be and nevertheless is incorruptible into the future, is in no way compatible with the opinion of the Philosopher. For the Philosopher explicitly proves, *On the Heavens* 1, that everything eternal into the future is eternal into the past, and conversely.[225]

158. Moreover, he did not posit that the intellectual soul is produced by generation, as these people concede, but that it comes from outside, but not by creation, since it was a principle for him that nothing comes to be from nothing; therefore the intellectual soul from eternity preceded the composite.

159. Again, since the Philosopher posited that man's resurrection in numerical identity is impossible, and since it is posited with this that man has existed from eternity, as the Philosopher posited, it would follow that infinite souls would be frustrated from their goals for an infinite time and would endlessly naturally desire what it would be impossible for them to attain, namely their union with bodies, to which they are naturally inclined according to Catholics, and these doctors attribute this manner of arguing to the Philosopher.

160. Otherwise it is argued that this is not the opinion of the Philosopher, since the Philosopher did not posit that God immediately causes more than one effect and that he causes nothing immediately in lower things, except by means of intermediate causes.

161. But this is doubtful, since at the end of the little book *On Fortune* it seems

---

[222] See above, para. 83.
[223] See above, para. 145.
[224] See above, para. 146.
[225] Arist. *De caelo*, 1. 12, 281^{b}20–283^{b}33.

losophi quod bona fortuna sit a Deo immediate, homine nihil ad hoc per consilium rationis coagente.[226] Nec etiam corpora caelestia agunt ad hoc, quoniam non habent causalitatem super intellectum et actus eius. Similiter 6 *Ethicorum* approbat Philosophus dictum Agathon dicentis quod solo hoc privatur Deus: ingenita facere quae utique facta sunt.[227] Ergo Deus potest producere formam intellectivam, sed nullum agens naturale potest attingere intellectivam nostram ipsam inducendo, sed dispositive tantum, secundum eos qui tenent opinionem praedictam. Ergo Deus immediate inducit animam intellectivam vel inducere | potest, et hoc ex intentione Philosophi.

162. Alii autem concordant cum primis in secundo articulo dicentes quod non fuit de intentione Aristotelis quod intellectus unus numero sit in omnibus, sed discordant a primis et etiam a Commentatore in primo articulo. Dicunt enim quod Aristoteles fuit quasi perplexus in hac materia, et considerando principia generalia quibus utebatur magis videtur esse intentionis suae quod non sit incorruptibilis quam quod sit incorruptibilis.

163. Ad istam conclusionem probandam quattuor rationes adducunt, quarum prima est de 7 *Metaphysicae*, quae tacta est contra primam opinionem.[228]

164. Secunda est quod secundum principia Philosophi 'omne quod incipit esse desinit esse' in 1 *Caeli et mundi*, quae similiter prius posita est.[229]

165. Tertia ratio est, quia Philosophus in 1 *De anima* dicit de intellectu quod vel est phantasia vel non est sine phantasia,[230] et videtur velle quod quaecumque pars detur, non concludit ipsum esse sine corpore.

166. Quarta ratio superius tacta est[231] quod tales animae infinitae in perpetuo separarentur et starent separatae a suis perfectibilibus.

167. Et si arguitur contra istos per hoc quod Philosophus dicit, 2 *De anima*, quod intellectus separatur ab aliis sicut perpetuum a corruptibili,[232] dicunt quod hoc dicit pro quanto non utitur organo corporali, non quia habet operationem perpetuam.

168. Sed haec expositio, licet a multis data fuerit, valde tamen extorta est, scilicet quod Philosophus vocaret aliquid incorruptibile et sempiternum propter

1 quod . . . fortuna *om.* T || immediate] in *add.* T   2 rationis] rationum T   3 et] nec P   4 dicentis] dicentem T || solo hoc] *inv.* T   6 attingere] intelligere P   8 intellectivam] intellectiva P   11 Aristotelis] Philosophi T   13 considerando] *lectio incerta* T   14 utebatur] utebantur T || esse *om.* T   15 incorruptibilis] corruptibilis T   16 probandam] *suppl. i.m.* P || quattuor] cum *add. et del.* P || adducunt] faciunt P   17 primam] aliam P   18 quod¹] quae P   19 in *om.* T || est] sunt P   20 ratio est *om.* T || Philosophus . . . dicit] 1 De anima dicit Philosophus T   21 videtur velle] verisimile T || quod] quia T   23 ratio *om.* T || superius . . . est] est superius tacta scilicet T || tales *om.* T || animae infinitae] *inv.* T || in *om.* T   24 perfectibilibus] perfectionibus T   25 arguitur] arguatur T || per . . . quod] quia T   27 dicit] pro tanto *add.* T   29 valde tamen] *inv.* T || extorta] exorta P   30 Philosophus . . . aliquid] aliquid Philosophus vocaret T || incorruptibile] in se corruptibile T || et *om.* T || sempiternum] vel perpetuum *add.* T

from the words of the Philosopher that good fortune is immediately from God, with man contributing nothing to this by the counsel of reason.[226] The celestial bodies, too, do not do anything to cause this, since they do not have causality over the intellect and its acts. Similarly, in *Ethics* 6 the Philosopher approves the claim of Agathon when he says that God is deprived only of this: to undo things that have already happened.[227] Therefore God can produce an intellectual form, but no natural agent can attain our intellectual soul by inducing it, but only by producing a disposition to it, according to those who hold the opinion previously stated. Therefore God immediately induces the intellectual soul or can induce it, and this is in accord with the conception of the Philosopher.

162. Others, however, agree with the first ones in the second article and say that it was not the conception of Aristotle that the intellect is numerically one in all men, but they disagree with the first ones and also with the Commentator in the first article. For they say that Aristotle was as it were perplexed in this matter, and considering the general principles which he used it seems to be more his conception that it is not incorruptible than that it is incorruptible.

163. In order to prove this conclusion they adduce four arguments, of which the first is from *Metaphysics* 7, which was touched on when I argued against the first opinion.[228]

164. The second is that according to the principles of the Philosopher 'everything which begins to be ceases to be' in *On the Heavens* 1, which is likewise posited earlier.[229]

165. The third argument is that the Philosopher in *On the Soul* 1 says concerning the intellect that either it is imagination or it does not exist without imagination,[230] and he seems to want to imply that whichever alternative is chosen, it does not lead to the conclusion that it exists without body.

166. The fourth argument was touched on above,[231] that such infinite souls would be separated perpetually and would remain separate from their perfectible things.

167. And if it is argued against these people by means of that which the Philosopher says, *On the Soul* 2, that the intellect is separated from the other things just as a perpetual thing from a corruptible,[232] they reply that he says this inasmuch as the intellect does not use a bodily organ, not because it has perpetual operation.

168. But this exposition, although it has been given by many people, is nevertheless very forced, namely that the Philosopher would call anything incorruptible

---

[226] Arist. *EE* 7. 14, 1248^{b}2–4.
[227] Arist. *NE* 6. 2, 1139^{b}9–11.
[228] See above, para. 145.
[229] See above, para. 157.
[230] Arist. *DA* 1. 1, 403^{a}8–10.
[231] See above, para. 159.
[232] Arist. *DA* 2. 2, 413^{b}24–7.

hoc quod non utitur organo. Similiter, si intellectiva sit forma corruptibilis secundum intentionem Aristotelis, ergo secundum intentionem eius erit generabilis, quod concedunt, licet per accidens, nec aliter corrumpitur alia forma, ut patet ex 7 *Metaphysicae*.²³³ Sed forma quae est generabilis et corruptibilis in materia est forma materialis, secundum intentionem Aristotelis, quia forma ex hoc quod transmutabilis, est materialis. Transmutatio enim omnis est ratione materiae. Ulterius omnis forma sic materialis extenditur ad extensionem materiae. Et hoc secundum intentionem Aristotelis probo: Aristoteles in fine 8 *Physicorum* probat quod virtus in magnitudine non potest movere per tempus infinitum.²³⁴ Et in sua demonstratione supponit quod omnis virtus in corpore dividitur sic quod totius est maior virtus quam partis, et super hoc fundatur sua demonstratio. Ergo cum per istos intellectiva sit forma corporis et ex corpore dependens, sequitur secundum intentionem Aristotelis ex hoc quod sit extensa. Aliter enim responderetur faciliter ad demonstrationem Philosophi dicendo quod non oportet, licet virtus movens per tempus infinitum sit in corpore sicut forma dependens ex corpore et perficiens ipsum, quod propter hoc extendatur, ita quod maior virtus sit in toto quam in parte, et sic demonstratio eius nulla.

169. Si autem concedatur conclusio quod intellectiva sit extensa in nobis per accidens saltem, nec aliter sensitiva extenditur, sequitur quod | potentia eius sit extensa, quia per istos potentia animae non est alia res ab eius substantia. Sed omnis potentia extensa sive extendatur per totum corpus, ut tactus, sive per partem solum ut alii quattuor sensus, est organica. Ergo intellectus materialis est potentia organica, quod ipsi negant.

170. Iterum, si esset extensa, non esset conversiva supra se. Consequentia et falsitas consequentis patent | per Proclum.²³⁵

171. Iterum, omnis forma extensa et corporalis per consequens vel est forma complexionalis vel superaddita complexioni per Philosophum, 3 *De anima*.²³⁶ Sed intellectiva non est forma complexionalis, quia sic causaretur ex quattuor elementis concurrentibus ad invicem, quod non est verum ⟨etiam⟩ de anima sensitiva, nec est superaddita complexioni, quia sic esset organica.

172. Praeterea, quod secundum intentionem Philosophi intellectus materialis sit incorruptibilis probatur ex 3 *De anima*, ubi quaerit quare intellectus noster non reminiscitur post mortem, in qua quaestione supponit quod anima manet corrupto

---

1 forma] corporis *add. et del.* P   2 erit generabilis] generatio P   3 licet] et P || corrumpitur... forma] corrumpuntur aliae formae T || ex *om.* T   5–8 quia... Aristotelis] *om. hom. et* 8 Physicorum *add.* T   6 Ulterius] *lectio incerta* P   8 probo] probatio T   10 corpore] magnitudine T   11 cum] *scripsimus*; *om.* T; et P   12 sequitur] quod *add. et del.* P   13 ex] ad P   14 licet] sit *add.* T   19 aliter sensitiva] *inv.* T   20 potentia... substantia] essentia animae non differt a potentia T   21 ut] nec P || per² *om.* P   22 solum *om.* T || materialis *om.* T   23 organica] organicus (*lectio incerta*) P   25 Proclum] processum P   26 corporalis... consequens] per consequens corporalis T   29 etiam] *supplevimus*; *om.* PT   31 quod *om.* P   32 quare] quia T

and eternal for the reason that it does not use an organ. Similarly, if the intellectual soul were a corruptible form according to the conception of Aristotle, therefore according to his conception it would be generable, which they concede, although by accident, nor is any other form corrupted in a different way, as is obvious from *Metaphysics* 7.[233] But a form which is generable and corruptible in matter is a material form, according to the conception of Aristotle, because a form is material because of the fact that it is transmutable. For all transmutation is because of matter. Furthermore, every form that is material in this way is extended with the extension of matter. And I prove this according to the conception of Aristotle: Aristotle at the end of *Physics* 8 proves that a power existing in magnitude cannot move for an infinite time.[234] And in his demonstration he assumes that every power in a body is divided in such a way that the whole has a greater power than a part, and his demonstration is founded on this basis. Therefore since according to them the intellectual soul is a form of the body and dependent on the body, it follows from this, according to the conception of Aristotle, that it is extended. For otherwise one could easily respond to the Philosopher's demonstration by saying that it is not required, although a power moving for an infinite time is in a body as a form dependent on a body and perfecting it, that because of this it is extended, so that there is a greater power in the whole than in a part, and so his demonstration would be null.

169. But if the conclusion is conceded that the intellectual soul is extended in us, at least by accident, and that the sensitive soul is extended in the same way, it follows that its potency would be extended, because according to them a power of the soul is not something other than its substance. But every extended power, whether it is extended throughout the whole body, as touch is, or through a part only, as are the other four senses, is organic. Therefore the material intellect is an organic power, which they deny.

170. Again, if it were extended, it would not be able to turn towards itself. The consequence and the falsity of the consequent are obvious according to Proclus.[235]

171. Again, every form that is extended and consequently corporeal is either a complexional form or superadded to the complexion according to the Philosopher, *On the Soul* 3.[236] But the intellectual soul is not a complexional form, because in that case it would be caused by the four elements concurring with each other, which is not true even of the sensitive soul, nor is it superadded to the complexion, because in that case it would be organic.

172. Moreover, that according to the conception of the Philosopher the material intellect is incorruptible is proved from *On the Soul* 3, where he asks why our intellect does not remember after death, in which question he assumes that the soul remains after the body is corrupted, otherwise there would be no doubt.

---

[233] Arist. *Metaph.* 7. 8, 1033^{a}24–^{b}26.
[234] Arist. *Phys.* 8. 10, 266^{a}10–^{b}6.
[235] Proclus, *Elem. theol.*, prop. 15, 'Omne quod ad se ipsum conversivum est incorporeum est' (p. 11); prop. 83, 'Omne sui ipsius cognitivum ad se ipsum omniquaque conversivum est' (pp. 43–4).
[236] Arist. *DA* 3. 4, 429^{a}24–7; cf. Aver. *In DA* 3, t. c. 6, 414. 16–23.

corpore, aliter nulla esset dubitatio. Et respondet quare hoc est, quia intellectus non intelligit sine phantasmate, quod non manet post mortem.[237]

173. Item, 16 *De animalibus*[238] vult expresse quod intellectus a deforis intrat, quia operatio sua nullo modo communicat operationi corporali. Sed si esset corruptibilis et per consequens generabilis, esset eductus de potentia materiae et non esset magis ab extrinseco quam aliae formae. Nam omnis forma nova secundum intentionem Philosophi per generationem et transmutationem naturalem in esse producitur. Nam creationem omnino negavit.

174. Rationes istius opinionis licet satis convincant iudicio meo hanc opinionem non esse consonam sententiae fidei et veritatis, tamen contra opinionem Commentatoris non concludunt. Prima enim ratio de 7 *Metaphysicae* soluta est prius.[239] Secundam rationem cum sua conclusione[240] concederet Commentator quod intellectus materialis est et incorruptibilis et ingenerabilis. Ad tertium[241] concederet Commentator quod intellectus non intelligit sine phantasmate nec est etiam sine corpore absolute, esse tamen potest sine hoc corpore vel illo. Et si addatur illud Philosophi quod ipsi adducunt, quod intellectus in nobis corrumpitur quodam interiori corrupto,[242] diceret ipse quod accipit ibi intellectum pro eius operatione, quae necessario corrumpitur ad corruptionem phantasmatum. Ad quartum[243] diceret quod non est nisi unus intellectus in omnibus, et ille numquam separatur a corporibus, quin sit actus aliquorum corporum.

175. Ad istum ergo articulum dico quod puto quantum ad utrumque articulum Aristotelem et Commentatorem esse eiusdem opinionis. Quantum ad primum credo quod intentio Aristotelis fuit quod intellectus sit incorruptibilis, ut deductum | est contra opinionem immediate praecedentem.[244] Et per consequens, cum per ipsum omne incorruptibile est ingenerabile, ut deductum est, sequitur quod secundum sententiam eius sit aeternus et ex parte ante et ex parte post. Et haec est sententia Commentatoris.

176. Quantum ad secundum articulum puto similiter quod eandem habuerunt opinionem, quoniam, licet nec Philosophus nec Commentator posuerint individua in genere substantiae, ubi distinguuntur solo numero, eadem specie, distingui per quantitatem seu per aliquid extrinsecum, sed quod Socrates per aliquid intrinsecum sibi de genere substantiae tam ex parte eius formae quam ex parte eius ma-

2 non²] ideo P   **3** Item *om.* P   ‖   vult expresse] *inv.* T   ‖   a . . . intrat] venit ab extrinseco T   **4** nullo] vero P *et corr. i.m.* in ullo   ‖   operationi corporali] *inv.* T   **5** eductus] educta P   ‖   et non] nec T   **6** nova] *om.* T   **7** transmutationem] generalem *add. et del.* P   **8** omnino] *corr. i.m. ex* omnis P   **9** convincant] *lectio incerta* P   **9–10** hanc opinionem] opinioni Aristotelis P   **10** consonam] consona P   **11** enim *om.* T   **14** Commentator] *scripsimus*; Philosophus PT   **15** hoc] isto T   **16** adducunt] addunt P   ‖   intellectus *om.* T   **19** est *om.* T   **23** Aristotelis fuit] *inv.* T   **25** per] secundum T   **26** sententiam eius] *inv.* T   ‖   est *om.* T   **29** posuerint] posuerit T   **30** substantiae *om.* P   ‖   ubi distinguuntur] nisi distinguantur T   ‖   solo numero] *om.* T *et sub add.*   ‖   numero] *suppl. i.m.* P   **31–32** intrinsecum sibi] *inv.* T   **32** eius¹ *om.* T   **32–106.1** formae . . . materiae] materiae quam ex parte formae eius T

And he responds why this is: because the intellect does not understand without a phantasm, which does not remain after death.[237]

173. Again, in *On the Animals* 16[238] he expressly wants it to be the case that the intellect enters from outside, because its operation in no way communicates with corporeal operation. But if it were corruptible and consequently generable, it would be elicited from the potency of matter and would not be more from outside than other forms are. For every new form, according to the conception of the Philosopher, is brought into being by means of generation and natural transmutation. For creation he absolutely denied.

174. Although in my judgement the arguments for this opinion are convincing enough that this opinion is not in harmony with the stated opinion of faith and truth, nevertheless they are not conclusive against the opinion of the Commentator. For the first argument from *Metaphysics* 7 was resolved earlier.[239] The Commentator would concede the second argument with its conclusion[240] that the material intellect is both incorruptible and ungenerable. In answer to the third[241] the Commentator would concede that the intellect does not understand without a phantasm nor even exist without body absolutely, but can exist without this body or that. And if there were added that point of the Philosopher's which these people cite, that the intellect in us is corrupted because something internal is corrupted,[242] he would say that there by intellect he means its operation, which is necessarily corrupted following the corruption of phantasms. In answer to the fourth[243] he would say that there is only one intellect in all men, and that is never separated from bodies, so that it is not the act of some bodies.

175. In answer to this article, therefore, I say that I think that regarding each article Aristotle and the Commentator are of the same opinion. Regarding the first I believe that the conception of Aristotle was that the intellect is incorruptible, as has been deduced in opposition to the immediately preceding opinion.[244] And consequently, since according to him every incorruptible thing is ungenerable, as has been deduced, it follows that according to his stated opinion it is eternal both into the past and into the future. And this is the stated opinion of the Commentator.

176. Regarding the second article I likewise think that they had the same opinion, since, although neither the Philosopher nor the Commentator posited that individuals in the category of substance, where they are distinguished only numerically, being of the same species, are distinguished by quantity or by anything extrinsic, but that Socrates is distinguished from Plato, both in terms of his form and

---

[237] Arist. *DA* 3. 5, 430ª23–5.
[238] See above, para. 143.
[239] See above, paras. 163, 156.
[240] See above, para. 164.
[241] See above, para. 165.
[242] Arist. *DA* 1. 4, 408ᵇ24–5.
[243] See above, para. 166.
[244] See above, paras. 162–73.

teriae distinguitur a Platone, tamen multitudinem individuorum sub eadem specie ⟨Philosophus⟩ non posuit nisi in corruptibilibus tantum. Et hoc propter hoc quod natura speciei non potest perpetuari in uno individuo. Videbatur enim sibi frustra ponere plura individua eiusdem speciei, ex quo tota perfectio speciei salvatur in uno individuo, nisi propter causam praedictam. Ulterius, ubi non posuit multitudinem individuorum, non posuit intentiones aliquas individuales superadditas speciei, quoniam frustra ponerentur. Et ideo dico quod in formis quae nec habent materiam partem sui quae est principium corruptionis, nec in esse dependent ex materia huiusmodi signata hac vel illa, sed habent esse perpetuum in identitate numerali, posuit Philosophus tantum unum individuum in una specie. Et haec est sententia Philosophi, 12 *Metaphysicae*,[245] ubi probat quod non sunt plures caeli, quia tunc essent plures motores, quod est falsum, quia non habent materiam. Dico ergo quod intentio Commentatoris est intentio Philosophi, ut apparet mihi, in hac materia.

⟨ARTICULUS 4: OPINIO THOMAE WYLTON⟩

177. De quarto articulo, quid mihi videatur dicendum ad quaestionem, dico quod intelligendo per intellectivam praecise formam quae est nobis principium cognoscendi quidditates rerum abstractas, quam cognitionem quilibet experitur in se ipso se habere, cum voluerit; intelligendo etiam per formam corporis humani formale principium in homine intrinsecum quo ab aliis speciebus specifice et ultimate distinguitur—non comprehendendo modum specialem quo informat, scilicet utrum inhaerentis vel alio modo, sed tantum in genere—dico quod evidenter convinci potest—et istam conclusionem convincebat Philosophus, 2 *De anima* ex hoc quod anima est quo vivimus, sentimus, movemur secundum locum et intelligimus—quod est principium intrinsecum nobis non ut materia, ut ipse inducit ibi, ex quo concludit quod est principium formale.[246] Et istud non minus convincit de anima intellectiva quam de aliis quod sit forma in nobis, quia per idem medium convincitur utrumque. Haec est etiam intentio Commentatoris ibidem. Concludit | enim in fine in exponendo Philosophum super illam litteram 'Quoniam quo vivimus et sentimus', scilicet in 24 commento 2 *De anima*,[247] quod anima est forma et corpus materia, et comprehendit intellectum sub anima, quoniam Philosophus numerat in textu intellectum in minore demonstrationis suae.

2 Philosophus] *supplevimus*; *om.* PT   5 individuo *om.* P   7 dico] dicendo P   8 sui] suam P || dependent] in esse *add.* P   9 materia huiusmodi] *inv.* T   12 plures] duo P   13 Commentatoris] in hac materia *add.* T   13–14 in . . . materia *om.* T   17 per intellectivam *om.* P || est] praecise *add.* T   18 cognoscendi] *scripsimus*; cognitionis PT || quidditates . . . abstractas] quidditatis rerum abstractarum T   21 comprehendendo] *corr. s.l. ex* comprehendere P   22 inhaerentis] inhaerenter T   24 anima] quia *add.* T   26 Et *om.* T   27 quam . . . nobis] quod sit forma in nobis quam de aliis T   30 et sentimus *om.* T || scilicet in] et est T || 24 commento] *inv.* T || 2] 3 P   31 quoniam] quantum T   32 minore] minori T

in terms of his matter, by something intrinsic to him belonging to the category of substance, nevertheless the Philosopher does not posit a multitude of individuals in the same species except in corruptible things only. And this is because of the fact that the nature of a species cannot be perpetuated in one individual. For it seemed to him pointless to posit several individuals of the same species, so that the whole perfection of a species is saved in one individual, except for the reason mentioned above. Furthermore, where he did not posit a multitude of individuals, he did not posit any individual intentions superadded to the species, since they would be posited pointlessly. And therefore I say that in forms which neither have a material part to them which is the principle of corruption, nor depend in being on matter of this sort, designated as this or that, but have perpetual being in numerical identity, the Philosopher posited only one individual in one species. And this is the stated opinion of the Philosopher, *Metaphysics* 12,[245] where he proves that there are not several heavens, since then there would be several movers, which is false, since they do not have matter. I say therefore that the conception of the Commentator is the conception of the Philosopher on this matter, as far as it appears to me.

⟨ARTICLE 4: OPINION OF THOMAS WYLTON⟩

177. Concerning the fourth article, what would seem to me necessary to be said in answer to the question, I say that by understanding by the intellectual soul precisely the form which is our principle of cognizing the abstract quiddities of things, the cognition which everyone experiences in himself that he has, when he wants to experience that; also by understanding by the form of the human body the formal principle intrinsic in man by which he is specifically and ultimately distinguished from other species—by not taking into account the special way by which it informs, namely either of something inhering or in another way, but only in general—I say that it can be established evidently—and the Philosopher established this conclusion, *On the Soul* 2, starting from the notion that the soul is that by which we live, sense, move with respect to place, and understand—that it is a principle intrinsic to us, not as matter, as he argues by induction there—from this notion he concludes that it is a formal principle.[246] And he establishes this no less concerning the intellectual soul than concerning other things that it is a form in us, since both things are established by the same means. This is also the conception of the Commentator in the same place. For he concludes at the end of his expounding of the Philosopher on that text 'Since that by which we live and sense', namely in comment 24, *On the Soul* 2,[247] that the soul is form and the body matter, and he encompasses the intellect under the soul, since the Philosopher numbers the intellect in his text in the minor premiss of his demonstration.

[245] Arist. *Metaph.* 12. 8, 1074ᵃ31–8.
[246] Arist. *DA* 2. 2, 413ᵇ11–414ᵃ14.
[247] Ibid. 414ᵃ4; Aver. *In DA* 2, t. c. 24, 165. 67–8.

178. Et ideo qui imponunt Commentatori quod ipse posuit intellectum materialem non esse principium intrinsecum formale in homine, per quod tamquam per partem sui intelligit, sed quod homo solum esset compositum ex anima | sensitiva et corpore tamquam ex principiis intrinsecis, et quod illud compositum intelligeret per copulationem intellectus materialis ad ipsum, qui tamen intellectus non est pars hominis, sed extrinsecum per se subsistens, qualitercumque poneretur illud simul secundum situm cum phantasmate hominis, salva pace, haec non fuit intentio Commentatoris, ut prius satis declaratum est.[248] Nec credo quod aliquis intelligens in illa opinione aliquem colorem videre possit quod aliquis intelligeret et experiretur se intelligere per principium elicitivum et receptivum huius actus non existens in ipso, sed in alio supposito. Qualitercumque enim angelus intimaret se mihi, et simul secundum situm esset cum intellectu meo, et ipse angelus videret Deum, per hoc ego nullam cognitionem haberem quam prius non habui. Intelligere enim quod est actus est actus immanens et informans intelligentem, et ideo implicatio contradictionis est quod aliquis intelligat nisi vel sit intellectus, qui est immediata potentia receptiva actus intelligendi, vel quod intellectus sit pars eius.

179. Si autem per intellectivam non solum intelligatur forma per quam intelligimus quidditates rerum abstractas, sed cum hoc comprehendamus conditiones eius alias quas catholici ei attribuunt, scilicet quod sit de novo producta simul cum individuo cuius est forma, et tamen quod sit aeterna ex parte post, dico, cum Adam in statu innocentiae et Salomon post in cognitione naturali viae ad multas veritates rerum naturalium cognoscendas habuerint intellectum elevatum, quas nos non cognoscimus nec ex naturalibus convincere possumus, dico quantum ad illos, nescio si istam veritatem per rationem naturalem convincebant vel convincere potuerunt. Quantum tamen ad philosophos nescio aliquem qui per rationem naturalem convincit nec etiam ponit. Quantum autem ad me, dico quod licet illam opinionem absque aliqua dubitatione credam veram esse, ipsam tamen per rationem naturalem convincere nescio—gaudeant illi qui convincere eam sciunt—sed sola fide teneo.

---

1 quod] *corr. ex* quoniam P   3 compositum] compositus T   7 situm] scitum T   9 possit] potuisset P   10 huius] istius T   11 existens] existentis T   12 et ipse *om.* P || angelus] autem *add.* P   14 informans] intellectum *add. et del.* P   15 est *om.* P   18 non . . . intelligatur] intelligatur non solum T   20 eius] enim T   21 sit] est P || aeterna] simul *add.* T   22 Adam *om.* P   24 possumus] possimus T   25 naturalem] convincere possunt *add. et del.* P || convincebant vel *om.* T   26 tamen *om.* P || nescio aliquem] nullum scio T   27 naturalem] eam *add.* T || convincit] convincat T || ponit] *scripsimus;* posuit P; ponat T || Quantum] quanto (*lectio incerta*) T   29–30 sed . . . teneo *om.* T

178. And therefore those who attribute to the Commentator that he posited that the material intellect is not a formal intrinsic principle in man, by which he understands as if by a part of himself, but that man would be only a composite of the sensitive soul and the body as if out of intrinsic principles, and that this composite would understand by the conjoining of the material intellect with him, which intellect is however not a part of man, but something extrinsic and subsisting by itself, in whatever sort of way this would be posited simultaneously according to position with the phantasms of man, with all due respect, this was not the conception of the Commentator, as was satisfactorily explained earlier.[248] Nor do I believe that someone who perceives some persuasive force in this opinion could see that someone would understand and experience himself as understanding by an elicitive and receptive principle of this act that does not exist in himself, but in another supposit. For in whatever sort of way an angel might intimate himself to me, and simultaneously according to position would be with my intellect, and the angel himself would see God, by this I would have no cognition which I did not have before. For to understand, which is an act, is an act immanent in and informing the one who understands, and therefore it implies a contradiction that someone understands unless either he is the intellect, which is the immediate receptive potency of the act of understanding, or the intellect is a part of him.

179. But if by the intellectual soul were understood not only the form by which we understand the abstract quiddities of things, but in addition to this we were to encompass its other conditions which Catholics attribute to it, namely that it is produced anew simultaneously with the individual whose form it is, and nevertheless that it is eternal into the future, I say, although Adam in the state of innocence and later Solomon in natural cognition in this life had an intellect elevated to the cognizing of many truths about natural things, truths which we do not cognize and cannot establish by natural means, I say regarding them, I do not know whether they established this truth by natural reason or whether they could establish it. Regarding the philosophers, however, I do not know anyone who establishes this by natural reason nor anyone who even posits it. But regarding myself, I say that although I believe without any doubt that this opinion is true, nevertheless I do not know how to establish it by natural reason—let them rejoice who do know how to establish it—but I hold it by faith alone.

---

[248] See above, paras. 95, 124, 134.

⟨ARTICULUS 5: AD RATIONES PHILOSOPHORUM ADVERSUS VERITATEM FIDEI⟩

180. Teneo igitur indubitanter quod opinio Averrois erronea est et falsa, et ideo ad eius rationes primo et postea ad rationes Philosophi quae videntur concludere | contra veritatem fidei secundum ordinem respondeo.

181. Et ad quarum solutionem praemitto quod secundum sententiam tam Aristotelis quam Commentatoris, ut supra dictum est,[249] ista convertuntur: formam aliquam numerari in diversis suppositis eiusdem speciei et esse formam materialem extensam ad extensionem materiae. Istud autem principium apud eos negamus.

182. Tunc ad primam rationem Commentatoris[250] concedo quod hic intellectus materialis est intellectum in potentia. Et cum infertur ex hoc quod est motivum intellectus, dico quod intelligendo per motivum intellectus activum quod natum sit reducere intellectum de potentia essentiali ad actum, nego. Et ad probationem,[251] cum accipitur quod intellectus materialis est ⟨in⟩ potentia sic ad omnem formam materialem, dicendum quod verum est ⟨quantum ad formam⟩ corporalem eductam de potentia materiae, cuiusmodi forma non est intellectus. Si autem per motivum intellectus intelligatur quodcumque obiectum intelligibile ab intellectu nostro, sic non est inconveniens concedere quod idem moveat se. Intellectus enim meus singularis potest cognoscere quidditatem intellectus abstractam ab hoc intellectu et illo; ad illam tamen cognitionem non devenit nisi praecedente abstractione facta a sensibilibus. Et ideo dicit Philosophus, 3 *De anima*,[252] quod intellectus intelligit se sicut alia, quia in eius cognitionem devenire non potest nisi praecedente abstractione specierum ab istis corporalibus, per quas species ipsa corporalia intelliguntur.

183. Ad secundum[253] dico quod non sequitur quod idem reciperet se. Et ad probationem, ubi stat vis rationis, quod ipse supponit quod, ubi intellectum et intellectus sunt idem, [quod] cognitio media est eadem, hoc est falsum etiam secundum ipsum, quoniam ipse posuit quod intellectus materialis, quando est in dispositione adeptionis, intelligit se, ut prius declaratum est.[254] Tamen non potest dicere quod intellectio illa sit eadem res cum intellectu materiali. Nam intellectus materialis secundum ipsum est aeternus, et illa intellectio est nova.

184. Dicetur: si extrema sint idem, medium erit idem; sed intellectio est me-

---

4 et *om.* T   5 secundum] per T || respondeo] respondendo P; *lectio incerta* T   6 Et *om.* T || secundum *om.* P   7 supra . . . est] dictum est supra T   13 intellectus² *om.* T || activum] actuum P   15 in] *supplevimus*; *om.* PT   16 quantum . . . formam] *supplevimus*; *om.* PT   19 enim] autem T   19–20 singularis] singulariter P   20 cognoscere] intelligere T || intellectus *om.* T || et] ab *add.* T   22 3 *De anima om.* P   23 sicut] et *add.* T   26 reciperet] recipet T   27 ubi¹] *corr. ex* verbi P || ubi²] si T   27–28 intellectum . . . intellectus] intellectus et intellectum T   28 quod] *delevimus*; *scrips.* PT || cognitio] cognitione P || media] materiae P   31 Nam . . . materialis *om. hom.* P   32 illa intellectio] *inv.* T   33 sint] sunt T || idem¹] eadem T *et* et *add.*

⟨ARTICLE 5: IN ANSWER TO THE ARGUMENTS OF THE
PHILOSOPHERS IN OPPOSITION TO THE TRUTH OF FAITH⟩

180. Therefore I hold indubitably that the opinion of Averroes is erroneous and false, and therefore I respond in order to his arguments first and afterwards to the arguments of the Philosopher which seem to be conclusive against the truth of faith.

181. And for the solution of these I make the preliminary point that according to the stated opinion both of Aristotle and of the Commentator, as was said above,[249] these things are equivalent: that some form is numbered in different supposits of the same species and that it is a material form extended according to the extension of matter. But we deny this claim, which they take to be a principle.

182. Then in answer to the first argument of the Commentator[250] I concede that this material intellect is something understood in potency. And when it is inferred from this that it is something capable of moving the intellect, I reply that when something capable of moving the intellect is viewed as something active that is apt by nature to lead the intellect from essential potency to act, I deny it. And to the proof of this,[251] when it is understood that the material intellect is in potency in this way to every material form, it must be replied that it is true regarding the corporeal form elicited from the potency of matter; but the intellect is not that kind of form. But if by something capable of moving the intellect is understood any object whatever that is intelligible to our intellect, in this way it is not an absurdity to concede that the same thing moves itself. For my singular intellect can cognize the quiddity of an intellect abstracted from this intellect and that; but it does not attain this cognition except by a previous abstraction made from sensible things. And therefore the Philosopher says, *On the Soul* 3,[252] that the intellect understands itself just as it does other things, because it cannot attain cognition of itself except by a previous abstraction of species from these corporeal things, by which species corporeal things themselves are understood.

183. In answer to the second argument[253] I say that it does not follow that the same thing would receive itself. And as to the proof, where the force of the argument is, I say that he assumes that where the understood thing and the intellect are the same, the intermediate cognition is the same, and this is false even according to him, since he posited himself that the material intellect, when it is in a state of accomplishment, understands itself, as was explained earlier.[254] However, he cannot say that that understanding is the same thing as the material intellect. For the material intellect according to him is eternal, and that understanding is new.

184. It will be said: if the extremes are the same, the intermediate will be

---

[249] See above, para. 88.
[250] See above, para. 87.
[251] See above, para. 89.
[252] Arist. *DA* 3. 4, 430^{a}2–3.
[253] See above, para. 90.
[254] See above, e.g. paras. 76, 82.

dium copulans intelligibile cum intellectu. Potest dici uno modo quod intellectio non est medium inter intelligibile et intellectum, sed est effectus causatus ex intelligibili et intellectu ad invicem approximatis sicut ex causa eius totali. Aliter potest dici, cum dicitur, si extrema sint idem, quod medium est idem cum extremis, verum est de medio copulante extrema ad invicem in esse naturae, non intentionaliter solum. Sed intellectio non copulat intelligibile cum intellectu nisi intentionaliter.

185. Ad tertium[255] dicendum quod non sequitur quod cognosceret rem ut hoc, nec quod non distingueretur a sensitiva, quoniam virtus sensitiva, quia organica est, ideo intentio recepta in ipsa non solum est singularis in essendo, sed etiam in repraesentando. Non sic autem de intellectu, quoniam licet intellectus meus singularis sit, non tamen est organicus et extensus ad extensionem organi, propter quod reflexivus est super se, et intentio in eo recepta, licet sit singularis in essendo, est tamen universalis in repraesentando.

186. Sed istud non videtur solvere, quoniam illud quod nec determinat sibi universalitatem nec particularitatem non est causa artans potentiam aliquam ad cognitionem particularis tantum. Sed res materialis corporalis nec determinat sibi universalitatem nec particularitatem. Ergo virtus sensitiva ex hoc quod est virtus corporalis et materialis, non erit causa quare sensus solum cognoscit singulare. Et per consequens sola singularitas in sensu est causa quare sensus solum cognoscit singulare. Et eadem est causa de intellectu, si individuetur et numeretur ad numerationem corporum. Maior est manifesta. Indeterminatum enim ad aliqua non est causa determinandi | ad alterum eorum ad quae se habet indifferenter. Minor etiam est manifesta. Nam quidditas rei materialis est primum obiectum intellectus nostri ex intentione Philosophi, 3 *De anima* ibi: 'Quoniam autem aliud est magnitudo'.[256] Accidit ergo rei materiali corporali universalitas vel particularitas.

187. Confirmatur ratio, quoniam virtuti sensitivae ex hoc quod est virtus corporalis et organica repugnat solum quod [non] cognoscat separata secundum esse a corpore et materia. Sed quod [non] cognoscat universale, dummodo sit corporale et sensibile, hoc non repugnat sibi quia virtus corporalis, sed solum quia singularis. Et credo quod istud principaliter movet Commentatorem et eodem modo Philosophum ad ponendum quod intellectus noster non numeretur in diversis individuis, quia tunc non cognosceret universale.

2 est¹] intellectum *add. et del.* P   3 intellectu] intellectione (*lectio incerta*) T || sicut] sed P
4–5 cum¹ . . . verum] quod propositio vera T   5 ad invicem *om.* T   6 Sed . . . nisi] intellectio autem solum copulat T   7 ut] *corr. s.l. ex* in P   8 distingueretur] distinguatur T   9 etiam *om.* P   14 nec] non T || sibi] nec *add.* T   15 particularitatem] nec universalitatem *add. et del.* P
16 materialis] naturalis T   18 corporalis . . . materialis] materialis et corporalis T || erit] est T
19–20 solum . . . singulare] cognoscit singulare solum T   21 Indeterminatum enim] quia indeterminatum T   22 eorum] illorum T   23 obiectum] omnium P   24 autem *om.* T   25 corporali *om.* T
27 non] *delevimus*; *scrips.* PT   28 non] *delevimus*; *scrips.* PT   29 singularis] singulariter P   30 Et] *illegibile* T || credo . . . istud] istud credo quod T || movet] movit T || modo *om.* T

the same; but the understanding is the intermediate conjoining the intelligible thing with the intellect. It can be said in one way that the understanding is not an intermediate between the intelligible thing and the intellect, but is the effect caused by the intelligible thing and the intellect that have been brought near to one another, as by its total cause. In another way it can be said: when it is said that the intermediate is the same as the extremes, if the extremes are the same, this is true of the intermediate conjoining one extreme with the other in natural being, not only intentionally. But the understanding does not conjoin the intelligible thing with the intellect except intentionally.

185. In answer to the third argument[255] it must be said that it does not follow that the intellect would cognize the thing as this, nor that it would not be distinguished from the sensitive soul, since as the sensitive power is organic, an intention received in it is not only singular in being, but also in representation. But this is not the case with the intellect, since although my intellect is singular, it is not however organic and extended according to the extension of an organ, and because of this it is reflexive onto itself, and an intention received in it, although it is singular in being, is nevertheless universal in representation.

186. But this does not seem to solve the problem, since that which determines for itself neither universality nor particularity is not the cause that limits any power to the cognition only of what is particular. But a material corporeal thing determines for itself neither universality nor particularity. Therefore the sensitive power, for the reason that it is a corporeal and material power, will not be the cause of the fact that the sense cognizes only what is singular. And consequently only singularity in the sense is the cause of the fact that the sense cognizes only what is singular. And the cause is the same regarding the intellect, if it is individuated and numbered according to the numbering of bodies. The major premiss is manifest. For what is indeterminate with respect to some things is not the cause of determining with respect to one among those things to which it relates indifferently. The minor premiss is also manifest. For the quiddity of a material thing is the first object of our intellect according to the conception of the Philosopher, *On the Soul* 3, there: 'But since magnitude is something else'.[256] Therefore universality or particularity is accidental to a material corporeal thing.

187. The argument is confirmed, since for the reason that it is a corporeal and organic power it is only incompatible with the sensitive power that it should cognize things that are separate in being from body and matter. But that it should cognize a universal, as long as it is corporeal and sensible, this is not incompatible with it because it is a corporeal power, but only because it is singular. And I believe that this principally moves the Commentator and in the same way the Philosopher to posit that our intellect is not numbered in different individuals, because then it would not cognize a universal.

---

[255] See above, para. 91.
[256] Arist. *DA* 3. 4, 429^{b}10.

188. Ad istam rationem²⁵⁷ respondetur uno modo quod, licet intellectus noster sit individuatus, tamen habet potentiam abstractam.

189. Contra: potentia intellectiva vel est ipsa substantia animae vel immediatissime consequitur ipsam. Sed sive sic sive sic, sequitur, si anima individuetur, quod potentia individuatur.

190. Aliqui dicunt ad hoc quod anima intellectiva potest dupliciter considerari: uno modo ut actus corporis, alio modo ut supergreditur materiam. Primo modo individuatur, et ut sic non fundatur potentia intellectiva in ea. Secundo modo fundatur in ea, et ut sic non individuatur.

191. Istud est ficticium. Si enim potentia qua homo immediate intelligit non fundetur in anima hominis ut est eius actus et perfectio, sed secundum quod anima supergreditur, sequitur quod nullus intelligit in quantum homo, quoniam homo constituitur formaliter per animam intellectivam | non in quantum supergreditur corpus humanum, sed in quantum ex his fit unum sicut ex actu et potentia.

192. Praeterea, quid intelligunt per supergressionem illam? Vel aliquem excessum in perfectione, ratione cuius non est proportio inter ipsam et materiam, vel quod non habet conditiones corporis quas aliae formae habent, puta extensionem, corruptibilitatem et huiusmodi. Non est dare primum, cum per essentiam ex ipsa et materia fiat unum per se. Nec potest dici quod secundum partem est actus et secundum partem actum supergreditur, cum sit indivisibilis. Et per consequens, ex quo per essentiam est actus et perfectio materiae, secundum se totam proportionatur materiae, et per consequens nullo modo sic supergreditur. Si intelligant secundo modo, bene volo quod sit incorruptibilis, et nec extensa per se nec per accidens. Tamen singularis est et individua sicut virtus extensa. Ergo quantum ad cognitionem universalis tantam repugnantiam habet sicut sensus.

193. Praeterea, intellectus possibilis in diversis suppositis numeratur necessario, quoniam sive ponatur esse idem cum substantia animae sive accidens, semper sequitur quod numeretur secundum numerationem animae. Cum ergo potentia qua immediate homo intelligit sit individuata et singularis sicut sensitiva potentia, ita quod quantum ad singularitatem non est differentia, videtur quod homo per intellectum possibilem non intelligit nisi singulare.

194. Praeterea, oportet concedere quod species recepta in intellectu possibili sit singularis in essendo et numerata in diversis suppositis sicut species recepta in virtute sensitiva. Ex hoc probo quod erit singularis in repraesentando, quoniam quaero a quo habet species universalitatem illam in repraesentando? Certum est

---

4 sequitur] quod *add.* T   **5** individuatur] similiter T   **7** ut² *om.* P   **8** fundatur] fundetur P   **10** immediate intelligit] *inv.* T   **11** fundetur] fundatur T || anima hominis] eius anima T   **15** quid] quicquid T || aliquem] a materiae P   **17** quod] quia P   **18** Non . . . primum] Primum non potest dari T   **20** partem *om.* P   **23** et *om.* T || extensa] nec *add.* T   **24** individua] *fortasse scribendum* individuata   **25** repugnantiam habet] *inv.* T   **28** secundum] ad T   **31** possibilem *om.* T; passibilem P   **34–35** quoniam quaero] quaero enim T   **35** species] illa recepta *add.* T

188. In response to this argument[257] it will be said in one way that, although our intellect is individuated, nevertheless it has abstract power.

189. To the contrary: intellectual power is either the very substance of the soul or follows it without any intermediate. But whether one way or the other, it follows that if the soul is individuated, its power is individuated.

190. Some say in answer to this that the intellectual soul can be considered in two ways: in one way as an act of the body, in another way as something that surpasses matter. In the first way it is individuated, and as such intellectual power is not founded on it. In the second way it is founded on it, and as such it is not individuated.

191. This is fictitious. For if the power by which man immediately understands were not founded on the soul of man as it is his act and perfection, but as the soul surpasses matter, it follows that no one understands in so far as he is man, since man is formally constituted by the intellectual soul not in so far as it surpasses the human body, but in so far as from these things one thing comes to be, just as from act and potency.

192. Moreover, what do they understand by this surpassing? Either some excess in perfection, because of which there is no proportion between itself and matter, or that it does not have the conditions of body which other forms have, that is extension, corruptibility, and properties of this kind. One cannot choose the first option, since essentially from the intellectual soul and matter a thing that is one thing by itself comes to be. Nor can it be said that in one part it is act and in another part it surpasses act, since it is indivisible. And consequently, since essentially it is the act and perfection of matter, it is proportionate to matter according to the whole of itself, and consequently in no way does it surpass it in this way. If they understand it in the second way, I gladly agree that it would be incorruptible, and neither extended by itself nor by accident. Nevertheless it is singular and individual just as an extended power. Therefore regarding cognition of the universal it is just as incompatible as sense.

193. Moreover, the possible intellect in different supposits is necessarily numbered, since whether it is posited to be the same as the substance of the soul or an accident, it always follows that it is numbered according to the numbering of the soul. Therefore since the power by which man immediately understands is individuated and singular just as the sensitive power is, so that regarding singularity there is no difference, it seems that by means of the possible intellect man understands only what is singular.

194. Moreover, it is required to concede that a species received in the possible intellect is singular in being and numbered in different supposits just like a species received in the sensitive power. From this I prove that it will be singular in representation, since I ask from what does a species have that universality in representation? It is certain that it has its universal or particular mode of represen-

---
[257] See above, paras. 186–7.

quod a quo habet esse effective, ab eo habet modum repraesentandi universaliter vel particulariter. Esse autem habet effective ab obiecto. Ergo modum repraesentandi habet ab eodem. Sed obiectum movens intellectum possibilem est phantasma. Nam phantasmata se habent ad intellectum possibilem sicut sensibilia ad sensum per Philosophum et Commentatorem, 3 *De anima*.[258] Cum ergo phantasmata sint singularia et in essendo et in repraesentando, ergo non causant speciem universalem.

195. Nec valet, si dicatur quod phantasmata in virtute intellectus agentis causa⟨n⟩t istam universalitatem, quoniam secundum sententiam catholicorum intellectus agens numeratur in diversis hominibus et individuatur sicut intellectus possibilis. Ergo et actus eius singularis est, et per consequens non erit causa speciei universalis, sed tantum singularis.

196. Sustinendo opinionem communem de intellectu possibili—quod non obstante quod sit singularis et numeratus in diversis suppositis, tamen primum obiectum movens ipsum est universale, nec intelligit singulare per propriam speciem singularis, sed solum indirecte—potest dici ad rationem quod species in intellectu possibili, licet | sit singularis in essendo, est tamen universalis in repraesentando. Et huiusmodi causa totalis est immaterialitas intellectus possibilis recipientis eam una cum virtute intellectus agentis, quae est virtus universalis in causando, licet singularis in essendo. Causa autem quare species existens in virtute sensitiva est singularis in repraesentando sicut in essendo est non materialitas absolute nec singularitas, sed hoc totum 'singularitas materialis'. Valeat quantum valere potest.

197. Credo tamen quod secundum opinionem veram concedenda sit conclusio huius rationis, quantum concludere potest, scilicet quod species quae causatur primo in intellectu possibili sit singularis et in essendo et in repraesentando, ita quod primum obiectum intellectus via generationis est singulare sensibile, licet universale sit primum eius obiectum, accipiendo 'primum' pro appropriato seu proprio. Quo modo autem intellectus possibilis primo recipit speciem singularis, postea tamen comparando diversa singularia ad invicem secundum illud in quo conveniunt, et quantum ad ea in quibus differunt, considerare potest ipsa praecise secundum illud in quo conveniunt sequestrando ea in quibus differunt, et hoc virtute intellectus agentis una cum virtute | eius propria, quia est virtus immaterialis,

---

1 quod *om.* T   **2** vel] seu T || habet effective] *inv.* T   **4** possibilem sicut *om.* P   **5** per] secundum T   **6** in² *om.* P   **8** phantasmata] phantasia (*lectio incerta*) T || in virtute *om.* T   **9** causa⟨n⟩t] causat PT; *correximus in* causant   **10** sicut] sed P   **13** possibili] scilicet *add.* T   **13–14** obstante] absolute (*lectio incerta*) P   **14–15** obiectum] *lectio incerta* P   **18** intellectus] *iter. et corr.* P   **20** essendo] et *add.* P   **21** sicut] sic P || est non] *fortasse scribendum* non est   **24** tamen *om.* P || secundum ... veram *om.* T || sit] est P   **25** huius] istius T   **27** obiectum *om.* T; omnium P   **28** eius obiectum] *inv.* T   **30** illud ... quo] illa in quibus T   **31** considerare] *lectio incerta* T || ipsa] ea T   **32** illud ... quo] ea in quibus T || ea] illud ab eis P || in² *om.* P

tation from that from which it effectively has its being. But it effectively has its being from the object. Therefore it has its mode of representation from the same thing. But the object moving the possible intellect is a phantasm. For phantasms relate to the possible intellect as sensible things do to the sense according to the Philosopher and the Commentator, *On the Soul* 3.[258] Therefore since phantasms are singular both in being and in representation, therefore they do not cause a universal species.

195. Nor is it valid, if it were to be said that phantasms in virtue of the agent intellect cause this universality, since according to the stated opinion of Catholics the agent intellect is numbered in different human beings and is individuated just like the possible intellect. Therefore its act is also singular, and consequently it will not be the cause of a universal species, but only of a singular.

196. In supporting the general opinion concerning the possible intellect—that notwithstanding that it is singular and numbered in different supposits, nevertheless the first object moving it is the universal, and it does not understand a singular by the proper species of the singular, but only indirectly—it can be said in answer to the argument that a species in the possible intellect, although it is singular in being, is nevertheless universal in representation. And the total cause of this state of affairs is the immateriality of the possible intellect, which receives it, together with the power of the agent intellect, which is a universal power in causation, although singular in being. However, the cause of the fact that a species existing in the sensitive power is singular in representation just as it is in being is not materiality absolutely nor singularity, but this whole 'material singularity'. Let this be accepted as valid until it is disproved.

197. I believe, however, that according to true opinion the conclusion of this argument should be conceded, as far as it can lead to a conclusion, namely that the species which is caused first in the possible intellect is singular both in being and in representation, so that the first object of the intellect in the way of generation is a singular sensible thing, although a universal is its first object, understanding 'first' in the sense of appointed or proper. But in what way the possible intellect first receives the species of a singular thing, but nevertheless afterwards by comparing different singular things with one another according to that in which they agree, and regarding the things in which they differ, can consider them precisely according to that in which they agree, setting aside the things in which they differ, and this by virtue of the agent intellect together with its own proper power, because it is an

---

[258] Arist. *DA* 3. 7, 431ᵃ14–15; Aver. *In DA* 3, t. c. 30, 468. 7–469. 11.

dixi in quadam quaestione quam determinavi de verbo singulari, qua quaerebatur 'An possibile sit formare verbum de singulari materiali'.²⁵⁹

198. Sciendum tamen est quod illi qui sustinent opinionem fidei, scilicet quod anima intellectiva numeratur in diversis suppositis et individuatur, non oportet quod admittant auctoritatem Philosophi et Commentatoris quantum ad intellectionem singularis in 3 *De anima*,²⁶⁰ ubi dicit quod singulare non intelligitur nisi per lineam reflexam, quoniam secundum sententiam eorum, cum anima non habeat aliquam singularitatem sub specie, sed solam singularitatem speciei, non esset secundum hoc proportio inter intellectum et speciem singularis, quae numeratur et multiplicatur in diversis individuis. Sed nos, qui ponimus intellectum individuari et numerari in diversis, salvare possumus proportionem inter speciem singularis et intellectum. Quantum enim ad singularitatem certum est quod est proportio, quia utrumque est singulare. Quantum ad materialitatem etiam est proportio, quia propter hoc quod intellectus est actus naturalis corporis, natus est recipere cognitionem suam a virtutibus sensitivis, quorum obiecta sunt corporalia et materialia. Et ideo inter intellectum et speciem singularis materialis est proportio secundum opinionem fidei, sed non secundum opinionem Commentatoris, quam puto esse opinionem Philosophi.

199. Sciendum etiam, cum dicimus quod Deus est quaedam substantia singularis, et Michael similiter, quod singularitas huius et illius | singularitas sub eadem specie atoma est 'singularitas' aequivoce dicta, et eodem modo est de intellectu materiali secundum intentionem suam. Sed in hoc posuit differentiam inter intellectum materialem et alias substantias immateriales quod, licet intellectus materialis non cognoscat singularia materialia directe recipiendo eorum speciem, quia sibi non proportionatur, tamen quidditatem rei materialis intelligit per intentionem abstractam a phantasmatibus virtute intellectus agentis, et hoc sibi competit quia est actus corporis. Sed ex alia parte posuit quod aliae substantiae separatae, quae non sunt actus corporum, sed solum uniuntur corporibus ut motores, nec intelligunt singulare materiale nec aliquid a corpore abstractum. Sed Deus solum cognoscit se. Aliae substantiae inferiores in cognoscendo se cognoscunt substantias superiores, sed nihil omnino inferius eis cognoscunt.

200. Ad aliud²⁶¹ primo videtur quod illud argumentum habeat aequalem ef-

1–2 in . . . materiali'] alias T   3 est *om.* T   5 admittant] admittat P   5–6 intellectionem] intellectum P   6 singularis] singulariter P || in *om.* T   8 sub] *suppl. s.l.* P || sed . . . speciei] *suppl. i.m.* P || esset *om.* T   9 quae numeratur *om.* P   11 salvare possumus] possimus salvare T   12 intellectum] intellectionem (*lectio incerta*) T || enim *om.* P || quod *om.* P   13 ad . . . etiam] etiam ad materialitatem T   15 sunt] corruptibilia *add.* T   17 sed] licet T   17–18 Commentatoris . . . Philosophi] Philosophi et Commentatoris T   20 quod] quia T || singularitas¹] singulariter P || huius] hoc P || illius *om.* P   21 est² *om.* T   22 posuit] ponit T   23 quod] quia T   24 recipiendo] accipiendo P   25 proportionatur] proportionantur T || intentionem] *corr. ex* intellectionem P   28 nec] non T   30 substantiae *om.* P   31 eis] eas T   32 habeat] habet P

immaterial power, I established in the question which I determined concerning the singular word, where it was asked 'Whether it is possible to form a word regarding a singular material thing'.[259]

198. Nevertheless it must be realized that for those who hold the opinion of faith, namely that the intellectual soul is numbered in different supposits and is individuated, it is not required that they should admit the authority of the Philosopher and the Commentator regarding the understanding of singular things in *On the Soul* 3,[260] where he says that a singular thing is not understood except by a bent line, since according to their stated opinion, the soul does not have any singularity below the level of species, but only the singularity of a species, and for this reason there would be in accordance with this no proportion between the intellect and the species of a singular thing, which is numbered and multiplied in different individuals. But we, who posit that the intellect is individuated and numbered in different things, can preserve the proportion between the species of a singular thing and the intellect. For regarding singularity it is certain that there is proportion, since both are singular. Regarding materiality there is also proportion, since for the reason that the intellect is an act of a natural body, it is apt by nature to receive its cognition from the sensitive powers, whose objects are corporeal and material things. And therefore between the intellect and the species of the singular material thing there is proportion according to the opinion of faith, but not according to the opinion of the Commentator, which I take to be the opinion of the Philosopher.

199. It must also be realized, when we say that God is a singular substance, and Michael similarly, that the singularity of this and the singularity of that in the same indivisible species is 'singularity' said equivocally, and the same goes for the material intellect according to his stated opinion. But in this he posited a difference between the material intellect and other immaterial substances that, although the material intellect does not cognize singular material things directly by receiving their species, because it is not proportionate to itself, nevertheless it understands the quiddity of a material thing by means of an intention abstracted from phantasms by the power of the agent intellect, and this agrees with it because it is the act of the body. But on the other hand he posited that other separate substances, which are not acts of bodies, but are only united with bodies as movers, understand neither a singular material thing nor anything abstracted from a body. But God only cognizes himself. Other lower substances cognize higher substances by cognizing themselves, but they cognize nothing at all that is lower than them.

200. In answer to another argument[261] it seems first that that argument has

---

[259] Wylton, *Quodlibet*, qq. 7–8, ed. Senko, 'Tomasza Wiltona Quaestio', 119.
[260] Arist. *DA* 3. 4, 429^{b}10–23; Aver. *In DA* 3, t. c. 9, 422. 34–55.
[261] See above, para. 92.

ficaciam contra Commentatorem, quoniam, licet ipse non ponat intellectum materialem numerari in nobis, ponit tamen intentiones actu intellectas multiplicari. Ponit enim diversas intellectiones de eodem obiecto in Socrate et Platone. Aliter quicquid intelligeret Socrates intelligeret Plato. Si ergo argumentum suum valeret ad probandum quod non sunt diversae intentiones intellectae in intellectu tuo et meo, quia tunc possit abstrahi tertia intentio communis et sic in infinitum, sic argui potest contra eum quod a duabus intellectionibus in Socrate et Platone potest abstrahi tertia et sic in infinitum.

201. Sed istud non valet contra Commentatorem. Nam Commentator non poneret intellectionem aliam secundum substantiam in intellectu Socratis et Platonis, sed eandem. Sed tamen non sequitur: intellectio lapidis est in intellectu Socratis, ergo Socrates intelligit lapidem, quoniam ad hoc quod Socrates denominetur 'intelligens lapidem' non sufficit quod intellectio lapidis sit in intellectu suo, sed cum hoc requiritur quod virtus phantastica Socratis sit in actu in cognoscendo lapidem. Unde, sicut nos ponimus quod eadem species firmata in intellectu nostro aliquando est principium cognoscendi rem extra secundum actum, puta quando virtus phantastica respectu eiusdem obiecti est in actu, quandoque non, scilicet quando virtus phantastica non est in actu, ita eadem intellectio nunc existens in intellectu meo copulata mihi per phantasmata existentia in me est mihi formalis ratio intelligendi obiectum extra, eadem autem intellectio non-copulata intellectui materiali per phantasmata mea, sed alterius est ratio intelligendi illi cui per sua phantasmata copulatur, sed non mihi.

202. Dico tamen ad rationem Commentatoris[262] quod non sequitur processus in infinitum in huiusmodi intentionibus. Cum illae species sint universales in repraesentando et solum singulares in essendo, solum sunt abstrahibiles ex ea parte qua sunt singulares, et non ex ea parte qua sunt universales, et hoc remanente eodem obiecto primo quod repraesentant. Dico ergo quod a specie hominis existente in intellectu meo et existente in mente alterius possum abstrahere speciem hominis non considerando ipsam ut est in hoc intellectu vel illo.

203. Et cum dicitur quod illa species abstracta est in intellectu singulari et per consequens est singularis,[263] dico, verum est quod est in essendo singularis, sed non alia singularitate quam eius a qua abstrahitur; et est universalis eadem universalitate in repraesentando et non alia qua est species universalis a qua abstrahitur.

2 intentiones] intellectiones T || intellectas] actu *add.* T   5 ad probandum *om.* T || intentiones] intellectiones T || tuo et] id est P   6–7 sic[2] ... potest[1]] eodem modo posset argui T   7 quod] quia T   9 contra] *suppl. s.l.* P   14 in cognoscendo] cognoscendi T   17 quandoque *om.* T   17–18 scilicet quando] *inv.* T   18 virtus phantastica] *inv.* P || actu] suo *add.* T   19 copulata] copulatur ita T || mihi[2]] enim T || formalis] formaliter T   20 ratio] est *add.* T   21 phantasmata mea] phantasma meum T   24 intentionibus] intellectionibus T   29 hoc intellectu] *inv.* T || vel] in *add.* T   31 est[1] *om.* T || est[2] ... essendo] in essendo est T   33 universalis] *lectio incerta* P || a *om.* P

equal efficacy against the Commentator, since, although he does not posit that the material intellect is numbered in us, he nevertheless posits that actually understood intentions are multiplied. For he posits different understandings of the same object in Socrates and Plato. Otherwise Plato would understand whatever Socrates understood. If therefore his argument successfully proved that there are not different understood intentions in your intellect and mine, because then a third, common intention could be abstracted and so on to infinity, it can be argued in this way against him that from the two understandings in Socrates and in Plato a third could be abstracted, and so on to infinity.

201. But this is not valid against the Commentator. For the Commentator would not posit an understanding that is different according to substance in the intellect of Socrates and of Plato, but the same. But nevertheless it does not follow: the understanding of a stone is in the intellect of Socrates, therefore Socrates understands the stone, since in order for Socrates to be denominated 'understanding the stone' it does not suffice that the understanding of the stone is in his intellect, but in addition to this it is required that the imaginative power of Socrates should be in act in cognizing the stone. Accordingly, just as we posit that the same species which is fixed in our intellect is sometimes the principle of cognizing an external thing according to act, namely when the imaginative power with respect to the same object is in act, and sometimes not, that is when the imaginative power is not in act, so the same understanding now existing in my intellect conjoined with me by means of the phantasms that exist in me is for me the formal principle for understanding the external object, but the same understanding when not conjoined with the material intellect by means of my phantasms, but by those of another, is the principle for understanding for him with whom it is conjoined by means of his phantasms, but not for me.

202. Nevertheless I say in answer to the argument of the Commentator[262] that an infinite regress does not follow in the case of these kinds of intention. Since these species are universal in representation and only singular in being, they can only be abstracted in so far as they are singular, and not in so far as they are universal, and this while there remains the same first object which they represent. Therefore I say that from the species of man existing in my intellect and existing in the mind of another I can abstract the species of man without considering whether it is in this intellect or that.

203. And when it is said that this abstract species is in a singular intellect and consequently is singular,[263] I say, it is true that it is singular in being, but not by any other singularity than that from which it is abstracted; and it is universal by the same universality in representation and by no other than that by which the species from which it is abstracted is universal. Accordingly, just as the quiddity

---

[262] See above, ibid.
[263] See above, ibid.

Unde, sicut quidditas rei materialis, quantumcumque abstrahatur per intellectum, non habet esse nisi in singulari, sic nec ista species abstracta.

204. Ad aliud,[264] quod scientia esset qualitas activa, non sequitur. Quo modo autem causetur scientia a doctore in discipulum non sicut a principali agente, sed sicut ab instrumentali—adiuvat enim doctor intellectum discipuli in ordinate proponendo conclusionem post principia ex quibus sequitur—habet dici in prologo primi *Posteriorum*.[265]

205. Ad ultimum argumentum Commentatoris[266] dictum est[267] quod cum hoc quod intellectus est substantia quaedam individuata stat quod cognoscit universalia et infinita, quod non est verum de sensu.

206. Ad rationem autem Philosophi in fine septimi *Metaphysicae*, per quam probat quod partes in composito quae manent toto corrupto sunt partes materiales, et per consequens in homine oporteret ponere aliud principium formale ab intellectiva,[268] dico, sicut prius dictum est,[269] quod non est simile in exemplo Philosophi, ubi partes remanentes habent eundem modum principiandi, non sic hic.

207. Et ad ultimam reductionem, cum quaeritur utrum illa unio quae requiritur ad esse hominis sit intra essentiam | vel extra,[270] dico quod extra. Et cum arguitur: ergo est posterior, et per consequens habens causam priorem in homine,[271] nego consequentiam. Exemplum: ad hoc quod ignis sit calefaciens aquam in actu, multa praesupponuntur, scilicet debita approximatio, remotio impedimenti etc., | quorum nullum est de intellectu essentiali ignis calefacientis in quantum huiusmodi, nec aquae in quantum est sub calefieri, necessario tamen requiruntur non tamquam consequentia actionem istam, sed aliquo ordine praecedentia. Sic dico hic.

208. Illa auctoritas duodecimi, ubi dicit quod nulla forma praecedit compositum, aliqua tamen sequitur,[272] dico quod in prima propositione, cum dicit quod nulla forma praecedit compositum, non comprehendit intellectivam, et hoc forsan quia non est univoce forma cum aliis. In secunda autem propositione comprehendit intellectivam. Si enim comprehenderet intellectivam utrobique, contradiceret hic ei quod dicit et probat ex intentione in 1 *Caeli et mundi*, ubi probat quod nihil est aeternum ex parte post quin sit aeternum ex parte ante et econverso.[273]

---

1 sicut] igitur T ‖ abstrahatur] abstrahitur T   **2** sic] *corr. s.l. ex* sed P   **4** discipulum] discipulo P   **5** sicut *om.* P ‖ in *om.* T   **6** principia ... quibus] principium ex quo T ‖ sequitur] sequuntur P   **7** primi *Posteriorum*] ubi post T   **9** cognoscit] cognoscat T   **9–10** universalia] alia T   **12** quae *om.* T   **13** in homine *om.* T ‖ ponere] aliquod *add.* T   **13–14** intellectiva] intellectu P   **14** quod] quia P   **17** vel] *lectio incerta* P   **18** habens] habet T   **21** quantum] est *add.* T   **22–23** necessario ... praecedentia *om.* T   **25–26** aliqua ... compositum *om. hom.* T   **26** forsan] forsitan T   **28** intellectivam[1] *om.* T   **29** in] *lectio incerta* T   **30** aeternum[2] *om.* T ‖ econverso] etc. *add.* T

of a material thing, however much it is abstracted by the intellect, does not have being except in a singular thing, so neither does this abstract species.

204. In answer to another argument,[264] that knowledge would be an active quality, it does not follow. But how knowledge may be caused by a teacher in a pupil not as by a principal agent, but as by an instrumental one—for the teacher helps the intellect of the pupil by putting forward in order the conclusion after the principles from which it follows—remains to be said in the prologue to the first book of the *Posterior Analytics*.[265]

205. In answer to the last argument of the Commentator[266] it has been said[267] that the fact that the intellect is an individuated substance is compatible with the fact that it cognizes universal and infinite things, which is not true of sense.

206. But to the argument of the Philosopher at the end of the seventh book of the *Metaphysics*, by which he proves that the parts in a composite which remain when the whole is corrupted are material parts, and consequently in man it would be necessary to posit a formal principle other than the intellectual soul,[268] I say, just as was said before,[269] that the case is not similar in the example of the Philosopher, where the parts that remain have the same mode of being a principle; not so here.

207. And in answer to the last reduction, when it is asked whether this union which is required for the being of man is internal to essence or external to it,[270] I say that it is external. And when it is argued: therefore it is posterior, and consequently has a prior cause in man,[271] I deny the consequence. Example: in order for fire actually to heat water, many things are presupposed, namely the necessary nearness, the removal of impediments, etc., none of which belongs to the essential conception of the heating fire in so far as it is heating, nor to that of the water in so far as it is subject to being heated, but they are necessarily required not as things that follow from this action, but as things that precede it in some order. So I say here.

208. To that authority of the twelfth book, where he says that no form precedes the composite, but some form follows,[272] I reply that in the first proposition, when he says that no form precedes the composite, he does not encompass the intellectual soul, and this perhaps because it is not univocally a form like the others. But in the second proposition he does encompass the intellectual soul. For if he encompassed the intellectual soul in both places, he would contradict here what he says and proves explicitly in *On the Heavens* 1, where he proves that nothing is eternal into the future unless it is eternal into the past and conversely.[273]

---

[264] See above, para. 93.
[265] We think that this is not a reference to a commentary by Wylton himself but to the *locus classicus* for the medieval discussion of this topic.
[266] See above, para. 94.
[267] See above, para. 196.
[268] See above, para. 145.
[269] See above, para. 146.
[270] See above, para. 152.
[271] See above, ibid.
[272] Arist. *Metaph.* 12. 3, 1070^{a}21–2.
[273] Arist. *De caelo*, 1. 10, 279^{b}17–280^{a}11.

INDEX AUCTORUM

ALBERT THE GREAT
In De anima (ed. C. Stroick, *Alberti Magni opera omnia*, vol. vii, Münster i.W., 1968)
  3, tract. 2, cap. 17: 56
  3, tract. 2, cap. 7: 104, 105, 106, 107, 121, 122, 123

ARISTOTLE
De anima (ed. W. D. Ross, Oxford, 1956)
  1. 1, 403^{a}8–10: 125, 165
  1. 2, 404^{b}8–15: 23
  1. 4, 408^{b}24–5: 174
  2. 1, 412^{b}4–6: 97
  2. 2, 413^{b}11–414^{a}14: 177
  2. 2, 413^{b}24–7: 167
  2. 2, 414^{a}12–14: 2
  2. 7, 418^{a}29–^{b}1: 27
  3. 4, 429^{a}22–4: 23
  3. 4, 429^{a}24–7: 171
  3. 4, 429^{b}10–23: 198
  3. 4, 429^{b}10: 88, 95, 186
  3. 4, 430^{a}2–3: 78, 81, 182
  3. 5, 430^{a}10–15: 50
  3. 5, 430^{a}23–5: 172
  3. 7, 431^{a}14–15: 194
  3. 8, 431^{b}21: 23
De bona fortuna (*Ethica Eudemia*) (ed. F. Susemihl, Leipzig, 1884)
  7. 14, 1248^{b}2–4: 161
De caelo (ed. P. Moraux, Paris, 1965)
  1. 10, 279^{b}17–33: 86, 208
  1. 12, 281^{b}20–283^{b}33: 157, 164
De generatione animalium (ed. H. J. Drosaart Lulofs, Oxford, 1965)
  2. 3, 736^{b}27–8: 143, 173
Ethica ad Nicomachum (ed. I. Bywater, Oxford, 1894)
  6. 2, 1139^{b}9–11: 161
Metaphysica (ed. W. Jaeger, Oxford, 1957)
  7. 8, 1033^{a}24–^{b}26: 168
  7. 13, 1038^{b}9–10: 105
  7. 13, 1039^{a}3–5: 108
  7. 17, 1041^{b}12–33: 145, 153, 154, 156, 163, 174, 206
  8. 5, 1045^{a}23–33: 108
  9. 8, 1050^{a}34–6: 1
  10. 10, 1058^{b}26–9: 50
  12. 3, 1070^{a}21–2: 143, 208
  12. 8, 1074^{a}31–8: 176
  12. 10, 1076^{a}3–4: 132
Physica (ed. W. D. Ross, Oxford, 1950)
  1. 7, 190^{a}17–21: 151
  8. 10, 266^{a}10–^{b}6: 168

AUGUSTINE
De civitate Dei (ed. B. Dombart and A. Kalb, 2 vols., Stuttgart, 1993)
  21. 2: 124

AVERROES
De substantia orbis (*Aristotelis opera cum Averrois commentariis*, vol. ix, Venice, 1562; repr. Frankfurt a.M., 1962)
  cap. 1: 85
In De anima (ed. H. Wolfson, D. Baneth, and F. Fobes, Corpus Commentariorum Averrois in Aristotelem, 6/1, Cambridge, Mass., 1953)
  1. 12: 141
  2. 24: 177
  2. 57: 10
  2. 67: 27
  3: 7, 8, 11, 41, 55, 69
  3. 1: 14, 40, 83, 85, 136
  3. 3: 141
  3. 4: 58
  3. 5: 9, 10, 11, 14, 21, 22, 23, 27, 32, 33, 38, 40, 45, 49, 55, 57, 83, 85, 87, 90, 91, 92, 93, 96, 97, 98, 99, 100, 101, 103, 106, 112, 114, 115, 116, 117, 118, 120, 136, 141, 182, 183, 185, 202, 203, 204
  3. 6: 171
  3. 9: 88, 95, 198

3. 14: 10, 48
3. 15: 81
3. 16: 81
3. 17: 24, 25
3. 18: 26, 27, 28, 49, 135, 138
3. 19: 13, 25, 29, 30, 31,
   42, 43, 79, 94, 205
3. 20: 34, 35, 39, 46, 47, 49, 55, 57,
   67, 83, 95, 111, 135, 136, 138, 156
3. 25: 11
3. 28: 10
3. 30: 194
3. 36: 36, 40, 60, 62, 63, 64, 65,
   66, 67, 68, 69, 77, 78, 79, 138

In De caelo et mundo (ed. F. J. Carmody,
*Averrois Commentaria magna in
Aristotelem*, vols. i–ii, Leuven, 2003)
   1. 5: 49
   1. 94: 88

In Ethicam ad Nicomachum (*Aristotelis
opera cum Averrois commentariis*, vol. iii,
Venice, 1562; repr. Frankfurt a.M., 1962)
   10. 8: 59

In Metaphysicam (*Aristotelis opera
cum Averrois commentariis*, vol. viii,
Venice, 1562; repr. Frankfurt a.M., 1962)
   5. 20: 55
   7. 2: 88

7. 23: 25
7. 60: 154
12. 17: 41, 69, 70, 77, 78
12. 36: 25
12. 39: 72, 73, 133
12. 44: 48
12. 51: 75

In Physicam (*Aristotelis opera cum
Averrois commentariis*, vol. iv, Venice,
1562; repr. Frankfurt a.M., 1962)
   prol.: 59
   7. 20: 55
   8. 4: 96
   8. 30: 43

PRISCIAN
*Institutionum grammaticarum libri
XVIII* (ed. M. Hertz, *Grammatici
Latini*, vols. ii–iii, Hildesheim, 1961)
   1. 17–18: 148

PROCLUS
*Elementatio theologica translata
a Guillelmo de Morbecca*
(ed. H. Boese, Leuven, 1987)
   prop. 15, 83: 170

THOMAS WYLTON
Quodlibet, qq. 7–8 (ed. W. Senko,'Tomasza
Wiltona Quaestio', 117–21)
   197

INDEX NOMINUM

Agathon 161

Albertus Magnus 56, 104, 121, 123

Alexander 11, 62

Aristoteles/Philosophus 2, 3, 4, 5, 23, 26, 27, 44, 50, 63, 76, 77, 78, 105, 122, 125, 140, 141, 142, 143, 144, 145, 146, 148, 149, 151, 153, 154, 156, 157, 159, 160, 161, 162, 164, 165, 167, 168, 171, 172, 173, 174, 175, 176, 177, 180, 181, 182, 186, 187, 194, 198, 206

Augustinus 124

Avempace 62, 64

Averroes/Commentator 4, 5, 7, 8, 10, 12, 13, 14, 16, 17, 23, 25, 26, 27, 30, 31, 32, 38, 40, 42, 43, 44, 45, 48, 49, 55, 59, 60, 61, 62, 63, 64, 66, 69, 70, 75, 76, 79, 80, 81, 82, 83, 84, 85, 88, 94, 106, 112, 120, 123, 124, 132, 133, 135, 137, 138, 139, 140, 141, 142, 147, 154, 155, 156, 162, 174, 175, 176, 177, 178, 180, 181, 182, 187, 194, 198, 200, 201, 202, 205

Avicenna 44

Empedocles 23

Magister Sententiarum 119

Plato 93, 105, 122

Priscianus 148

Proclus 170

Themistius 62, 135

INDEX VERBORUM POTIORUM

abhorrere 144
abicere 10
abiectio 10
absolute 21, 57, 67, 174, 196
absolutus 55, 58, 152
abstractio 81, 128, 136, 138, 182
abstractus 6, 13, 23, 26, 32, 42, 48, 55, 57, 62, 63, 67, 70, 78, 79, 81, 92, 120, 136, 141, 177, 179, 182, 188, 199, 203
abstrahere (*noun*) 28
abstrahere (*verb*) 92, 130, 135, 200, 202, 203
abstrahibilis 202
absurdus 107
acceptio 8, 83, 84
accidens 15, 20, 21, 64, 88, 111, 133, 134, 168, 169, 192, 193
accidentalis 6, 15
accidere 55, 64, 65, 75, 88, 123, 124, 186
accipere 54, 60, 64, 114, 125, 174, 182, 197
acquirere 19, 101, 102, 118
acquisitus 64, 76
actio 70, 77, 96, 125, 130, 207
active 64
activum (*noun*) 51, 137, 182
activus 30, 38, 39, 50, 93, 204
actualissimus 125
actualitas 22
actuare 15
actuatus 16, 76
actus 12, 13, 14, 20, 21, 24, 26, 27, 28, 30, 31, 40, 43, 50, 54, 55, 59, 60, 61, 64, 65, 72, 73, 74, 77, 78, 79, 81, 82, 95, 108, 111, 112, 124, 130, 134, 136, 137, 138, 141, 146, 148, 161, 178, 182, 191, 192, 195, 200, 201, 207
~ cognitionis 82
~ corporis 2, 95, 141, 144, 174, 190, 198, 199
~ deformis 132
~ immanens 1, 178
~ informans 178
~ intelligendi 1, 75, 114, 178

~ naturalis 54
~ primus 144
~ secundus 10
adaequatio 112
adaequatus 155
addiscere 93
adeptio 67, 68, 75, 76, 77, 82, 183
adeptus 8, 48, 61, 82, 136
adhaerere 124
adipisci 61
admiscere 72
admittere 198
admixtio 72
adunare 75
adunatio 75
adunatus 75
aequalis 73, 200
aequaliter 19, 147, 155
aequivoce 67, 141, 199
aeternaliter 124, 158
aeternitas 142
aeternus 11, 49, 96, 99, 111, 113, 132, 159, 183
~ ex parte ante 86, 175, 208
~ ex parte post 86, 175, 179, 208
agens (*adj.*) 8, 16, 17, 23, 24, 25, 26, 27, 28, 29, 30, 31, 32, 33, 34, 35, 36, 37, 40, 41, 42, 43, 44, 45, 46, 48, 49, 50, 54, 57, 60, 61, 64, 65, 66, 70, 72, 76, 77, 79, 80, 82, 89, 96, 111, 112, 113, 126, 128, 129, 130, 131, 135, 136, 137, 138, 195, 196, 197, 199
agens (*noun*) 24, 25, 30, 43, 49, 52, 53, 54, 61, 64, 113, 132, 161, 204
agere 43, 50, 51, 77, 132
albedo 21, 58
albus 18, 58
ambiguitas 63
analogia 54
analogus 53
angelus 178
anima 2, 7, 8, 10, 14, 20, 23, 25, 27, 32,

38, 39, 40, 41, 48, 49, 55, 56, 60,
66, 67, 69, 77, 78, 79, 81, 83, 85, 88,
95, 97, 100, 104, 122, 124, 125, 132,
141, 142, 145, 146, 148, 155, 159,
165, 166, 167, 169, 171, 172, 177,
182, 186, 189, 191, 193, 194, 198
~ humana 145
~ intellectiva 2, 6, 16, 32, 132, 144,
145, 161, 177, 190, 191, 198; (intellectiva) TITLE, 18, 19, 84, 85, 95,
115, 116, 124, 132, 141, 143, 145,
149, 151, 152, 153, 156, 158, 161,
168, 169, 171, 177, 179, 206, 208
~ rationalis 43
~ sensitiva 156, 171, 178
animal 83, 85, 95, 125, 136, 143, 173
animalitas 107
animatus 49
apparere 69, 73, 75, 176
appellatio 9
appetere 159
apponere 134
approbare 161
appropriatus 49, 80, 197
approximans 134
approximatio 19, 207
approximatus 134, 184
aqua 51, 207
ardere 134
arguere 3, 90, 92, 94, 96, 103, 104, 108, 116,
145, 146, 149, 151, 160, 167, 200, 207
argumentum 5, 113, 116, 152, 156, 200, 205
ars 25
artare 186
articulus 17, 48, 60, 142, 143, 144, 162, 175,
176, 177
artifex 25
artificialis 25
artificium 57
asinus 113
assimilare 10, 23, 25
assimilatio 23
assistens 45, 47, 64
assistentia 46, 64
assumere 124
atomus 199
attendere 45
attentio 19
attingere 82, 159, 161
attribuere 179
auctoritas 21, 22, 23, 45, 49, 73,
141, 143, 149, 156, 198, 208

augere 64
augmentatio 64

bos 57
brutum 6, 156

caelestis 103, 127, 161
caelum 49, 85, 86, 88, 127, 128,
131, 133, 157, 164, 176, 208
calefaciens 207
calefieri 207
carere 57
caro 95
catholicus 85, 95, 116, 124, 132, 142, 155,
159, 179, 195
causa 10, 31, 63, 64, 65, 91, 111, 118,
125, 131, 134, 138, 143, 152,
156, 176, 186, 195, 196, 207
~ agens 112
~ effectiva 111, 113, 134
~ finalis 134
~ materialis 147
~ media 160
~ partialis 113
~ per accidens 134
~ per se 64, 134
~ totalis 26, 60, 64, 113, 184, 196
causalitas 161
causare 25, 43, 60, 93, 137, 160,
171, 194, 195, 196, 197, 204
causatus 118, 184
clare 7, 60
clericus 59
coaeternus 74
coagens 161
cogitare 67
cognitio 6, 23, 60, 63, 64, 68, 69, 70, 71,
76, 82, 90, 91, 124, 130, 136, 138,
177, 178, 179, 182, 183, 186, 192, 198
cognitivus 79, 82
cognitum (*noun*) 23, 73, 90
cognitus 137
cognoscens 23, 73, 91
cognoscere 6, 10, 61, 62, 64, 73, 74, 76,
79, 82, 84, 91, 94, 138, 177, 179,
182, 185, 186, 187, 199, 201, 205
cognoscibile (*noun*) 79
cognoscitivus 27, 42
colligatio 136
colligere 82
color 20, 27, 45, 46, 47, 60, 80, 130, 178

colorate 156
comburere 134
combustibile 134
combustio 134
commendare 44
commentator (*common noun*) 59
commentum 7, 8, 9, 10, 11, 13, 14, 24,
    25, 26, 27, 28, 29, 30, 32, 33, 34, 35,
    36, 38, 39, 40, 41, 48, 49, 55, 57, 58,
    60, 62, 66, 67, 68, 69, 70, 72, 73, 75,
    77, 79, 81, 83, 85, 88, 95, 96, 111,
    133, 135, 136, 138, 141, 156, 177
commixtio 125
communicabilis 119, 122
communicare 173
communis 59, 97, 196, 200
communiter 127
comparare 29, 30, 120, 138, 197
comparatio 27, 67, 125
competere 199
complecti 125
complere 40, 64
complexio 171
complexionalis 171
complexus 59
componens 32
componere 16, 23, 35, 55, 107, 123, 132
compositio 47, 125, 134
    ~ hominis 3, 126, 152
compositum (*noun*) 6, 47, 55, 104, 117,
    121, 122, 124, 125, 143, 145, 146,
    147, 152, 153, 154, 178, 206, 208
    ~ corruptibile 125
    ~ materiale 125
compositus 32, 36, 55, 125, 132
comprehendens 132, 134
comprehendere 23, 62, 73, 124, 127, 177,
    179, 208
comprehensio 73
concludere 77, 165, 174, 177, 180, 197
conclusio 7, 10, 62, 84, 139, 156,
    163, 169, 174, 177, 197, 204
concomitans 152
concordans 142
concordare 5, 25, 77, 142, 162
concurrens 171
concurrere 113
conditio 6, 29, 123, 125, 179, 192
confinium 122
confirmare 2, 187
confirmatio 119
conformitas 122

congregare 39
coniungere 40, 65, 133
coniunctus 62, 67, 70, 82, 124, 125
connectere 132
connexio 132, 134
consequens 13, 20, 42, 43, 51, 59, 67, 76,
    81, 87, 92, 95, 96, 100, 114, 118, 126,
    132, 133, 143, 152, 154, 170, 171,
    173, 175, 186, 192, 195, 203, 206, 207
consequentia 88, 89, 90, 91, 92, 93, 96, 100,
    102, 170, 207
consequi 75, 128, 131, 152, 189
considerare 54, 162, 190, 197, 202
consilium 161
consistere 64, 70, 73, 76, 78, 136
consonans 148
consonus 132, 174
constituens 153, 154
constituere 9, 21, 39, 40, 112, 125, 149, 191
constitutio 152
constitutivus 149, 152
constitutus 153
contentus 121
contiguus 43
continuatio 66, 136
continuatus 39
continue 159
continuus 43, 128
contradicere 119, 208
contradictio 20, 92, 178
contrariare 119
contrarius 18, 19, 20, 27, 45, 49, 79, 88,
    102, 119, 135, 144
conveniens 56, 132
convenientia 29
convenire 6, 85, 92, 197
conversio 26, 124, 130
conversivus 170
convertire 181
convincere TITLE, 7, 174, 177, 179
copulans 184
copulare 11, 57, 61, 64, 65, 70, 83, 111,
    132, 133, 135, 136, 137, 138, 184, 201
copulatio 64, 111, 128, 131, 134, 135, 136,
    137, 138, 178
copulatus 63, 111, 124, 201
corporale (*noun*) 54, 88, 95, 125, 134, 182,
    187, 198
corporalis 88, 89, 122, 132, 141,
    167, 171, 173, 184, 186, 187
corporeitas 117
corporeus 111

corpus 2, 6, 52, 86, 95, 109, 111, 115,
    124, 125, 128, 131, 132, 133, 134,
    140, 141, 142, 143, 144, 145, 153,
    155, 159, 165, 168, 169, 172, 174,
    177, 178, 186, 187, 190, 192, 199
  ~ animatus 49
  ~ caeleste 103, 127, 161
  ~ corruptibile 117
  ~ humanum TITLE, 6, 84, 124,
    131, 132, 134, 155, 177, 191
  ~ mixtum 145
  ~ mobile 54
  ~ naturale 198
  ~ organicum 95, 125, 144
correspondens 25, 144
correspondere 94, 103, 118, 132
corrigens 41
corrumpere 143, 152, 168, 174
corruptibilis 50, 51, 57, 107, 112, 113, 116,
    117, 122, 125, 132, 134, 167, 168, 173,
    176
corruptibilitas 192
corruptio 143, 174, 176
corruptus 118, 151, 152, 155, 172, 174, 206
creare 132, 135, 137
creatio 142, 158, 173
credere 44, 64, 76, 95, 134, 175, 178, 179,
    187, 197
cumulus 124

dealbabilis 21
declarare 25, 28, 63, 66, 69, 124, 178, 183
declaratio 83
deducere 60, 102, 145, 175
defectus 149
deficere 134, 149
definibilis 125
definiens 3
definitio 9, 22, 97, 141
  ~ naturalis 22
deformis 132
demonstrare 29
demonstratio 125, 168, 177
  ~ 'propter quid' 152
denominare 201
denudare 9, 58, 64, 70, 72, 73
denudatus 58, 64, 70, 71, 73, 74, 76, 77, 138
dependens 168
dependentia 6, 95, 124, 125
dependere 57, 60, 95, 113, 124, 125,
    128, 129, 131, 133, 151, 176
depingere 10

describere 9
descriptio 12
desiderare 82
desinere 164
destruere 70, 155
determinare 8, 54, 67, 133, 186, 197
determinatio 8
determinatus 120, 132
deus 52, 53, 54, 73, 76, 119, 124, 128,
    131, 132, 160, 161, 178, 199
devenire 182
diaphanum 27, 33, 45, 60, 80
dies 64
differens 58
differentia 10, 12, 29, 30, 31, 42,
    74, 107, 123, 125, 193, 199
  ~ corporalis 132
  ~ individualis 121
  ~ specifica 3
differre 50, 51, 83, 85, 197
difficilis 63, 97, 124
difficultas 18
dignitas 60
dignius 62
directe 199
disciplina 67
discipulus 93, 204
discordare 85, 86, 162
discurrere 7
disponere 132
dispositio 27, 61, 67, 68, 75, 80, 81, 132,
    183
dispositive 161
dispositus 64
dissimilis 45
dissolutus 145, 148
distans 109, 132, 133
distincte 19
distinctio 7, 114, 119, 125
distinctus 104, 105, 109, 112, 132, 133, 156
distinguere 1, 6, 10, 12, 14, 18, 24, 40, 83,
    85, 91, 92, 95, 120, 122, 136, 176, 185
diversus 7, 8, 57, 58, 62, 84, 102, 107,
    110, 114, 118, 119, 120, 122,
    132, 133, 136, 181, 187, 193,
    194, 195, 196, 197, 198, 200
dividere 168
divinus 110, 119, 133
doctor 60, 142, 145, 159, 204
doctrina 60, 93
domus 25
dubitatio 32, 50, 63, 96, 97, 172, 179

dubius 161
ducere 24

educere 6
eductus 88, 116, 122, 141, 173, 182
effective 25, 194
effectivus 64, 111, 113, 134
effectus 68, 113, 138, 160, 184
efficacia 200
efficiens 25, 60
efficere 77, 104
efficax 144, 147
elementum 125, 145, 146, 152, 153, 154, 171
elevare 125
elevatus 179
elicitivus 178
ens 9, 14, 23, 30, 53, 112, 125, 127, 132
entitas 149
equus 57
erroneus 142, 180
esse (*noun*) 28, 88, 95, 107, 123, 125, 131, 133, 136, 141, 151, 152, 173, 176, 184, 187, 194, 203, 207
~ perpetuum 176
~ per se 6
~ reale 23
~ verum 112
essendo (in) 91, 185, 194, 196, 197, 202, 203
essentia 9, 20, 74, 146, 152, 192, 207
essentialis 15, 24, 43, 182, 207
essentialiter 55, 125, 129
evasio 10
evidens TITLE
evidenter 27, 174
evidentia 62, 88
excellere 6
excessus 192
exclusus 156
exemplariter 25
exemplum 103, 113, 115, 119, 120, 130, 146, 156, 206, 207
exequi 67
exigere 132, 134
existens 58, 64, 67, 103, 130, 178, 196, 201, 202
existere 156
experiri 1, 18, 19, 177, 178
exponens 4, 28, 30, 142
exponere 5, 6, 7, 8, 56, 84, 140, 142, 177
expositio 31, 56, 84, 168

expositor 4, 63, 154
extendere 112, 168, 169
extensio 141, 168, 181, 185, 192
extensus 88, 141, 168, 169, 170, 171, 181, 185, 192
extortus 168
extremum 90, 132, 134, 184
extrinsecus 130, 152, 173, 176, 178

facere 5, 28, 56, 60, 97, 125, 143, 161
faciliter 89, 156, 168
factus 161, 182
fallacia 114
falsitas 170
falsus 7, 50, 58, 92, 93, 96, 100, 112, 121, 127, 176, 180, 183
felicitas 73, 78, 82, 136
ficticius 108, 109, 111, 124, 132, 142, 191
fictus 132
fides 116, 174, 179, 180, 198
fieri 6, 116
fiducia 66
finalis 125, 128, 134
finis 24, 27, 35, 40, 49, 56, 64, 66, 68, 70, 77, 79, 83, 85, 95, 124, 132, 135, 138, 145, 156, 159, 161, 177, 206
forma TITLE, 3, 6, 16, 20, 25, 32, 33, 36, 40, 42, 43, 48, 49, 55, 60, 61, 64, 65, 66, 67, 77, 79, 80, 82, 84, 88, 95, 99, 104, 105, 108, 115, 116, 117, 121, 122, 124, 125, 126, 132, 133, 137, 138, 143, 145, 146, 148, 151, 152, 154, 156, 168, 173, 176, 177, 179, 181, 182, 192, 207
~ absoluta 152
~ abstracta 48, 120
~ accidentalis 15
~ adaequata 155
~ argumenti 113, 116
~ artificialis 25
~ assistens 47
~ complexionalis 171
~ corporalis 88, 89, 171, 182
~ corporea 111
~ corporis 6, 84, 140, 145, 168, 177
~ corruptibilis 168
~ educta de potentia materiae 88, 116, 122, 141, 182
~ extensa 171, 181
~ hominis 6, 145, 152
~ illuminans 64
~ illustrans 64, 72
~ imaginabilis 64

~ immaterialis 103
~ individua 133
~ individuata 88
~ informans 6, 27, 43, 47, 48, 49, 60, 84
~ inhaerens 45, 60
~ intellectiva 161
~ intelligibilis 16, 24, 56, 58
~ irradians 64
~ limitata 110
~ materialis 9, 22, 88, 89, 90, 168, 181, 182
~ non inhaerens 6, 124
~ propria 61, 64, 79, 155
~ rationis 65
~ repraesentans 77
~ repraesentativa 79
~ respectiva 152
~ separata 103, 141
~ singularis 10
~ subsistens 124
~ substantialis 15, 16, 104, 145
~ totius 153, 154
~ universalis 10
formale (*noun*) 3, 57, 156
formalis 1, 85, 123, 126, 146, 148, 156, 177, 178, 201, 206
formalissime 152
formaliter 191
formare 18, 94, 197
frustra 57, 176
frustrari 159
fundare 114, 152, 168, 190
fundatus 20

gaudere 179
generabilis 50, 57, 168, 173
generalis 162
generans 111, 133, 134
generare 60, 64, 66, 119
generatio 40, 64, 113, 122, 136, 138, 143, 158, 173, 197
genus 20, 24, 50, 52, 53, 54, 58, 107, 123, 127, 176, 177
~ analogum 53
~ logicum 52, 53
~ physicum 50, 51, 53
~ principiandi 156
glossare 142
gradus 58, 82

habituatus 59, 60, 64, 82

habitus 8, 10, 40, 59, 60, 64, 65, 70, 82, 124, 137, 138, 141
~ cognitivus 82
~ intellectivus 55
~ moralis 59
~ scientificus 59, 82
~ speculativus 59, 65
haeccitas 95, 115
homo 1, 3, 6, 14, 40, 53, 57, 61, 66, 79, 82, 83, 85, 86, 87, 88, 94, 95, 97, 98, 100, 102, 104, 107, 113, 114, 115, 117, 118, 121, 122, 123, 124, 125, 126, 129, 130, 132, 136, 145, 148, 149, 150, 151, 152, 153, 156, 159, 161, 177, 178, 191, 193, 195, 202, 206, 207
humanitas 107, 153
humanus 6, 70, 84, 95, 120, 124, 131, 132, 134, 136, 144, 155, 177, 191

idea 76
identitas 159, 176
ignis 43, 51, 134, 207
ignorantia 10
illimitatio 110
illimitatus 133
illuminans 64
illustrans 64, 72
imaginabilis 64,
imaginari 72, 125
imaginatio 95, 125
imaginativus 83, 118
imaginatus 28, 57, 64, 136
imago 76
immanens 1, 178
immateriale (*noun*) 62, 122, 123, 132
immaterialis 62, 103, 138, 197, 199
immaterialitas 25, 196
immediate 15, 21, 132, 138, 145, 160, 161, 175, 189, 191, 193
immediatus 21, 178
immiscibilitas 29
immixtus 23
immutabilis 111
immutare 27, 46
impassibilitas 29
impedimentum 207
imperfecte 64, 82
imperfectum (*noun*) 60
imperfectus 125
implicans 92
implicare 20
implicatio 178

INDEX VERBORUM POTIORUM

imponere 4, 158, 178
impossibilis 70, 90, 102, 110, 125, 159
incipere 25, 142, 157, 164
inclinare 159
inclinatio 6, 95, 124, 125
incomplexus 59
inconveniens 90, 91, 92, 98, 99, 123, 132, 182
incorporale (*noun*) 134
incorruptibilis 40, 50, 51, 57, 85, 86, 88, 100, 108, 112, 116, 117, 122, 142, 143, 155, 157, 162, 168, 172, 174, 175, 192
indeterminatus 186
indifferenter 186
indirecte 196
individuabilis 123
individualis 121, 132, 176
individuans 122
individuare 88, 107, 186, 189, 190, 195, 198
individuatus 88, 95, 107, 123, 188, 193, 205
individuum (*noun*) 11, 57, 58, 88, 105, 132, 133, 155, 176, 179, 187, 198
individuus 133, 192
indivisibilis 192
indubitanter 180
inducere 132, 161, 177
inductive 44
inductus 132
ineffabilis 124
inesse 133
inferior 48, 50, 51, 70, 76, 128, 132, 160, 199
inferius (*adv.*) 17, 29, 48
inferre 87, 182
infinitas 92
infinitus 92, 94, 152, 159, 166, 168, 200, 202, 205
informans 6, 27, 43, 47, 48, 49, 60, 84, 178
informare 27, 43, 48, 76, 177
informatus 59
infundere 132
infusio 132
ingenerabilis 57, 86, 174, 175
ingenitum 161
ingredi 67
inhaerens 6, 45, 60, 64, 124, 177
inhaerentia 152
inhaerere 6, 47, 64, 124
innascibilis 119
inniti 62, 149
innocentia 179
innotescere 7

innuere 136
innumerabilis 132
inpingere 23
inquirere 5, 7
inquisitio 60
insistere 83
instans 40, 136
instantia 30
instrumentalis 204
instrumentum 60
intellectio 64, 68, 70, 71, 73, 74, 81, 118, 129, 136, 183, 184, 198, 200, 201
intellectivus 55
intellectualis 59
intellectualiter 54
intellectum (*noun*) 60, 64, 70, 71, 72, 75, 87, 136, 137, 182, 183
~ speculabile 137
~ speculativum 64, 67, 72, 96, 112, 113
intellectus (*adj.*) 26, 28, 57, 59, 60, 77, 89, 112, 136, 138, 200
intellectus (*noun*) 1, 7, 8, 9, 10, 11, 14, 18, 23, 26, 27, 31, 35, 39, 40, 41, 49, 55, 56, 57, 59, 64, 67, 70, 71, 72, 73, 75, 76, 81, 82, 83, 84, 85, 86, 87, 92, 93, 94, 95, 98, 112, 114, 115, 118, 119, 120, 124, 125, 135, 136, 141, 143, 147, 161, 162, 165, 167, 172, 173, 174, 175, 177, 178, 179, 182, 183, 184, 185, 186, 187, 188, 197, 198, 200, 201, 202, 203, 204, 205
~ abstractus 13
~ adeptus 8, 48, 61, 82
~ agens 8, 16, 17, 23, 24, 25, 26, 27, 28, 29, 30, 31, 32, 33, 34, 36, 37, 40, 41, 42, 43, 44, 45, 46, 48, 49, 50, 54, 57, 60, 61, 64, 65, 66, 70, 72, 76, 77, 79, 80, 82, 89, 96, 111, 112, 113, 126, 128, 129, 130, 131, 135, 136, 137, 138, 195, 196, 197, 199
~ coniunctus 62, 70
~ essentialis 207
~ in habitu 8, 40, 59, 60, 64, 65, 70, 82, 124, 137, 138
~ in potentia 41, 135
~ materialis 8, 9, 10, 11, 12, 13, 14, 15, 16, 18, 20, 21, 22, 23, 24, 25, 26, 27, 29, 30, 31, 32, 33, 34, 36, 37, 40, 42, 43, 45, 46, 48, 49, 54, 55, 57, 58, 60, 61, 62, 63, 64, 65, 67, 68, 69, 70, 71, 72, 73, 74, 76, 77, 78, 79, 80, 81, 82, 83, 84, 85, 86, 88, 89, 90, 91, 95, 97,

134 INDEX VERBORUM POTIORUM

98, 99, 100, 102, 103, 104, 105, 107, 110, 111, 113, 118, 120, 121, 124, 125, 126, 128, 130, 131, 134, 135, 136, 137, 138, 140, 142, 155, 156, 157, 169, 172, 174, 178, 182, 183, 199, 200, 201
~ passibilis 8
~ passivus 8, 83
~ possibilis 9, 40, 42, 54, 193, 194, 195, 196, 197
~ primus 1
~ separatus 118
~ singularis 182, 203
~ speculativus 8, 40, 55, 57, 59, 82, 96, 112, 136
~ verus 142
intelligens 1, 19, 59, 70, 77, 85, 178, 201
intelligentia 49, 70, 73, 95, 127, 128, 131
intelligere (*noun*) 12, 23, 54, 82, 97, 125, 129, 130, 131, 178
intelligere (*verb*) 1, 2, 4, 6, 9, 22, 23, 26, 27, 30, 31, 45, 48, 49, 50, 55, 59, 61, 62, 63, 64, 65, 67, 70, 71, 72, 73, 74, 75, 76, 77, 78, 79, 80, 81, 82, 83, 84, 89, 112, 114, 121, 124, 125, 128, 135, 136, 137, 138, 141, 143, 154, 172, 174, 177, 178, 179, 182, 183, 191, 192, 193, 196, 198, 199, 200, 201
intelligibile (*noun*) 70, 81, 82, 130, 184
intelligibilis 15, 16, 20, 24, 26, 56, 58, 76, 81, 92, 136, 138, 182
intendere 76, 153
intentio 7, 21, 22, 25, 57, 67, 69, 70, 72, 77, 78, 95, 125, 132, 157, 162, 168, 185, 199, 202, 208
~ abstracta 23, 26, 55, 57, 78, 81, 136, 199
~ Aristotelis 44, 162, 169
~ Averrois 7, 82
~ Commentatoris 12, 13, 16, 17, 23, 25, 40, 42, 44, 70, 75, 79, 84, 141, 176, 177, 178
~ communis 200
~ formae materialis 9, 22
~ formae universalis 10
~ imaginata 28, 57, 64, 136
~ individualis 176
~ individui 88
~ intellecta 26, 28, 57, 59, 60, 112, 136, 138, 200
~ intelligibilis 15, 20, 24, 76, 92
~ media 136
~ obiecti 23

~ Philosophi 2, 3, 77, 78, 144, 154, 161, 172, 173, 175, 176, 186
~ rei materialis 21, 82
~ speciei 88
~ speculativa 57
~ universalis 21, 25, 26, 55
intentionaliter 23, 184
interior 174
intimare 178
intrare 173
intrinsece 132
intrinsecus 85, 126, 129, 130, 152, 156, 176, 177, 178
invenire 60, 63, 75, 110, 125, 133
irradians 64
irradiare 64
iudicare 94
iudicium 174

labor 63
laborare 4
laicus 59
lapis 125, 201
libellus 161
liber 11, 13, 32, 69, 141, 142
limitatus 110, 133
linea 198
littera 177
locus 41, 62, 109, 132, 133, 141, 177
logicus 52, 53
lucere 130
lumen 27, 43, 45, 47, 60, 64, 76, 80, 89, 112, 136
lux 27, 33, 45, 46, 60

magister 86, 94, 119
magnitudo 67, 88, 95, 168, 186
manens 58, 149
manere 107, 143, 145, 146, 147, 148, 149, 151, 152, 153, 154, 172, 206
manifestus 24, 84, 88, 141, 186
manus 115
materia 4, 6, 7, 10, 15, 16, 25, 30, 32, 41, 43, 47, 50, 51, 55, 56, 60, 63, 67, 69, 76, 77, 84, 85, 88, 111, 116, 121, 122, 124, 125, 132, 133, 141, 142, 143, 145, 146, 148, 149, 151, 152, 153, 156, 162, 168, 173, 176, 177, 181, 182, 187, 190, 192
~ determinata 132
~ hominis 151, 152

~ prima 10, 12, 156
~ propria 43
~ signata 176
materiale (*noun*) 62, 76, 78, 79, 122,
    123, 125, 132, 156, 198, 199
materialis 1, 8, 9, 10, 11, 12, 13, 14, 15, 16,
    18, 20, 21, 22, 23, 24, 25, 26, 27, 29,
    30, 31, 32, 33, 34, 35, 36, 37, 40, 42,
    43, 45, 46, 48, 49, 54, 55, 57, 58, 60,
    61, 62, 63, 64, 65, 67, 68, 69, 70, 71,
    72, 73, 74, 76, 77, 78, 79, 80, 81, 82,
    83, 84, 85, 86, 88, 89, 90, 91, 95, 96,
    97, 98, 99, 100, 102, 103, 104, 105,
    107, 110, 111, 113, 118, 120, 121,
    123, 124, 125, 126, 128, 130, 131,
    134, 135, 136, 137, 138, 140, 142,
    146, 152, 155, 156, 157, 168, 169,
    172, 174, 178, 181, 182, 183, 186,
    196, 197, 198, 199, 200, 201, 203, 206
materialitas 196, 198
medium (*noun*) 27, 43, 47, 58, 64,
    132, 134, 135, 136, 177, 184
medius 90, 132, 136, 160, 183
membrum 7
mens 14, 25, 202
metaphysicus (*noun*) 68
miraculum 124
mixtus 11, 141, 145, 146
mobile (*noun*) 52, 54, 103
mobilis 54
modus 10, 19, 23, 30, 32, 48, 49, 54, 60,
    65, 66, 70, 75, 79, 82, 84, 91, 112,
    124, 131, 132, 137, 138, 141, 148, 157,
    173, 177, 184, 187, 188, 190, 192, 199
    ~ loquendi 38, 49
    ~ ponendi 7, 95
    ~ principiandi 146, 206
    ~ repraesentandi 194
moralis 59
mors 124, 172
motivum (*noun*) 7, 21, 87, 112, 182
motor 48, 52, 103, 131, 133, 176, 199
motrix 131
motum (*noun*) 87, 89
motus (*noun*) 22, 25, 40, 54, 55, 64, 65,
    70, 82, 124, 128, 131, 133, 137
motus (*adj.*) 30, 43
movens 25, 30, 43, 48, 49, 52, 54,
    89, 127, 131, 168, 194, 196
movere 14, 18, 52, 64, 67, 83, 85, 87, 89,
    96, 127, 131, 133, 136, 168, 177, 182,
    187

multiplicabilis 57, 132
multiplicare 57, 198, 200
multiplicatio 57
multiplicatus 57
multipliciter 6
multitudo 75, 176
mundus 49, 86, 88, 112, 157, 164, 208

nascibilis 119
natura 6, 9, 12, 13, 21, 22, 25, 28, 58,
    67, 82, 83, 95, 124, 125, 127,
    132, 133, 134, 136, 137, 152, 184
    ~ corporalis 122
    ~ corruptibilis 122
    ~ differentiae 123
    ~ divina 110
    ~ generis 107, 123
    ~ humana 95, 120, 124
    ~ illimitata 133
    ~ incorruptibilis 122
    ~ individuata 123
    ~ limitata 133
    ~ speciei 176
    ~ specifica 155
    ~ spiritualis 122
naturale (*noun*) 179
naturalis 4, 6, 20, 22, 24, 54, 95, 124, 125,
    130, 132, 136, 141, 144, 161, 173, 179,
    198
naturaliter 60, 63, 64, 76, 134, 138, 159
natus 6, 18, 46, 64, 136, 182, 198
nauta 103
navis 103
necessario 20, 21, 101, 113, 114, 123,
    124, 125, 130, 152, 193, 207
necessarius TITLE, 27, 81, 122
necesse 24, 60, 70, 122, 135, 152, 156
necessitas 24, 132
    ~ naturae 127
    ~ naturalis 130
negare 26, 76, 124, 133, 152, 169, 173, 181,
    182, 207
nescire 179
nomen 8
nominare 117
notitia 60, 118
numerabilis 90, 123, 132
numeralis 142, 159, 176
numeraliter 119
numerare 86, 90, 107, 114, 119, 123, 136,
    142, 144, 177, 181, 186, 187, 193, 195,
    198, 200

numeratio 86, 88, 114, 133, 142, 144, 186, 193
numeratus 87, 88, 133, 194, 196
numerositas 133
numerus 22, 58, 86, 92, 94, 98, 102, 104, 107, 110, 115, 119, 123, 132, 133, 136, 145, 152, 162, 176

obiectum 18, 23, 46, 76, 89, 112, 136, 137, 138, 182, 186, 194, 196, 197, 198, 200, 201, 202
obliviscens 101
oblivisci 101, 102
operari 125, 141
operatio 128, 131, 136, 173, 174
~ corporalis 173
~ finalis 125
~ perfectissima 61, 131
~ perpetua 167
~ prima 128, 131, 138
opinans 102
opinio 5, 7, 55, 85, 96, 102, 104, 119, 122, 132, 135, 143, 145, 146, 149, 161, 163, 174, 175, 176, 178, 179
~ Aristotelis 5, 145
~ Averrois 5, 180
~ catholica 85, 95, 116, 124, 155, 157
~ Commentatoris 124, 142, 174, 198
~ communis 196
~ Empedoclis 23
~ fidei 198
~ Philosophi 142, 157, 160, 198
~ Platonis 122
~ Themistii 135
~ vera 85, 86, 197
oppositus 6, 119, 124, 140
oratio 112
orbis 48, 85
ordinate 204
ordo 6, 13, 15, 21, 28, 92, 123, 124, 125, 132, 134, 180, 207
organicus 95, 125, 141, 144, 169, 171, 185, 187
organum 141, 167, 168, 185

pars 5, 85, 95, 121, 132, 133, 134, 136, 139, 154, 165, 168, 169, 176, 178, 192, 199, 202, 206
ex ~te ante 86, 157, 175, 208
ex ~te post 86, 157, 175, 179, 208
~ affirmativa 67

~ formalis 1
~ hominis 1, 178
~ materialis 95, 152, 206
~ medii 58
~ septentrionalis 57
~ terrae 57
~ universi 132, 134
partialis 113
particulare (*noun*) 105, 112, 121, 186
particularis 86, 105, 132
particularitas 186
particulariter 194
passibilis 8
passio 10
passive 10
passivum (*noun*) 51, 137
passivus 8, 18, 30, 38, 39, 83
passum 30
pati 10, 51
patiens 30, 43, 52, 53
perfecte 19, 61, 64, 65, 69, 82, 137
perfectibile (*noun*) 103, 124, 132, 133, 144, 155, 166
~ primum 95, 120, 124
perfectio 10, 11, 14, 33, 40, 45, 46, 48, 58, 64, 95, 103, 108, 136, 137, 138, 141, 155, 176, 191, 192
~ abstracta 120
~ finalis 128
~ formalis 85
~ informans 48
~ humana 70
~ prima 14, 83, 85, 97, 104, 114, 136, 141
~ propria 144
~ secunda 97, 114
~ ultima 73, 74, 156
perfectum (*noun*) 60, 62
perfectus 30, 59, 60, 61, 64, 65, 75, 82, 95, 124, 125, 131, 138, 156
perficere 10, 15, 16, 34, 48, 82, 133, 134, 141, 145
perficiens 43, 168
peripateticus 44, 62
perpetuare 176
perpetuus 128, 131, 134, 166, 167, 176
perplexus 162
persona 119, 132
pertinere 54, 68, 91
pes 115
phantasia 164
phantasma 26, 27, 57, 67, 113, 114,

118, 119, 124, 128, 130, 136, 138, 172, 174, 178, 194, 195, 199, 201
phantasticus 64, 118, 130, 136, 201
philosophia 57
philosophus (*common noun*) 3, 4, 6, 23, 179
Platonicus 122
pluralitas 88
ponderare 23, 49
pondus 7
possibilis 9, 12, 13, 14, 15, 18, 20, 21, 40, 42, 54, 67, 74, 193, 194, 195, 196, 197
possibilitas 9, 21, 66, 69, 70
posterior 137, 143, 152, 204, 207
potentia 9, 10, 11, 20, 21, 22, 26, 28, 30, 40, 41, 50, 54, 58, 64, 70, 71, 72, 73, 74, 76, 77, 81, 82, 87, 89, 108, 124, 135, 138, 146, 148, 152, 169, 182, 186, 189, 191, 193
~ abstracta 188
~ activa 50
~ animae 20, 169
~ cognitiva 79
~ cognoscitiva 27, 42
~ essentialis 24, 43, 182
~ extensa 169
~ intellectiva 189, 190
~ materiae 6, 88, 116, 122, 141, 173, 182
~ naturalis 20
~ organica 169
~ passiva 18
~ receptiva 1, 50, 58, 178
~ sensitiva 18, 19, 95, 193
potentialitas 71, 73, 74
praecedens 71, 175, 182, 207
praecedere 99, 131, 135, 138, 143, 158, 208
praedicatum (*noun*) 119
praeparatio 125
praesens 27, 45
praesentare 18
praesentia 46
praesentatus 19
praesupponere 15, 59, 114, 136, 138, 207
praesuppositus 89
praetendere 23
principium 9, 32, 37, 40, 60, 61, 63, 64, 65, 67, 79, 105, 122, 124, 125, 127, 129, 138, 149, 150, 152, 153, 156, 158, 164, 176, 181, 204, 206
~ activum 30, 93
~ agendi 51
~ cognoscendi 6, 79, 84, 177, 201
~ constituens 153

~ constitutivum 149, 152
~ elicitivum 178
~ formale 123, 126, 146, 148, 156, 177, 178, 206
~ formalissimum 152
~ generale 162
~ individuans 122
~ intrinsecum 129, 130, 152, 177, 178
~ materiale 123, 156
~ motus 22
~ movens 25, 30, 43
~ passivum 30
~ primum 60
~ productivum 25
~ reductivum 54
~ simplex 125
principalis 7, 30, 84, 128, 139, 142, 204
principaliter 187
privare 161
privatio 151
probans 62
probare 1, 39, 40, 50, 53, 55, 70, 73, 77, 83, 89, 91, 92, 145, 151, 152, 153, 157, 163, 168, 172, 176, 194, 200, 206, 208
probatio 33, 182, 183
probatus 29
procedere 5, 7, 10, 96, 111
processus 92, 145, 152, 202
producere 158, 161, 173
productio 40
productivus 25
productus 113, 179
proficere 82
prohibere 113, 119, 133
prologus 59, 204
promittere 63
propinquus 125
proportio 192, 198
proportionaliter 60
proportionare 192, 199
propositio 18, 30, 58, 60, 94, 208
proprie 61
proprietas 6, 119
proprius 18, 31, 43, 61, 64, 77, 79, 96, 111, 125, 137, 144, 155, 196, 197
prosperitas 70
purus 1, 12, 13, 14, 15, 20, 21

quaerere 134, 152, 172, 194, 197, 207
quaesitum (*noun*) 69
quaestio 5, 14, 67, 79, 83, 85, 172, 177, 197
qualitas 20, 93, 204

quantitas 88, 176
quidditas 6, 54, 84, 95, 120, 122, 133, 152, 156, 177, 179, 182, 186, 199, 203
quiescere 133

ratio TITLE, 2, 7, 16, 24, 29, 50, 53, 55, 57, 60, 62, 64, 65, 72, 76, 87, 92, 96, 104, 105, 106, 107, 111, 115, 117, 119, 121, 123, 124, 126, 127, 136, 137, 138, 139, 144, 146, 147, 149, 152, 155, 156, 161, 163, 165, 166, 168, 174, 180, 182, 183, 187, 188, 192, 196, 197, 202, 206
~ considerandi 53
~ intelligendi 136, 201
~ naturalis 4, 132, 144, 179
~ propria 18
~ quidditatis 133
~ singularitatis 133
rationabilius 132, 133
rationalis 3, 43
realis 23
realiter 23, 24, 83, 152
receptio 10
~ transmutabilis 10
receptivum (*noun*) 21, 102
receptivus 1, 50, 54, 58, 90, 118, 178
receptum (*noun*) 58, 91
receptus 185, 194
recessus 125
recipere 10, 15, 16, 21, 22, 23, 24, 26, 56, 58, 64, 80, 90, 91, 135, 183, 197, 198, 199
recipiens 49, 58, 91, 196
recitare 5, 7
reducens 46, 50
reducere 7, 24, 26, 50, 90, 91, 92, 98, 182
reductio 127, 207
reductivus 54
reflexivus 185
reflexus 198
regio 67
regula 125, 152
relatio 55
relucere 67, 68
remanens 202, 206
reminisci 93, 118, 124, 172
remotio 207
remotus 125
repraesentans 77
repraesentare 91, 185, 194, 196, 197, 202, 203
repraesentativus 76, 79

repugnantia 192
repugnare 13, 21, 78, 92, 187
res 6, 10, 27, 31, 74, 78, 84, 94, 99, 112, 116, 130, 149, 150, 151, 152, 169, 183, 185, 197, 199, 201
~ abstracta 63, 67
~ corporalis 186
~ materialis 21, 22, 23, 45, 78, 81, 136, 138, 186, 199, 203
~ naturalis 24, 179
~ vera 151
respectivus 58, 152
respectus 24, 25, 30, 48, 49, 57, 60, 66, 81, 119, 124, 125, 132, 148, 156, 201
respicere 91
respondere 21, 45, 62, 112, 117, 146, 156, 168, 172, 180, 188
responsio 64, 148, 156
resultans 153
resultare 55, 56
resurrectio 159
retinere 123

salvare 56, 176, 198
sanctus 6
scientia 10, 19, 31, 42, 55, 67, 68, 79, 93, 101, 118, 122, 204
scientificus 59, 82
scire 8, 26, 27, 54, 60, 62, 70, 71, 82, 85, 88, 93, 135, 179, 198, 199
scitum (*noun*) 31, 42, 79
scribere 23, 69
sempiternus 157, 168
sensibile (*noun*) 182, 194
sensibilis 187, 197
sensitivus 18, 19, 60, 83, 95, 117, 125, 156, 169, 171, 178, 185, 186, 187, 193, 194, 196, 198
sensus 18, 91, 169, 186, 192, 194, 205
sententia 23, 31, 69, 70, 76, 77, 78, 86, 88, 119, 136, 137, 141, 155, 174, 175, 176, 181, 195, 198
sentire 2, 4, 140, 144, 177
separabile (*noun*) 124
separabilitas 29
separare 166, 167, 174
separatim 156
separatio 145
separatum (*noun*) 88, 124, 187
separatus 13, 48, 61, 62, 63, 64, 65, 67, 68, 69, 70, 71, 73, 74, 76, 77, 79, 81,

103, 108, 118, 124, 125, 127, 128,
    138, 141, 145, 146, 148, 156, 166, 199
septentrionalis 57
sequela 128
sequi 20, 22, 26, 30, 37, 42, 43, 48, 58, 60,
    63, 79, 89, 90, 93, 97, 98, 100, 101,
    107, 113, 114, 115, 117, 118, 127,
    128, 129, 130, 133, 136, 145, 152,
    156, 159, 168, 169, 175, 183, 185,
    189, 191, 193, 201, 202, 204, 208
signatus 57, 176
similis 27, 32, 60, 124, 128, 131, 146, 156,
    206
similitudo 45
simplex 23, 75, 125
singulare (noun) 87, 95, 121, 186,
    193, 196, 197, 198, 199, 203
singularis 10, 11, 49, 91, 94, 95, 104, 105,
    120, 182, 185, 187, 192, 193, 194,
    195, 196, 197, 198, 199, 202, 203
singularitas 28, 120, 133, 186, 193, 196, 198,
    199, 203
singulariter 39, 49
situs 178
sol 43, 50, 51, 113, 130
sollicitido 19
solutio 181
solutus 144, 174
solvere 16, 18, 65, 186
specialis 177
species 1, 40, 57, 58, 60, 77, 80, 88, 91,
    92, 95, 107, 120, 122, 123, 124, 127,
    132, 133, 136, 156, 176, 177, 181,
    182, 194, 196, 197, 198, 199, 201, 202
    ~ abstracta 92, 203
    ~ animalis 125
    ~ atoma 199
    ~ composita 132
    ~ hominis 116, 121, 136, 202
    ~ intelligibilis 92
    ~ media 132
    ~ singularis 195, 196, 197, 198
    ~ universalis 194, 195, 203
specifice 1, 6, 85, 177
specificus 3, 132, 133, 155
speculabilis 137
speculari (noun) 131
speculatio 128
speculativum (noun) 64
speculativus 8, 36, 40, 55, 57, 59, 64, 65,
    67, 68, 72, 82, 96, 112, 113, 136
spiritualis 122

spiritus 124
status 76, 77, 82, 179
studere 19
studium 19
subiectum 36, 60, 112, 125
subsistens 13, 32, 37, 40, 44, 108, 109, 122,
    124, 126, 178
subsistere (noun) 6, 124
subsistere (verb) 124, 155
substantia 30, 32, 37, 40, 43, 44, 53, 70, 71,
    73, 74, 76, 82, 85, 88, 126, 127, 132,
    138, 169, 175, 189, 193, 199, 201, 205
    ~ abstracta 13, 32, 70
    ~ aeterna 49, 111
    ~ corporea 1
    ~ immaterialis 103, 138, 199
    ~ incorruptibilis 40
    ~ separata 13, 48, 61, 62, 63, 64, 65,
        67, 68, 69, 70, 71, 73, 74, 76, 77,
        79, 124, 125, 127, 128, 138, 199
substantialis 6, 15, 16, 71, 104, 145, 156
successio 155
successive 114
sufficere 26, 53, 58, 125, 201
sufficiens 26
superadditus 95, 122, 133, 171, 176
supergredi 190, 191, 192
supergressio 192
superior 48, 70, 73, 76, 82, 128, 132, 138,
    199
superius (adv.) 29, 42, 144, 166
suppositum (noun) 43, 71, 95, 107,
    110, 114, 119, 120, 122, 133, 136,
    155, 178, 181, 193, 194, 196, 198
susceptivus 119
sustinere 146, 196, 198
syllaba 145, 146, 148

tabula 10
tactus (noun) 169
tangere 69
tenere 5, 7, 62, 94, 142, 161, 179, 180
terminare 111
terminatio 10
terminatus 82, 124
terminus 5, 64, 65, 70, 137, 138
terra 57
textus 23, 177
theologus 76
totalis 26, 60, 64, 113, 184, 196
totaliter 64, 133

totum (*noun*) 82, 149, 153, 154, 168, 196, 206
totus 1, 95, 125, 133, 154, 169, 176, 192, 196
tractatus 85
transferre 28
transire 107
translatio 23
transmutabilis 10, 113, 168
transmutare 10
transmutatio 10, 56, 168, 173
trinitas 133

uniformiter 138
unio 60, 111, 124, 150, 151, 152, 159, 207
unire 40, 49, 60, 61, 124, 131, 132, 199
unitas 114, 124, 132
~ analogiae 54
~ numeralis 142
unitus 152
universale (*noun*) 112, 120, 122, 123, 187, 196, 197, 205
universalis 10, 21, 22, 25, 26, 55, 94, 107, 141, 185, 192, 194, 195, 196, 202, 203
universalitas 28, 186, 194, 195, 203
universaliter 71, 194
universum 123, 132, 134
univoce 208
usus 6, 48
uti 7, 8, 49, 122, 167, 168

vagus 120
valere 51, 116, 117, 152, 154, 195, 196, 200, 201
variare 58

venire 143, 158
verbum 57, 69, 161, 197
vere 40, 60, 125, 126
verificare 119
veritas 44, 112, 174, 179, 180
verus 12, 31, 71, 85, 86, 112, 116, 118, 119, 120, 122, 124, 140, 142, 151, 171, 179, 182, 184, 197, 203, 205
via 124, 159, 179, 197
videre 5, 7, 16, 17, 18, 19, 27, 45, 46, 47, 50, 56, 62, 77, 78, 80, 107, 109, 119, 130, 133, 135, 143, 161, 162, 165, 176, 177, 178, 180, 186, 193, 200
vigere 4
virtus 38, 39, 49, 64, 85, 94, 141, 168, 192, 195, 196, 197, 199
~ abstracta 62
~ cognitiva 79
~ cognoscitiva 42
~ corporalis 141, 186, 187
~ imaginativa 83
~ immaterialis 62, 197
~ intellectualis 59
~ phantastica 64, 118, 130, 136, 201
~ sensitiva 83, 125, 185, 186, 187, 194, 196, 198
vis 24, 183
visibilis 27, 60
visus (*noun*) 27, 46
vivere 2, 144, 177
vocalis 148
vocare 9, 10, 71, 72, 168
voluntarie 60
voluntas 129
voluptas 73